THE HUNTING & FISHING CAMP BUILDER'S GUIDE

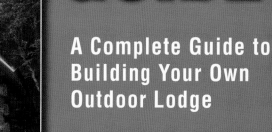

A Complete Guide to Building Your Own Outdoor Lodge

MONTE BURCH

Skyhorse Publishing

Skyhorse Publishing books may be purchased in bulk at special discounts for sales promotion, corporate gifts, fund-raising, or educational purposes. Special editions can also be created to specifications. For details, contact the Special Sales Department, Skyhorse Publishing, 307 West 36th Street, 11th Floor, New York, NY 10018 or info@skyhorsepublishing.com.

Skyhorse® and Skyhorse Publishing® are registered trademarks of Skyhorse Publishing, Inc.®, a Delaware corporation.

Visit our website at www.skyhorsepublishing.com.

10 9 8 7 6 5 4 3 2 1

Library of Congress Cataloging-in-Publication Data is available on file.
ISBN: 978-1-61608-466-0

Printed in China

Acknowledgements:
Thanks to the folks at *Extreme How-To Magazine* for allowing the use of some of my previously published articles. For more information visit www.extremehow-to.com

Photography Credits:
All photos and drawings by the Monte Burch except the following:
Courtesy of – Bosch: 17; Logosol: 25, 26, 44; Wood-Mizer: 26; The Engineered Wood Association: 50; Johns Manville: 118; Owens Corning: 118; Formica Corporation: 135; Gastineau Log Homes: 138, 140, 141, 144-145, 184; iStockphoto: 104, 146-147, 170, 180, 183, 216; Vermont Castings: 177

Introduction

A piece of land in the wilderness and a hunting or fishing cabin or lodge is the dream of many an outdoor man or woman. The cabin or lodge may be a simple, one-room log construction, or a fancy lodge suitable for housing several hunting guests in luxury. This book illustrates how to design and construct standard stick-construction lodges, log buildings, pole and post-and-beam structures. Also covered are the necessities such as foundation construction, fireplaces and wood stoves, finishing inside and out, insulating and other details. Additions that can make the lodge more enjoyable, such as porches, decks and sunroofs are also covered. Full plans are also included for building a shooting house, ladder stand and other projects for your hunting club or property. Even rustic furniture construction is covered so you can furnish your cabin in an outdoor décor.

A great deal of the enjoyment of hunting and fishing property is "building it yourself." I hope you enjoy the information in this book and use it to create your very own hunting or fishing get-away.

Contents

Land, Plan & Design

Above: A hunting or fishing camp can be as simple as a small cabin in the woods or lakeside, or a mansion-size lodge for a hunt club or extended family enjoyment.

Hunt and fish camps can be as simple as a one-room log or even "tarpaper" shack. More than one such camp consists of an old trailer hauled to the site. On the other hand, I've been in lodges bigger and much fancier than the average home. The first step is the land, whether it's a large timberland holding for deer and turkey hunting, a marsh or slough for waterfowling, a rolling upland area for upland and deer hunting, or a property located near a choice fishing site. Before plunking down the money for your dream hunting lodge, it always pays to do a bit of planning and assessment.

"The hunting is fantastic," is often a major selling point of any rural lands these days. The real estate agent, however, may not really have any idea of the hunting situation. It's extremely important to determine the true potential of the property before buying. Marginal properties can often be managed for better hunting and fishing. If the property is bought for hunting or fishing, ideally you should have the opportunity to actually hunt or fish there to determine its potential. Fishing is usually possible, however, when buying land out of the prime hunting season, scouting may have to suffice. You may find the ideal property that has been managed for the hunting or fishing you desire. Well managed hunting and fishing property will have a higher value and price than more marginal land, even in the same region.

- How much can you afford not only to purchase, but to manage for wildlife?

- How much does the land cost?   • How much will insurance and taxes add to the cost?

- Will you live on the land, or is this a weekend or hunting retreat?

- What type of wildlife are you interested in?

LAND

In some cases your specific desires may not be compatible with the property, even under intensive management. For instance, deer hunting may be your passion, but the property has soil conditions that will make it hard to produce deer foods. On the other hand, a management condition that can improve deer hunting would be a property with old, mature timberlands. Although these do not produce the proper amounts of food and cover to sustain much of a deer herd, by doing timberland management you can improve habitat for deer, as well as wild turkeys and other wildlife. You may also desire a pond, lake or wetland for fishing and/or waterfowl hunting. It's important to determine if creating a pond is feasible, or possible.

If you dream of owning your own wildlife haven, the first step is to **set goals and make a plan.** How much can you afford not only to purchase, but to manage for wildlife? How much does the land cost: how much will insurance and taxes add to the cost? Will you live on the land, or is this a weekend or hunting retreat? What type of wildlife are you interested in? Often the habitat and management for one species will also be suitable for others.

We were very lucky when we purchased our land back in the 70's. Located "where the Ozarks meets the prairie," as a nearby small town describes the area, the property is extremely diversified, with hardwood timber, open prairie, a creek and a small marsh. We've added six ponds and numerous food plots.

Two tools are valuable in determining wildlife potential in a property you are looking to buy—a topographical map and an aerial photo. The **topographical map** can show the topography, or whether the land is sloping, hilly, flat, or mountainous. Marshes, streams and lakes as well as other features are also shown. The **aerial photo** illustrates the vegetation and other features. A **county plat map** can tell you who owns land you're interested in or the neighboring lands. Other factors you should consider include the average yearly rainfall, availability of water, soil types and average weather conditions. Some wildlife management practices are only successful when you have the proper rainfall and soils.

Another important factor is, can the land be monetarily productive as well as managed for wildlife? Usually, a well-managed ranch, farm, pine plantation, or timberland can be both a money-maker and a wildlife haven. Some studies show well-

When acquiring land, it's important to match the land type and capability to your hunting or fishing interests.

An aerial photo and topographical map are invaluable for determining wildlife habitat and the potential for future habitat management.

You will have to put your feet on the ground to make the final determination of whether you wish to purchase the land. The best bet is to actually hunt the property.

If the property has woodlands, a timber cruise can help determine wildlife habitat and management potential. You can do this yourself or hire a professional.

managed timberlands can be, over the long run, more profitable than investing in the stock market.

Although an aerial photo or topo map can be used in determining the potential of the land, **you'll need to put your feet on the land** as well. Don't hesitate to ask for help. Hunting land experts are available for hire and free advice is also available from state and federal wildlife agencies. Begin by contacting the state fish and wildlife agency. You may also wish to contact the Natural Resources Conservation Service (NRCS), county Soil Conservation Service (SCS), county Extension Service and state and private foresters.

With the aerial photo you can make a general assessment of habitat and wildlife potential. There are seven broad habitat types you can mark on the aerial photo. These include:

1. **Upland woodland,** forests or areas overgrown with trees with a canopy greater than 10 percent.
2. **Bottomland hardwoods,** or forested bottomlands or wood swamps. This may also include tree-lined oxbows.
3. **Pasture and hay lands,** including native prairies.
4. **Croplands,** or fields planted to row crops and small grains.
5. **Old fields, agricultural fields** or pasture abandoned for more than two years and having less than ten percent canopy of overstory trees.
6. **Non-forested wetlands** such as ponds, potholes, marshes, sloughs, low-wet grassy areas and shallow, water-logged depressions.
7. **Riparian corridors** or those areas lining rivers and streams.

Outline any of these categories that apply and estimate the acreage of each habitat type. Now it's time for fieldwork. With the photo and a notebook in hand, walk the property and examine the different areas. Make notes on the suitability of existing habitats for your desired species, as well as possible improvement practices. Again, an expert in the field can be a great help.

Woodlands

Deciduous woodlands are important habitat for many species. Estimate the percentage of black and white oak groups in the forest, since they are the most important mast-producing trees. Also, determine the size class, as defined by the **diameter at breast height (DBH)**. These classes include: old growth, or trees greater than sixteen inches (DBH); saw timber, or trees greater than nine inches (DBH); pole-timber, or two to nine inch (DBH); and regrowth, zero to two inch (DBH). You should also determine the amount of canopy, as this has a great effect on food availability. An **open canopy** has less than fifty percent coverage. A **"closed" canopy** has greater than fifty percent coverage. The latter results in less productive mast trees, and indicates thinning needed. Also look for nest and roost trees and determine their percentage or the number available. These include either dead or live trees greater than six inches DBH with obvious cavities. Determine the density and makeup of the forest understory. If there are more than four stems per square yard, walking can be difficult for deer and turkeys, but provides great ruffed grouse areas.

In pine plantations look for proper thinning. A pine monoculture doesn't provide as much quality habitat unless it's interspersed with other types of cover and food sources.

Croplands

Determine the current or past cropping rotations, including rotations into grass. Also determine land fertility and if there are existing **Crop Reserve Programs (CRP)**. The latter can sometimes offset some of the cost of purchasing land. The crop history can also be a help in determining feasibility of food plots for deer and turkeys.

Uplands

Uplands can be an invaluable habitat for many wildlife species, including wild turkeys, deer, quail, pheasants and rabbits. But they must have certain qualities. Estimate the amount of dense or shrubby areas, brush piles, rock piles, fallen logs and other cover. Include dense, shrubby draws extending into at least fifty percent of a field. Also examine the borders of the

DOING YOUR HOMEWORK

- **Determine the size class of the trees, as defined by the diameter at breast height (DBH).**

- **Establish the density and makeup of the forest understory.**

- **Determine the number of nest or roost trees.**

- **Determine the normal or past cropping rotations, including rotations into grass.**

- **Determine land fertility and if there are existing Crop Reserve Programs (CRP).**

- **Identify and estimate the percentage of legumes.**

It's also important to determine the succession age of grasslands, old fields and other upland areas.

field for the amount of **"edge" cover**. These include hedgerows, overgrown fencerows and strips of vegetation between habitat types. Note whether the edges are straight or irregular. Determine the number of nest or roost trees (these include either dead or live trees greater than 6 inches diameter at breast height (DBH) with cavities, including coniferous trees such as pine or red cedar). These are all used for nesting by doves.

A careful examination of the **vegetative cover** can also indicate suitable habitat for specific species. Vegetative cover less than twenty percent will not supply enough cover and food for most species. **Canopy coverage** of shrubs and herbaceous vegetation that is 6 inches to 4 feet tall is preferred by whitetail deer. Cover 6 to 18 inches tall is preferred by other species including turkeys, rabbits and quail. If the area has more than sixty percent coverage of shrubs and herbaceous vegetation, however, it may be too thick for ground-nesting birds and small mammals to walk through. Note the **types of cover**, cool-season grasses, warm-season grasses, legumes or a mixture of plants.

Pasture and Hay Lands

In pasture and hay lands, determine **past grazing or haying pressure** on the area, as well as any flooding or burning. Moderate pressure leaves three to six inches of cool-season grasses and eight to twelve inches of warm-season grasses over winter. Identify and estimate the percentage of legumes, including clovers, in the grasslands. Finally, take note of the grassland species, along with existing forbs.

Wetlands

Wetlands are not wetlands without seasonal water. Determine the fall and winter water availability. *Note: many waterfowl wetlands are artificially flooded each fall, requiring water availability for pumping or flooding.* Estimate the amount of **land that can be flooded** from one to eighteen inches deep either naturally or manually. If it is more than eighteen inches, puddle ducks can't tip up to feed. Also determine the types and estimate the **percentage of existing wetlands plants**, as well as the percentage of winter cover in the form of woody and/or emergent plants that can provide winter protection.

With this assessment you will be able to determine what wildlife habitat is available and what management practices may be suitable for the property. You may discover that some practices are not suitable for the property and don't meet your expectations. But, you may also discover your land is capable of attracting and holding a number of wildlife species. With the right property, money and hard work, you can manage the habitat for a wide variety of species or manage for your preferred species.

After you've assessed the habitat types on your property, it's useful to also **determine the percentage of habitat types** within a two-mile radius of your land. This allows you to manage for wildlife in conjunction with habitat surrounding you; perhaps offer something that is not already available. Management can consist of any number of techniques for timberlands, uplands and wetlands.

If this sounds like an advanced wildlife management class, it is. As

The range of designs for hunting lodges, cabins or homes is unlimited. The lodge shown is on the Prairie Sky Ranch in South Dakota.

you can guess, an expert's advice can be invaluable, even if you have to pay for it. With a handful of tree, grass and plant identifying books, an aerial photo, topo map, a notebook and plenty of time, however, it's possible to do it yourself. And, it's an enjoyable experience that can really provide an in-depth knowledge of your land and how to manage it for wildlife.

Don't let this advice deter you from the possibility of purchasing your dream hunting and fishing land.

SITE YOUR LODGE

Properly locating your building site is extremely important. Your first thoughts will probably be about the "view." Most hunting and fishing camp lodges or cabins are located to take advantage of the view, whether a sweeping valley, majestic mountains or a scenic lake or river. Other factors, however, must also be considered. The first is subsurface ground conditions. If you're building anything more than a simple cabin, you should probably have a geological and soil condition report. And, in fact, the building codes in some areas may require it. Earthquake prone areas may also require a seismic report. These tests will be used to determine proper building support as well as what excavation problems may occur. For instance you will need to know if the soil is made up of sand, clay or rock. If rock, are they solid ledges of rock that may require blasting? This can be very expensive. Even if the local codes don't require these tests, it's a good idea to at least do some testing yourself. Dig a number of

THE REAL EXPECTATIONS OF RURAL LIVING

- Consider access to utilities, including sewer, water, electricity, phone service and heating gas.

- Check the county and local zoning rules on septic or sewer systems.

- Check out local schools.

- Contact the county collector's office for taxes.

- Consider the availability and quality of medical services.

- Check out the amenities like the nearest shopping areas.

- Consider if the peace and quiet of country living is really for you.

holes around the building site down through the topsoil and into the subsoil. Then use a long steel bar to probe deeper to determine any problems. You should also consider safety factors for your building site. For instance, steep hillsides of clay may be prone to mudslides. Other hazards include falling rocks, if sited too close to a rocky cliff, large trees with dead branches can also be a hazard, but are more easily controlled. Tornadoes, high tides, high winds and danger of wildfires can all be hazards you should at least check into and consider.

The next factor is how much excavation will be required. Bulldozer work can run from $60 to well over $100 an hour and extensive excavation can be costly. Consider not only what vegetation you want removed, but also what you want to retain.

You should also think about the location of the lodge in relation to solar exposure. Ideally, in northern areas, you'll want to position the living area, kitchen and dining room on the south side in order to receive more winter sun. Bedrooms located on the western side won't receive that early-morning sunlight. If an attached garage is part of your plan, you may wish to position it on the north to provide a windscreen in the winter. Or you may wish to position the open garage door on the south. For hotter climes a garage on the west side will add protection from afternoon sun. Porches should be positioned to take advantage of the climate, whether north or south. You may wish to have a porch on the east for that morning coffee and to watch the sunrise.

Another factor is access to the building site from the nearest public road. Some folks want to be as far back in the wilderness as possible, and that's not a bad thing, but building and maintaining a lengthy road can be quite costly, so that cost must be considered as well. In northern climates, avoid steep slopes. They can be a real problem in icy weather. If you must build a road through another person's property to reach your site, make sure to have a proper easement contract drawn up by a lawyer.

Another very important factor is utilities. In all but remote areas, electricity will be available, but if you plan to build a distance from the nearest service line, it can be extremely costly. In instances where the service must be brought some distance you will probably have to pay to have the service brought to your site. Make sure you understand the maintenance procedures of the utility line. You should also check into telephone, cable, and in some instances water and sewage.

PLAN

In some instances you may eventually decide to reside on the land. Living the rural lifestyle can be extremely satisfying, great for your health and the country is a great place for children and grandchildren. And there's the wildlife. After over thirty years of wildlife management, we have created a wildlife haven on our property. Our entire family, including kids and grandkids, nieces and nephews, as well as friends enjoy hunting deer, turkeys, squirrels, rabbits, upland birds and waterfowl. Our ponds also furnish fishing recreation as well as frogging fun and places for family picnics. We see wildlife from our home and office windows every day, and there are binoculars strategically placed in almost every room for nature watching. Not that we don't enjoy the cities, our travels take us to major cities each year. They are great places to visit, but we don't want to live there.

You can enjoy great things from rural life if you understand your expectations.

Even in the most remote of rural areas these days, the availability of services is expanding exponentially. This is a result of the increased migration from the urban areas to **"farmettes"** or parcels of 20 acres or less. Most of these "farmettes" are located on or near a major road or highway and within commuting distance of metropolitan areas. This migration is almost a duplicate of the "back to the land" movement of the late '60s. The difference is the upward scale of the land buyers. Travel the back roads to find true rural living.

Let's look at the real expectations of rural living. The first consideration is utilities, including sewer, water, electricity, phone service and heating gas availability. Some services may already exist on the property; **"undeveloped" property** will require the addition of all services. The cost can be fairly hefty to run power lines. For water you may have to drill a well, and that can also be costly depending on the depth necessary for a dependable water supply. You should also check with county and local zoning rules on septic or sewer systems. In the case of some backwoods hunting camps, you may not desire sewer or running water. I can tell you, however, that's mighty unhandy on a daily basis, and not nearly as romantic as it sounds.

Check out local schools. While you may not have school-age children, the rating of the schools can make a difference in land values and taxes. For the most part rural taxes are less than urban and suburban tax rates, but not always. Check the county collector's office for taxes, as well as any proposed increases. A very important factor for many, especially retirees, is the availability and quality of medical services. If you have serious health problems and the nearest first-responder is many miles away, you may want to rethink

Floor plans, designs and blueprints are available from numerous sources. Shown is a simple 24 x 24 foot lodge floor plan.

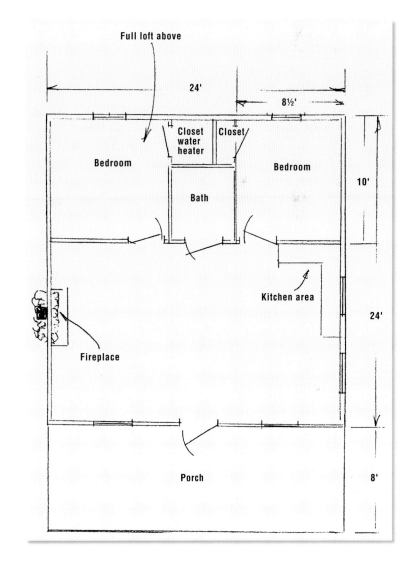

*One of the most popular features of many hunt camps is
a trophy room, or trophy wall.*

the area you want to move to.

And then there are the amenities. If the nearest shopping area is some distance away you'll have to learn to organize your stays. If you're used to popping into the supermarket or hardware store on a daily basis, do you really want to shop only once a month?

One of the expectations of country living is the peace and quiet. Solitude is a great source of enjoyment to many, but not everyone enjoys days alone. Rural neighbors can be and in many instances are great friends, but there is a difference. More than one retired urban couple has discovered rural life boring, a sense of great loss without the constant touch with their circle of friends. Divorces are not uncommon when one partner is comfortable with this new way of life and the other isn't.

DESIGN

It's also important to determine what, where and how you will build your hunting or fishing camp lodge. First, determine your finances, and what you can afford. Then add about 5% for those "things that can go wrong," for instance digging a well may cost more than you budget, or bringing electricity to a site can be costly. Hundreds of plans are available for any number of buildings from various plan companies. If considering a log building, lots of kits are available that you can assemble yourself, or have built.

Before you start building your cabin consider your needs. How often will you use your hunting or fishing camp? If you plan short visits during hunting season or weekend fishing trips, with a relatively small party, a smaller, more economic structure, with "rustic" facilities may be the best choice, offering basic requirements for sleeping and cooking. On the other hand, if you plan long stays and plan to use your camp as vacation property, a larger, "home-like" structure with "modern conveniences" might be in order.

The next step is to carefully design your lodge. A one-room log cabin doesn't take a lot of planning, except for fireplace or stove location. If the lodge is part of a several-owner hunting or fishing camp, you'll need to design rooms that will comfortably sleep several people with a bathroom between and a large combination eating/living area. In many instances a lodge can also benefit from **"outdoor living" areas** such as decks, enclosed porches, and built-on sheds for holding firewood.

One item in many hunting lodges is **a trophy room**, especially in the more upscale lodges. A trophy room not only offers a pleasant area for admiring trophies and reliving the experience, but also helps you share with others. These rooms bring the outdoors in, especially to those who haven't experienced the thrill and challenge in collecting trophies as well as to friends who have. Properly designed, a trophy room can also be a great area for simply relaxing alone and for entertaining.

A trophy room makes a very personal statement, and should be well planned. Most trophy rooms will change as trophies are collected. This must be taken into consideration in the initial planning. Begin the planning stage by determining the trophies you currently wish to display. **Hanging trophies**, or mounted heads, requires specific amounts of space, not only simply for the exact size of the mount, but also wall space around each so they aren't crowded. **Larger heads**, such as elk, caribou or moose, require a lot of wall height to display a trophy rack. **Full-size trophies**, such as bear, deer or elk require a great deal of floor space. Any of these larger trophies, however, can be the center of your room. Use scaled paper for each wall on which you wish to hang trophies and also for the floor. Measure the trophies and make a rough, but scaled sketch of each. Then cut out the sketch for each trophy. Mark the wall length and height on the scaled paper and arrange the trophy cut-outs. Shift the trophies around, making a wall arrangement plan on paper. This makes it easy to mount the heads in the proper position.

It's especially important to have a solid hanging support for larger heads. If possible, locate all trophy wall mounts over studs. Fastening through wallboard alone may eventually cause problems. Use a stud finder when hanging, or mark the stud locations when building or remodeling. Another option is to install 2 x 6 blocking between the studs and flush with their outside edges in the trophy locations as indicated by your scale drawing.

Taxidermy of mounted heads has become increasingly more versatile. These days the forms used for mounting heads have a great deal of variety, including pedestal mounts that are designed to be mounted on floor or wall pedestals. These mounts can add more versatility to your overall room design.

Rather than just hanging the heads around the room, you may wish to create **a "theme" wall**. This might include a focal point trophy head, surrounded by photos relating to the hunt as well as objects or souvenirs from the hunt or area. A number of similar heads, for instance four or five deer heads, can be hung in a group with the monster as the center focus.

Lighting is a major key to properly displaying trophies. As trophies change you may wish to also rearrange the lighting. **Track lighting** is one method of achieving the versatility needed. Each wall should be covered by individual tracks. **Overhead lights** should be used for general illumination as well as outlets for reading lamps in the sitting areas. All lighting should be dimmable for greater versatility. **Skylights** can be used to bring natural light into the room, and provide more of an "outdoor" feel.

The **scaled floor plan** also allows you to design "viewing" areas for the trophies. If the area is to be used for entertaining, the scaled floor plan can be used not only to determine seating areas, but also to locate entertainment areas as well as locations for a wet bar with refrigerator, ice machine, wine cooler or the equipment you deem essential. A small bathroom with sink and toilet is a necessity. A shower could be included for convenience after a hunting trip or if the area will ever be used as a small apartment or simply for resale value. Once the basic plan is formulated, use the scaled floor plan to measure furniture to be purchased, make scale cut-outs and "arrange" furniture on paper before purchasing.

A trophy room can also include a work area as well as bookshelves. You may, however, wish to create a separate "study" or library room. An office or study can provide an area for quiet reading or relaxing. Equipped with a hide-a-bed, this room can become a "guest" room. Again use the scaled paper and "design" this room to suit your needs. Perhaps you would like a fly-tying bench or table, a display case for outdoor collectibles, or a work space for repairing outdoor gear. Maybe you just want a "traditional" study/library with lots of bookshelves and a place for "quiet time." If this room is to be used for working or sleeping, consider closing it off with a door.

You may also wish to add a zero-clearance fireplace or small stove to the study or trophy room. One of the most popular room additions these days is a gas-operated, zero-clearance fireplace or stove.

You can build a hunting lodge with nothing more than a axe. Our forbearers did, but it is hard work and takes quite a bit of time and skill. These days you're unlimited in the tools you can use, depending on the type of lodge, access to electricity, your pocketbook, skills, type of lodge construction and desires. For instance, building a log-only lodge requires different tools than a standard stick construction lodge. And, if you're doing electrical, plumbing, sheetrocking, rockwork fireplaces and other chores, you'll need even more tools. We'll start with the most commonly used tools and progress through the "specialty" tools, including tools for log-construction and building your own lodge furniture.

Many a cabin has been built in the back woods with nothing more than a sharp axe, but these days a wide range of tools is available to help you make a better constructed lodge easier.

HAND TOOLS

We'll start with "primitive" hand tools, or those that can be used for standard construction, as well as those that can be used for post-and-beam. Primitive doesn't mean many of these tools are not available these days as new tools, but some old tools can also be found quite economically at flea markets and garage sales. New purchased tools should be top quality as poor quality tools will not last as long, dull quicker and cause more strain and effort.

Hammers are, of course, very important construction tools. You can get by in most instances with a quality 16 oz. carpenter's curve-

BASIC CABIN BUILDER'S HAND WOODWORKING TOOL KIT

- Hammers
  (Framing & Finishing)
- Handsaws
  (Crosscut & Ripping)
- Level (4-ft.)
- Tape Measure (25 ft.)
- Framing Square
- Blumb Bob & Chalk Line
- Utility Knife
- Axe
- Chisels
- Miter Box & Saw
- Brace & Bits
- Jack Plane
- Screwdrivers

Handsaws can be used for cutting framing or finish work. A medium coarse crosscut with 8 points to the inch is a good choice. It is possible to construct a stick-frame building with nothing more than hand tools.

Handsaws

Many a house was built with nothing more than handsaws and they can still be invaluable for building your lodge or for other construction around the camp. Handsaws are available in several sizes, with different cuts, depending on the teeth per inch, and as cross cut or rip saws. Again, you can get by with only one handsaw, and a good choice would be a medium coarse crosscut, with 8 points to the inch. If you intend to do much finish work, a finer toothed, hollow ground or **taper ground saw** can also be helpful. Handsaws are also available as **"ripping" saws** that are used to rip or cut with the grain instead of across it. They cut like chisels, not like knives as do crosscut saws. A 5-½-point saw is the best all-around choice.

Levels and Measuring Tools

Levels are a necessity, and again they're available in several sizes. A 4-foot model is the standard for precise framing. Smaller, 24 inch models will suffice, but you may need a straight edge or level board for leveling longer spans. You will also need a string or level for laying out footings, foundations or concrete slabs. A good steel tape measure is also necessary, and a 25 footer is a good choice for an all-around tape. A 100 foot tape is best, however, for laying out buildings. A framing square is required for laying out rafters and stair stringers and for checking the squareness of a joint. A smaller combination square can be used to mark boards to be cut. A T-bevel is used for marking angle cuts. And you'll need a plumb bob and chalk line.

Hammers are available in several sizes, ranging from 12-ounce finishing hammers (left) to 20-ounce framing hammers (right).

claw hammer. For framing, however, a heavier, 20 oz. straight claw hammer will do a better job without undue tiring. In fact, many of these are sold as **"framing hammers."** Depending on the amount of "finishing," you intend to do, you may also wish to have a 12 oz. **"finishing hammer."** These little hammers are great for installing trim, building cabinets and other light-duty chores. If you're going to be using hammers for working chisels and gouges for timbers or logs, you'll need a heavy-duty **"blacksmith's" hammer** or small sledge. Do not use carpenter's hammers for this chore as they can chip or break if used to strike other metal tools, and can cause a serious injury. These can range from 1 up to 3 or 4 pounds. Always wear safety glasses when doing these chores.

A variety of measuring tools are required, these include a tape measure, level, a framing square, plumb bob, chalk line and line level.

Woodworking Tools

In addition to the tools mentioned, several other woodworking tools can be helpful. These include a jack plane, chisels for notching studs and cutting mortise-and-tenons and a utility knife. Pry bars can be used for pulling nails and prying nailed boards loose. A brace and bits can also be used for hand boring of holes. Make sure the brace is double-acting, or works when rotated in either direction. A wood miter box and back miter saw makes it easier to cut and install trim. A handful of other tools can also be handy, including a variety of screwdrivers, wrenches and ratchets.

Additional woodworking tools, such as hand planes, chisels, pry bars, wrenches, screwdriver and pliers will also be a considerable help.

LOG & POST AND BEAM TOOLS

Both post and beam and log construction require specialized tools. The first is a good chain saw.

Chain Saws

Chain saws are the ultimate tool for some, the ultimate nightmare for others. Chain saws are actually neither. Once considered the primary tool of professional loggers, ranchers and farmers, chain saws became a popular homeowner tool when Robert McCulloch introduced the first lightweight model back in the late 60's. Since that time chain saws have become increasingly popular with homeowners. Of course they're also used by numerous professionals including arborists and loggers. Chain saws can be used around the camp for tree pruning, storm cleanup, cutting firewood, felling trees and even creating rough carpentry projects such as fences, fence posts and others.

One of the most important tools for the hunt camp builder is a good chain saw.
Actually with a chain saw and a little skill you can build just about
anything from buildings to furniture.

A chain saw can also be a best friend to wildlife. Most timberlands benefit from **Timber Stand Improvement** or **TSI**. TSI often involves selective cutting or thinning of the trees to encourage growth of selected trees. The result of the thinning is more and better mast crops and more sunlight reaching the forest floor. Both of these improve the timberlands for all types of wildlife. And, chain saws can be used to clear shooting lanes for stand hunting, build turkey and deer blinds as well as waterfowl blinds.

Chain saws are available in a wide variety of sizes including bar lengths and engine power, as well as in electric and gasoline powered models. Before choosing a chain saw, first consider the uses you will need it for. **"Will the saw be used primarily for trimming, felling, cutting or all of those chores?"** asks Charlie Durand, manager of sales and training at John Deere Consumer products

in Moline. Charlie also asks how often the saw will be used—regularly, occasionally or intensively. Chain saws are basically available in three sizes: mini, mid- and heavy-duty. The mini's, also called light-duty, range from 30 to 40cc with bar lengths ranging from 12 to 14 inches. Mid-range saws range from 40 to 60cc with bar lengths from 16 to 24 inches. Professional, or heavy-duty saws range from 60 up to 120cc and have bar lengths up to more than most homeowners can fathom. And it requires the muscles to use them. For the most part you should select the saw not only on the engine size, but the diameter of wood you would most often be cutting. With proper use, you can safely cut logs with diameters almost double the length of the bar.

Chain saws are available as **electric** or **gasoline powered**. Outdoorsmen will get the most benefit from the gasoline models because they're more versatile and aren't "tied to a cord." Consumer-use chain saws come in three basic sizes: light-duty, medium-duty use, and professional saws. The medium-duty use saws are for the most part the best choice for outdoorsmen. These saws will fell most trees and do most other chores, yet they're light weight enough to easily transport and use, even by the less experienced. Fitted with a 16-inch bar, it will handle even the bigger chores easily.

It's also important to pick a **quality chain saw**. Chain saws must take a lot of abuse, even with the best of use, and durability is important. Many of today's quality saws also have numerous other features that make them much easier to start and run than earlier models. Newer safety features make them safer as well. For instance, Stihl's anti-vibration system eliminates vibration felt through the handle, reducing user fatigue. The Quad Power engine provides increased power and fuel efficiency over the standard two-port design. In addition, an electronic ignition system with timing advance allows for quicker, easier starting. Stihl also offers some of the easiest to control machines. A master control lever directs several major functions including on/off switch, choke and fast-start positions. I regularly test chain saws and a couple of other features I like about the Stihl models are the fuel/oil fill caps and chain tension adjuster. The fuel and oil caps have lift-up handles making it easy to remove the caps even with heavy leather gloves on.

Purchasing a quality chain saw, however, is only the first step. Chain saws, like many tools, can be extremely dangerous if misused. Safety begins with **proper maintenance**. Keep the chain sharp; it's easier on both you and the saw. Make sure the chain has the proper tension and the chain brake is working. The chain should not move while the saw is idling. Never modify the chain brake; it is designed to prevent dangerous kickback.

Always **wear protective gear** and clothing. This begins with eye and ear protection. A hard hat should also be worn. Logger's helmets combine these features. You should also wear leather gloves. Sturdy, steel-toed boots and protective chaps can also prevent problems if you happen to brush the moving chain against your legs or feet.

Chain saws are available in several sizes, with the cc and bar length the deciding factors. A mid-sized saw (40 to 60cc) with a 16- to 20-inch bar will handle most camp chores, including tree felling.

Features

The **oiling system** is extremely important as oil must lubricate the bar as the chain rides over it. The better the bar is kept lubricated, the longer the chain and bar will last. Oilers are available as automatic, which delivers oil to the bar at a given amount, or automatic/adjustable which allows you to adjust the amount of oil depending on the job. The Stihl automatic system is designed to reduce oil consumption as much as 50 percent. Both Echo and John Deere offer automatic/adjustable oilers on their chainsaws. John Deere Pro models and Echo saws also have a no-oil-at-idle feature which means you aren't wasting oil during idling.

Chain saws take a lot of abuse and they must be used and maintained properly. Keeping proper **tension** on the chain is important for both safety and efficiency. As the saw runs, it may loosen or tighten.

Always wear protective gear when operating chain saws.

For adjustment, most saws have two nuts that must be removed or loosened. A large tension screw located behind the bar is then used to maintain proper tension. You'll need the appropriate wrench and screwdriver. A number of saws these days, including Craftsman, Poulan, some Husqvarna and Echo models have the adjustment on the bar itself, a much easier method than having to locate and adjust the tension screw. Stihl has a side-access chain tensioner on some models which allows you to adjust through the sprocket cover. The company, however, goes one step further with some of their models, featuring an exclusive "no-tools-required" Quick Chain Adjuster. To adjust the tension, simply loosen a dial on the side, adjust the tension by turning a top-mounted knob, and then retighten the side dial.

Many modern-day chain saws also offer numerous safety features older saws didn't have. Some, however, don't offer all safety features. When shopping, look for these features: A chain guard that will catch the chain should it slip off during operation. Hand guards to prevent accidentally touching the moving chain should your hand slip off the handle. A rear hand guard also protects your hand if the chain happens to come off the bar. A safety interlock feature is found on some saws. The interlock utilizes two triggers on the handle to prevent accidental operation of the throttle. If you don't hold the throttle lock-out in place with your hand, the saw won't start or run.

The most dangerous occurrence in chain saw use is **kickback,** a reaction that happens when the moving chain near the upper quadrant of the nose contacts a solid object. The action of the chain cutting force creates a rotational pull on the saw in the direction opposite the movement of the chain. The force created can fling the bar up and back in an uncontrollable arc, mainly in the plane of the bar. This makes the bar move back toward the operator and can cause severe injury.

Chain brakes are the first step in preventing kickback. Chain brakes are available as two types: manual and inertial. Manual chain brakes must be activated by hand. Inertia chain brakes are the safest as they operate by the force of the saw being thrown backwards and can be hand-activated if necessary. Inertial brakes are found on most recent models from John Deere, Echo, Makita, Jonsered, Husqvarna, Shindaiwa, Tanaka and Craftsman. Stihl was the first to offer a chain brake. Some of their models have two-way and some three-way chain brakes. They are activated by inertia, by the hand guard, and also with the interlock lever by removing the hand from the rear handle.

Some consumer saws these days offer a safety tip on the end of the bar to prevent insertion of the bar end into a cut and also help prevent kickback. Most nonprofessional saws also are available with low kickback chains. These chains can serve to reduce kickback by as much as 75 percent as compared to a non-kickback chain.

Additional Features

Those of us who used chain saws 25 years ago really appreciate the ease of starting and handling of today's saws. **Purge-pump-equipped carburetors** are found on many saws. This extends starter life by limiting the number of pulls needed to start the engine. Most will start on the first or second pull when gasoline is pumped into the carburetor before starting. The larger saws from John Deere, Stihl, Jonsered and Husqvarna also feature **decompression valves**. These reduce the pressure needed to pull the starter rope. Stihl, Jonsered and Husqvarna saws also feature a single-start control

It's important to keep the chain sharpened and properly adjusted. Some saws, such as the Stihl model shown above, offer easy chain tension adjustment.

that simplifies cold starting and prevents flooding. Most of today's saws also feature some sort of vibration isolation. These **vibration isolators** or dampening systems help to reduce operator fatigue and also help the chain saw last longer. Today's saws also feature easy-to-use and conveniently located controls. Stihl features one switch that does it all, on/off, choke and fast-start.

How to Use

Modern chain saws have become relatively easy to use and extremely efficient. They can also be extremely dangerous, however. According to statistics from the Consumer Products Safety Commission, each year nearly 100,000 injuries occur involving the use of chain saws. These injuries can be drastically reduced with proper safety training and by following a little advice from the experts. According to Tim Ard, President of Forest Applications Training, Inc., and instructor and co-founder of the Game of Logging,

When using a chain saw, it is important to check the chain brake often to make sure it is working properly.

PROPER CHAIN SAW MAINTENANCE

- **Keep the chain sharp.**

- **Make sure the chain has the proper tension and the chain brake is working.**

- **Never modify the chain brake.**

the chain saw has been deemed as one of the most hazardous tools in the workplace where tree removal, repair and storm cleanup work is performed. As a 25-year veteran of the outdoor power equipment industry, Ard instructs almost 7,000 people annually in chain saw safety and application throughout the U.S. Husqvarna is a major sponsor of his courses, supporting hands-on safety training. Ard feels most users are unaware of the potential uses and dangers of chain saw operation and suggests these six safety tips:

1. **Select the right size saw.** A mid-sized saw is right for cutting wood on the ground. One with a bar of 16 to 20 inches offers good maneuverability without being too heavy. For smaller limbs and chores, a light-weight, high-speed saw is recommended.

2. **Wear appropriate protective gear.** By far, the most overlooked aspect of tree felling safety is proper apparel, without which no felling job should be undertaken. A properly outfitted operator should wear protective chaps or rugged pants, eye and ear protection, protective footwear, work gloves and a helmet. Always avoid loose-fitting clothing.

3. **Inspect the saw before use.** Ensure the chain brake is clean, that the brake band isn't worn, and that both the inertia and manual activation of the chain brake are in proper working condition. The chain should be sharpened and should exhibit proper tension.

4. **Start safe.** A chain saw is safest to start on the ground. Be sure nothing is obstructing the guide bar and chain. To make sure the saw sits securely on the ground, place your right foot in the rear handle.

5. **Carefully plan your cutting job.** Avoid hazards such as dead limbs, electric lines, roads and bystanders (work at a safe distance, but never work alone). Evaluate wind direction and lean of the tree.

6. **Protect yourself against "kickback."** Never modify or remove the chain brake. It is designed to reduce the effect of "kick-back" and prevent possible injury.

Make sure you read and understand the user information from your saw manufacturer's instruction manual before using the saw.

Basic Chores

Chain saws are commonly used for several specific **wood-cutting** chores. I've also used an electric chain saw for butchering a beef, and my dad used a small chain saw to cut ice from his pond in the winter to water the livestock. I've also used a chain saw to rough cut framing for remodeling chores. Most common uses include **pruning** or trimming trees, **felling** trees, **limbing** or cutting limbs off felled trees, and **bucking** or cutting trees or limbs into lengths desired. The latter can be for firewood, saw logs or in the case of storm damaged trees, sometimes simply to make the pieces small enough to haul away. When pruning, trimming or limbing, do not reach above

Chain saw mills, such as the Logosol M7 shown here, use a chain saw and special ripping chain for the cuts. A wide variety of milling tools are available these days making it easy to mill logs into boards, planks or beams right on the spot.

chest height, and don't reach far out to make cuts, especially on ladders. When on the ground, regardless of the chore, make sure you maintain a safe, stable stance.

Always make sure the chain is sharp and the tension is set properly. A dull chain is hard on both you and the saw and can cause you to apply pressure. With proper tension, the chain should not move while the saw is idling. Fuel or re-fuel the saw in a safe place on bare ground where nothing is burnable, then move the saw to another location before starting. Place one foot in the rear handle guard and make sure nothing obstructs the chain and the chain is not touching the ground before starting.

MILLING TOOLS

If you have the timber, milling your own wood for post-and-beam, log construction or standard or pole construction is a great way to build your lodge or outbuildings, as well as accessories. These days beams

and construction boards can be cut fairly easily using either a chain saw or **portable bandsaw mill**. Sawing logs into planks, or milling, is most often done by commercial stationary saw-mills. In large-scale operations the logs are skidded or pulled to a load-ing yard. With today's portable chain saw or bandsaw mills the logs can often be milled in place. For a fee a sawyer will bring a portable band-saw mill to your property and saw the log. One-man bandsaw mills are also available for do-it-yourself mill-ing operation. Both chain saw and bandsaw mills have grown in pop-ularity with landowners and wood "scroungers." **Chain saw mills** are the most economical.

The Logosol M7, one-man por-table sawmill consists of a sturdy anodized, extruded aluminum frame onto which logs are rolled. The entire mill weighs only 115 lbs., and can easily be carried by one person and transported even on a car roof rack if necessary. It is easily set-up right at the log site. The log

Granberg produces a number of chain saw mills including the Alaskan MK-III shown here. These mills are basically metal rails fastened to the log to guide the saw chain.

Portable bandsaw mills, such as the TimberKing model shown here, are fully working sawmills, but tend to be much safer than circular saw mills. In addition, the thin bandsaw blade doesn't waste as much material.

Wood-Mizer even has a portable model that can be folded up and stored along a garage wall.

The Logosol Log House Moulder allows you to mill logs into beams with one, two, three or even four flat sides.

is placed on one or two log shelves which can be moved up and down. One end of the log is held in place by a spiked bumper. The chain saw runs on a straight guide rail and saws the log very accurately and extremely smoothly.

The Jonsered SM2095 Chain Saw Mill is powered by their largest chain saw, a 94cc 2095 Turbo. The chain is guided on a mill with two 10-foot rail sections, providing an effective cutting length of 17 feet. The mill utilizes a saw carriage that runs on rails at ground level, making it easy to set up the log without heavy lifting. Precision controls let you mill the type of lumber you want, from siding to thick structural beams.

Granberg has a number of economical chain saw mills, including their Alaskan MK-III, Alaskan Mark III KC2 and their Mini Mill II as well as a Small Log Mill. These are basically rails that are fastened to the log and the chain saw guided by the rails. The Mini Mill II is basically a lightweight edger and saw mill.

Also from Logosol is their Log House Moulder, an accessory for their saw mills. The machine allows you to mill round logs into beams with one, two, three or even four flat sides and in a wide range of log shapes, typically used by kit-built or manufactured log homes. You can even create dado and splined joints with the machine.

Portable bandsaw mills such as the TimberKing models have become increasingly popular. Not only can these mills be towed to a logging site, but they are much safer and easier to use than circular mills. Rather than a huge spinning circular saw blade, these machines utilize a heavy-duty bandsaw blade. The thin bandsaw blade doesn't waste as much material, and if you're cutting for rough projects, the surface is smooth enough to use without further working. The smallest of the TimberKing models is the 1220. It will handle logs up to 12-feet long and up to 29-inches in diameter. With a 15-horsepower, electric start Kohler engine, the price of the mill plus the transport package is a little over $6,000. Although this may sound expensive, processing a few choice logs can more than make up the price. You can also farm-out milling to pay for the machine.

Wood-Mizer also has a full line of portable bandsaws, including one small model that breaks down and is easily stored inside a garage against a wall, taking up very little space.

LOGGING TOOLS

In addition to the milling tools a number of other specialty logging and log working tools are required. The first is an **axe**, and a variety of axes are available. A single-bit is the best choice for most work, and a single-

bit felling axe is used for felling trees, if you are inclined to do all work by hand. A double-bit axe is more versatile, especially if you sharpen one side to a finely honed, narrow "felling edge" and the opposite blade to a more blunt edge for working knots or splitting chores. The head will weigh from 3.5 to 4 pounds. The axe handle should be from 26- to

An essential for the hunt-camp builder is a good axe. These are available in either single or double-bit styles.

Special tools are requided for log and post-and-beam construction. Shown are some of the author's collection, including a broadaxe, froe, adzes, log chisel, hand auger, timber framer's slick, brace and bits and some old-time logging saws.

30-inches in length and of a good grade hickory. A smaller, lightweight 1-½ pound axe with a 19-inch handle is handy for limbing. A carpenter's hatchet can also be handy for many lighter chores. A broad axe has one flat face with the blade ground on the tapered side. This is used for hewing logs into beams. A broad hatchet is used for trimming and smoothing chores. An adz can also be used for smoothing and hewing logs. Two head styles are available, a curved and straight. The curved head, also called a "gutter adz" is used for smoothing the inside round areas for log construction.

Other log or post and beam hand tools include heavy-duty chisels and socket gouges for shaping logs or beams, and cutting and cleaning mortises and other joints. A draw knife is necessary for removing bark as well as for other trimming chores. A bark peeling spud makes this chore easier, but you will still probably have to do some clean-up with the debarking drawknife. A froe is used for making your own split shakes and for other splitting chores. A hand auger can also be used for boring holes for pins and other chores, if you prefer to do it all in the old-fashioned, traditional manner. Log dogs are required for holding logs for marking and cutting. These can be purchased or you can easily make them from reinforcing rod. A scriber is needed for scribing logs for chinkless construction. This can also be purchased or you can build your own.

Moving heavy logs also requires some special equipment. If you have a tractor with a front bucket you can use the bucket to push and roll logs around, but even small logs can be too heavy for many tractors to safely lift with a bucket. A number of tractor skidders are available or you can use a lift and loading tongs to lift one end of the log up for dragging. ATV logging tools are also available, including arch haulers. You can roll and move logs with a peavey or cant hook. A peavey has a sharp point on the end to jab into the log, while a cant-hook has a flatter end. Two people can also tote small logs using a lug hook (log carrier). A come-along can also be used to pull logs into place.

For lifting logs up for walls, you can build a coffin-hoist.

POWER TOOLS

Although they're pretty well taken for granted these days, cordless power tools are a marvel of our age. For instance, I have used a Bosch **cordless miter saw** all day long on the job, merely changing batteries a time or two throughout the day. Drill/drivers were the first cordless power tools and are still the most popular, but these days the range of tools without the tethering cord, is growing rapidly. Following are some of the newest and hottest.

After nine years of research and development, Milwaukee Electric Tool Company introduced the most powerful battery powered tools with their V28 **lithium ion battery** technology. The 28-volt battery delivers increased power and up to twice the run time of traditional 18-volt models, yet the battery weighs slightly less. This breakthrough technology has allowed Milwaukee to introduce new tools like the world's first cordless band saw, yet powerful enough for every day professional use. The V28 line also includes a hammer-drill, circular saw, Sawzall reciprocating saw, impact wrench, work light and battery charger. The V28 technology

A cant-hook or peavey is used to roll logs in place. A come-along or winch can be used to pull and hoist logs.

This cordless variable-speed, reciprocating saw has a jigsaw-type blade and a handle that allows the saw to be used comfortably on vertical surfaces. Battery technology has produced this and other cordless tools that will run all day, do powerful chores and weigh much less than their corded counterparts.

opens the potential for many formerly "corded" products to go cordless. A built-in fuel gauge tells you how much run time is available, while consistent fade-free power throughout the discharge cycle ensures the last job is as powerful as the first.

The Bosch Four-Piece 18-Volt Cordless Combo Kit is the first to feature two "Bluecore" batteries and a 30-minute Dual-Bay Charger. The technology boasts 50-percent more battery life and half the charge time. Positioned between individual cells, "Bluecore" cooling rods absorb and dissipate potentially damaging heat within the battery for extended cycle life—the number of charges each battery will hold. The addition of the 30-minute dual-bay charger, which also utilizes a micro-processor to read the internal battery temperature and optimize the charging process, replaces the standard one-hour single-bay charger. Now, you can charge two batteries simultaneously and in half the time. All "Bluecore" batteries and 30-minute chargers are compatible with current and previous generation tools, batteries and chargers. The combo kit includes the 18-volt Brute Tough hammer drill/driver, 6½-inch circular saw, reciprocating saw and flashlight.

Makita has their MXT **Cordless Drill** Series featuring extreme power, durability and performance. The 3-speed, all-metal gear transmission delivers great torque and efficiency for a choice of light, heavy-duty and extreme applications. Makita's exclusive Shift-Lock driver system locks out the clutch with one touch and quickly shifts from drill to driver modes for superior power and operator efficiency. 3-speed, variable speed and reversible gearing options are also available in the MXT Series and includes a 14.4V and 18V, ½-inch driver-drill kit; 18V, ½-inch hammer driver-drill kit and four 18V Combo Kits. Designed for professional results, the MXT Series has a high-power, two-piece D-31 motor which uses a rare earth magnet for maximum power, efficiency and serviceability. Combo kits include: driver-drill, reciprocating saw; drill-driver, reciprocating saw, circular saw and flashlight; drill-driver, reciprocating saw, metal circular saw and flashlight; drill-driver, reciprocating saw, circular saw, metal circular saw, jig saw, blower and flashlight.

Makita has increased performance and ergonomics on their **cordless impact driver**. With torques of 1,240 and 1,110 inch-pounds. they both tout an impressive 00-3,200 impacts per minute. At 6½-inches, they are the most compact in their class.

Ryobi has tools and accessories in their extremely popular 18-Volt One+System including a Right Angle Drill, Trimmer, Corner Cat finishing sander, Caulk and Adhesive Gun, and In-Vehicle Charger. The One+ 18-volt tools use the same battery platform as all previous and future Ryobi 18-volt tools, making the system interchangeable.

Ryobi has a seven-piece Renovator Combo Kit and a 10-piece Workshop Combo Kit for those serious about home improvements and renovations. The Renovator Kit includes their 18-volt Torque IV drill/driver which allows users to flip a switch and quickly change between drilling and driving modes, eliminating the need to twist the clutch (torque) ring back and forth between the two modes. The Renovator Combo Kit also includes other 18-volt tools: Laser Circular Saw, Reciprocating Saw, Corner Cat Finish Sander, Jig Saw, Tuff Sucker (wet/dry vac) and Flashlight. All come in a durable carrying bag with two 18-volt batter-

ies and a one-hour charger.

The Ryobi Workshop Combo Kit includes a wider variety of 18-volt power tools for home improvement and repair projects inside and out. Tools included are: Torque IV9 Drill/Driver, Right Angle Drill, Impact Driver, Laser Circular Saw, Reciprocating Saw, Jig Saw, Chain Saw, Corner Cat Finish Sander, Tuff Sucker (wet/dry vac) and Flashlight.

Ridgid has excellent tools including their 9.5v Pivoting Screwdriver and 18v adhesive caulk gun. The Pivoting Head Screwdriver offers best in class torque of 100 inch pounds and a variable speed of 0-525 RPM. It features a compact Pivoting Body, allowing use in pistol grip and screwdriver orientation. 16 settings for driving and drilling offer great versatility. A variable speed reversible switch allows for easy starting and driving. A ¼-inch Quick Coupler provides quick bit changes and the driver can be used with existing Ridgid Rapid Max chargers.

The Ridgid 18-volt **Cordless Adhesive/Caulk gun** can handle a wide variety of jobsite applications. It is designed to use 10.1- or 30-oz. tubes of caulk, construction adhesive or roofing sealer. The dual capacity tube holder does not have special fittings or attachments needed to go from one size tube to the other, saving workers time. It has an adjustable speed control that allows for consistent bead application, which enhances the quality of work and means less need for clean up or call backs at the end of the job. It also features a lock-off button to prevent any accidental start-ups that would lead to drips. A heavy duty joist follower aids in adhesive application to studs and joists, and a conveniently attached piercing tool prevents having to look for a nail or wire to get the tube started. The compact battery pack provides plenty of power and comes with a Rapid Max charger, which is capable of charging the battery pack in only 20 minutes.

The Hitachi power tools DMR series of cordless tools includes **impact drivers** and **impact wrenches**, ranging from 9.6- to 18-volt. These tools range from 930 in.-lbs. of torque in the 9-volt impact driver to 1,950 inch-pounds in the 18-volt impact wrench. This allows reduced end-user fatigue as they essentially power themselves through the toughest materials with ease. Equipped with high-capacity batteries, the tools can run longer with fewer charges. The electronic feedback control switch saves time and effort by providing equal torque and rpm in both forward and reverse. An externally accessible carbon brush and replaceable armature greatly increase tool life, limiting down time and saving money. The heart of the DMR line is the industrial grade, two-piece motor with heavy gauge copper coils that makes them extremely powerful and long lasting. Hitachi's unique Cool Flow system provides a steady stream of air to the motor, allowing the impact to run harder and longer, minimizing the risk of burnout. Also in the DMR line are the Hitachi 18- and 14-volt cordless hammer drills. Extremely flexible, they can be set in drill mode to tackle drilling applications, driving mode for fastening applications or hammer mode to hammer drill in concrete and stone. Both feature a keyless chuck, a 22-stage slip clutch, and come equipped with Hitachi's patented five-position belt hook and

an integrated LED work light.

The Hitachi DVF3 series of 18, 14.4- and 12-volt **cordless power drills** are designed to meet the need for compact and lightweight drills that have the power and durability to stand up to tough jobs at a competitive price, they feature two-piece magnet motors and deliver 400 inch-pounds, 300 inch-pounds, and 230 inch-pounds. All three come with two 1.4Ah batteries that ensure longer run time and fewer charges. All offer 2-speed transmissions controlled by a one touch speed shift knob that allows you to select speed needed. They also feature an aggressive, ergonomic design coupled with no-slip rubber grip.

Power tool combination kits are popular sellers among do-it-yourselfers and professionals. But not all combo kits serve both DIY and professional tool user's needs. The Craftsman Custom Combo (C3) program allows you to mix and match power tools and accessories to create your own custom kits for your specific chores. The C3 system revolves around the Craftsman 19.2 Volt Drill-Driver, which is powered by Ni-Cd batteries. For instance you might want a cordless drill, a circular saw and a nailer for home remodeling projects. A hobbyist, on the other hand might desire a jigsaw, trim saw, drill-driver and a pair of battery packs to finish a weekend project. The program actually allows you to "choose your tool—build your own system" without having to purchase separate tools and battery packs. The centerpiece of the combo kits, the 19.2 Volt Drill/Driver, has a two-speed gear box (0-400/0-1,400 rpm), a 24-position clutch to adjust speed and torque and a maximum torque of

420 inch-pounds. The cordless drill's T-handle design features a comfortable overmold grip, while its ½-inch keyless single-sleeve chuck with automatic spindle lock provides single-handed, rapid-bit-changing capabilities. The reversible drill also features LED worklights to illuminate the work area and two bubble levels to enable accurate horizontal and vertical drilling. Other tools that can be added include the **Cordless Trim Saw** with Laser Trac, **Cordless Nailer** that fires staples in six different lengths, **Cordless Jigsaw** with four orbital settings and a saw base that tilts 45 degrees for left or right bevel cutting. The entire list includes a drill-driver, worklight, fluorescent worklight, hand vac, charger, dual-port charger, jigsaw, two battery pack combo, trim saw with Laser Trac, reciprocating saw, in-car charger, a sander, impact driver, right-angle drill, hammer drill, planer, spiral saw and a laminate trimmer.

DeWalt has a first-of-its kind 6-in-1 **driver for power drills and drill drivers**. The innovative tool allows you to quickly change and store six different drivers in one unit, eliminating the need for rechucking to change bits. The patented, easy to use, "flip and drive" design is ideal for installation jobs, furniture assembly, HAVAC jobs and electrical applications. Multiple combination bit sets and sizes are available ranging from Phillips, square drive and square recessed to nut driver, Torx and a slotted driver. The driver is equipped with pro-grade nutsetters and an engineered tip design that helps to reduce stripping.

Also from DeWalt is an 18V Heavy-Duty Steel **Framing Screwdriver**. Designed to deliver increased levels of speed, runtime and durability is it

An air compressor and air nailers can make many chores quick and easy, from framing to siding to roofing to adding trim.

able to perform a variety of fastening applications for commercial dry-wall, MRO, mechanical, HVAC and metal roofing and siding installations. The DC668KA is designed with an innovative Versa-Clutch system that allows you to regulate the amount of initial turning power to ensure the fastener is properly seated and to help prevent stripping the threads.

Air Tools

If you have power to the site, air tools, such as framing nailers, coil nailers and roofing nailers, can cut a great deal of the work, and even make building easier and more precise. An air compressor such as the Porter-Cable 150 Job-site model can provide power for two tools at once.

Stationary Power Tools

Stationary power tools can be a great help for a number of building chores. Jobsite **miter saws**, such as the Rigid Exactline Compound miter saw, are great examples.

A planer moulder allows you to plane planks into lumber and even create your own moulding designs.

Supported on their Miter Saw Utility Vehicle Support they can be used for quickly and precisely cutting framing materials, siding and flooring strips. The Repeat-A-Cut Fence and stop block make it easy to cut all pieces to precise lengths. The Bosch 24-volt cordless model is an excellent choice for working in areas where there is no electricity. With a pair of batteries you're set to go all day. Small jobsite table saws are also handy for ripping materials. The Woodmaster planer/moulder can be used to plane materials to thickness, as well as create your own molding to suit the décor. A jointer is also necessary for jointing or smoothing the edges of rough-sawn lumber.

LAYOUT TOOLS

For laying out the building you'll need string, string level, short-handled sledge and a big right-angle triangle. The latter can be shop-made or purchased. A laser level makes it even easier to lay out the building. A plumb bob is needed as well.

ELECTRICAL AND PLUMBING TOOLS

A pair of **linesman's pliers**, **combination stripper/crimper** and **power testing light**, along with a variety of screwdrivers with insulated handles are necessary for electrical work. A pipe cutter, flux, solder and propane torch are used for soldering copper pipe. A flange tool and cutter, along with wrenches are used for flexible

If you get into trimming and other interior chores, stationary power tools, such as a table saw can be a great help.

copper tubing. A hacksaw is used for cutting plastic pipe.

CONCRETE AND MORTAR TOOLS

The tools needed for concrete work include **woodworking tools** for building forms. A hammer, hand crosscut saw, portable circular saw, measuring tape, square, level and string level, along with a small sledge and a maul are required for building the forms. A pry bar is needed for disassembling the forms. A builder's transit or a laser level can make it easy to level or place a form to grade. **Concrete preparation tools** are also required. The tools needed depend on the jobs you will be doing. Shovels and hoes are required for moving the liquid concrete around. Rubber hip boots are needed for wading in the wet concrete. For small jobs a wheelbarrow or mixing box are required for mixing the materials. A mortar hoe with holes in it makes it easier to mix the materials. A power mixer can also be mighty handy for small- to medium-sized jobs.

Concrete finishing tools include a screeding board that is longer than the pour to pull the concrete off and level it with the form edges. A tamper can also be helpful in settling concrete in the forms. Other essential finishing tools include: an edger, groover, magnesium or wooden float, finishing trowel, pointing trowel, cement broom and a water hose. For larger projects such as floors or slabs, you'll need a bull float with a bracket. The Marshalltown models include their Auto-Just or RotaLeveler. Marshalltown also makes it easy for the beginner with a Concrete Apprentice Tool Kit. It includes: fin-

If you do your own electrical work you'll need the proper tools for the job.

Concrete and mortar chores also require specialized tools.

ishing trowel with DuraSoft handle, magnesium float with DuraSoft handle, wood float, groover, curved end edger, margin trowel, Marshalltown "Tips" book, all included in a sturdy canvas tool bag. For large projects, you may wish to rent a power trowel. The materials in concrete can irritate the skin. Wear long-sleeved shirts, pants and gloves.

Materials

Several years ago my wife Joan and I spent a week's vacation on Lake of the Woods in Canada. In addition to the great walleye angling we enjoyed exploring many of the numerous islands near our island lodge. One of our "finds" was a trapper's line cabin. It was open so we went in and found a cache of storable food, wood and whatever the trapper needed to stay in the cabin. I really don't know how old the cabin was, but some references in a journal found in the cabin with notes from those that had stayed or visited dated back to the turn of the century. The old log cabin was slowly sinking into the earth, but still sturdy. Inside there was just enough room to stand without bumping your head. The roof was log framed and covered with a mixture of tarpaper, branches, moss and I really don't know what-all. Another exploring trip, a side trip during an elk hunt in Idaho, resulted in finding a gold-miner's cabin, again constructed of logs. This old home was in fine shape, and again it dated in the 1800's. The cabin was on private land, and my guide delighted in showing off the old cabin. It was still completely furnished down to a lead bathtub.

Above: Logs have been traditional cabin and lodge material for the ages and they are still a great choice.

Logs in one form or another have been a traditional building material for ages, and are still very popular. If available, they require nothing more than lots of hard work

- How do you determine the potential for logs or milled lumber in trees?

- What is involved in felling and limbing a tree? • How do you use a chainsaw mill?

- How long do you cure wood? • How to get the most use from a portable bandsaw mill?

- What are the choices in manufactured construction materials?

to construct a lodge or home. A **woodlot** or **timber stand** on your hunting property can not only provide wildlife habitat, but wood for constructing your lodge, furniture and other projects. And the trimming can result in firewood to heat your lodge. Not only can logs from the timberland be used, but the logs can be sawn into planks and other lumber that can also be used.

LOGGING

In most instances the first step is to make a timber cruise (walk) to determine the potential for logs or milled lumber, as well as to establish a wildlife management plan for your property. The two do work together; often removing some timber can result in better wildlife habitat. It's not a bad idea to have an expert help with this. Many state agencies have foresters that will do this chore for free, and any number of commercial foresters will do the chore for a fee.

If you do this yourself, a **forester's cruising stick**, or scale can be invaluable for this chore. They resemble a yardstick, but have scales for measuring trees and logs. For instance, you may desire to construct a log building. With the cruising stick you can determine how many logs of a specific diameter and length are available in tree form. Most sticks have three scales. One scale is used to measure tree diameter in inches at breast height (DBH). Another scale can be used for determining the number of logs of a specific length in a standing tree. The third scale is used to determine the board foot volume of a log.

To determine a tree's diameter, hold the cruising stick horizontally

If you have woodland, you may have logs to build your own lodge. A forester's cruising stick is used to determine the size of the standing trees and the logs, or board feet of milled dimension lumber they will produce.

against the tree at about 4½ feet above the ground and at arm's length. Determine the approximate center of the tree and then without turning your head, move your eyes to the left and shift the stick so the zero on the scale lines up with the left-hand side of the tree. Again, without moving your head, shift your eyes to the right and read the number of the right side of the tree. This is the diameter at breast height (DBH).

To determine the number of logs in a tree, first pace off the distance from the tree as indicated on the stick. Holding the stick vertically at arm's length, move it until the zero is at approximate stump height, usually about a foot above ground level. Without moving your head, shift your vision to the merchantable height. In typical logging this means a minimum of about 8 inches for saw logs, however, you may be more interested in diameter for building logs.

After determining the DBH and the number of saw logs in the tree, you can then use the board-foot

*Logging is hard and can be dangerous work. Make sure you follow all safety rules
for safe chain saw use, as well as those for felling, limbing and bucking trees.*

scale to determine the board feet in volume in a standing tree.

Logs for whole-log construction should be as straight as possible and from 8- to 12-inches in diameter. The logs should also be fairly uniform in size. Generally, the better logs for whole-log construction are found in fairly dense stands as they tend to be straighter, with fewer limbs. In most cases, logs should be at least 20 feet in length. You should also determine the species and amount or number of trees. Even a small log building will require around 50 logs. Some species are better than others for different types of construction. For instance pine, spruce and other conifers are the best choice for most **whole-log construction** as they are fairly straight, even in diameter or not unduly tapered and lighter in weight than others woods. Deciduous trees, such as oak, maple, ash and even walnut, can be used for whole log construction and were traditionally used with hewn log construction in many regions. These woods are much heavier and harder to work, but for the most part are longer lasting. The cedars, white and red, can also be used for some purposes. Any of the woods, and others such as sycamore, can be used as timbers, plank or sawn dimension lumber for construction. The latter is available in fairly large size saw logs and light in weight, but the wood tends to split and warp more than other materials.

Logging can be dangerous and is certainly hard work. If you are not experienced you may prefer to have a professional do this chore. With knowledge, attention to detail and observation of safety proceedures, however, you can do this, but it does require some heavy-duty tools.

You'll need a good quality chainsaw for the initial **logging operations**. A wide variety of models and sizes are available, but these days any name-brand chainsaw will do the job. Make sure you follow all safety rules as per the manufacturer's instructions.

General chainsaw safety rules:

1. **Inspect the saw** before each use. Make sure the chain is sharpened and has the proper tension. Make sure the chain brake is working.

2. **Plan your cutting job safely.** Avoid such hazards as electric lines, dead limbs, roads and bystanders. Check wind direction and the lean of the tree to be felled.

3. **Start the saw safely.** The safest method is to start it on the ground. Make sure the saw sits securely, the chain isn't touching the ground. Use your right foot on the handle

to hold the saw in place.

4. **Protect against "kick-back."** Don't modify or remove the chain brake. Always manually activate the chain brake when moving from cut to cut.

5. **Keep a stable, safe stance** while cutting.

6. **Do not saw above chest height,** nor reach far out with the saw.

7. **Wear protective gear including;** eye and ear protection, a helmet, work gloves and protective clothing. Avoid loose clothing.

It is very important to understand all of the the basic cuts. These include: felling, limbing and bucking.

FELLING

Felling a tree is considered the most difficult and dangerous task by many, and indeed it can be. The first step is to examine the tree to determine the direction of lean, if any. If in doubt, use a **string line** and **plumb bob** to see if the tree has any lean. Also examine the **crown**. Does one side have more or larger limbs? Then determine the wind direction. All of these factors have an influence on where and how the tree will fall. If at all possible, fell the tree with its natural lean. Examine for other problems—nearby buildings, other trees, power lines or any other obstacles. Clear the ground around the tree of all obstacles and make at least two escape paths with no obstacles that could trip you. Make sure all pets and people are kept away from the tree during cutting, but do not cut alone. The most common method of felling is with a notch and hinge. A **notch** is cut about two-thirds the way through the tree

trunk. First make a cut parallel to the ground, then a slanting cut downward to meet the first cut. Remove the wedge to create the notch. From the back of the tree, make another cut parallel to the ground and about two inches above the notch cut. Do not cut all the way through. Instead, leave a section of wood to act as a **"hinge."** This will help guide the fall of the tree and also prevent it from kicking back and upward when the limbs strike the ground. Never stand directly behind a tree being felled. A tree butt kicked back in this manner can kill you. Watch the tree and as soon as it begins to lean, remove the saw, shut it off and get away as quickly as possible. If necessary, leave the saw. If the tree leans a bit but doesn't fall, make a slight bit deeper cut from the back, but do not cut through the hinge. If the tree doesn't fall, use **plastic or wooden wedges** driven into the back cut to start it falling.

LIMBING

Once the tree is downed, the next step is to cut away the limbs to leave the final log. In valuable woods such as walnut, even the limbs can be important to the wood forager. Limbing can be as dangerous as felling due to the tension on the limbs from the weight of the tree. Begin limbing on the outer ends of the limbs. Cut the **upper branches** first if possible and work downward and back toward the trunk. If limbs are too high to reach, cut them off at the trunk to allow them to fall downward. The smaller branches and limbs are bucked at the same time they are limbed, cutting them into firewood or saw board lengths, depending on their diameter. Anything

Before felling a tree, examine it carefully to determine if it has any lean. Use a string and plumb bob to eye-ball the tree if necessary.

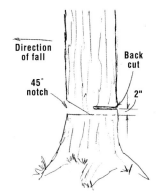

A notch and hinge is the most common method of felling.

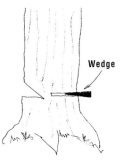

If necessary, plastic or wooden wedges can be used to help the tree begin to fall.

FELLING AND LIMBING

1. Clear all obstacles from around the tree to be felled.

2. Make a cut parallel to the ground, then a slanting cut down to meet the first cut.

3. Remove the wedge and make the back cut parallel to the ground and about two-inches above the notch cut. Do not cut all the way through, but leave a hinge.

4. As soon as the tree begins to lean move away quickly.

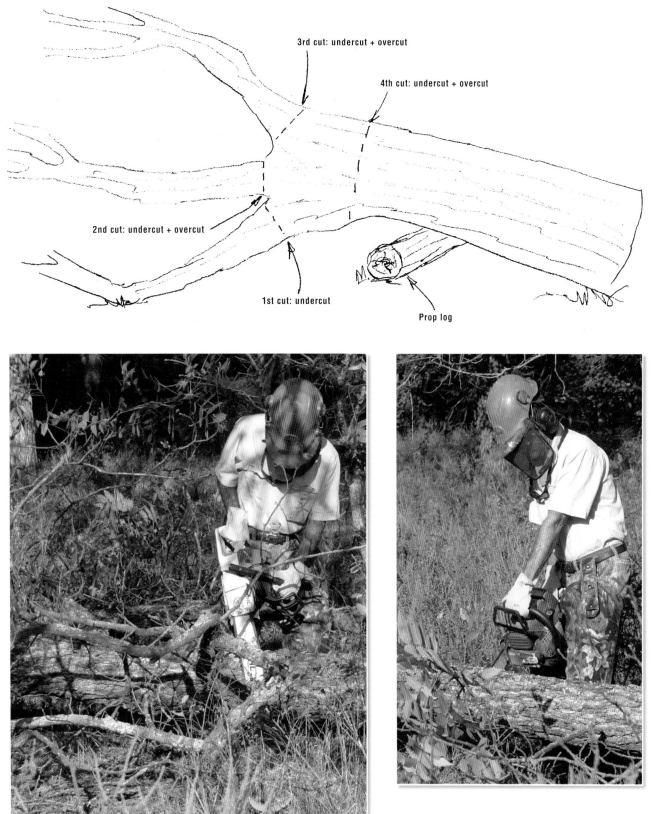

3rd cut: undercut + overcut

4th cut: undercut + overcut

2nd cut: undercut + overcut

1st cut: undercut

Prop log

5. *Use caution when removing the limbs. This can be dangerous due to tension on limbs that contact the ground from the weight of the trunk.*

6. *Once the limbs have been removed, the log can be cut into desired lengths for log construction or milling.*

A tractor, skidder or even ATV, such as the Polaris Ranger shown above, can be used to skid or drag the logs to the building or milling site.

12 to 16 feet. The most important factor, however, in home creation of lumber is **cutting the trunk** to get the most useable wood. This is especially so with crooked trunks. Even two 4-foot sections are better than wasting material in an 8-foot log because the log is crooked.

HAULING OUT OR SKIDDING

Getting logs from the woodlot to the site for whole log construction, or a sawmill for milling, takes a lot of hard work, and is also dangerous. Even small logs are amazingly heavy. For this reason portable bandsaw mills or chainsaw mills that can be transported to the logging site can be invaluable for milling logs.

A tractor, even a compact size, or a heavy-duty ATV or utility vehicle will handle most logs, if you use a **skidding sled**. This tool holds the front end of the log off the ground and allows for easier dragging. A **logging arch** is even better for this purpose and they are available in several sizes for use with ATV's, tractors or even by hand.

A **heavy-duty winch** on a vehicle or ATV can also be used to extract logs from ravines or other tough-to-get-to places. It can also be used for winching logs into place or for loading. It's extremely important to match the size winch to the vehicle. Pull ratings of the different sizes are in pounds, with the maximum pull rating on the first roll of cable on the drum. The pull rating decreases as you increase the number of layers.

Winches can be a great help, but also extremely dangerous. Make sure you know how to use them safely. Three different methods can be used

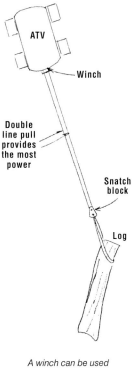

A winch can be used to extract logs from difficult areas.

less than 8 inches in diameter should probably be cut into firewood. Be extremely careful in cutting off the limbs the tree is resting on. A lot of pressure is applied to these limbs. When the pressure is released by cutting, the tree may drop suddenly, or even roll over. Make these cuts slowly and carefully from the bottom of the limbs to release tension and be ready to move quickly out of the way.

BUCKING

Bucking is cutting the tree into firewood, saw-log or construction log lengths. First **determine the length of logs** that can be milled or the lengths needed for a log building. This will depend on whether you have a mill, or plan to have the log milled by a commercial saw mill. In most instances this length will range from for rigging winches. A **straight-line, single-pull rigging** is the simplest, but also provides the least amount of pulling power. The cable is directed in a straight line to the object to be pulled. If you can't get a straight-line pull because of obstacles, you can use a **direction-change pull**. A snatch block anchored to a tree or other secure object with an anchor strap is used for this technique. If you need more power, a third method can be used. This is a **double-line, straight-line pull** with a **snatch block** located at the log. This will, however, reduce line speed. Make sure that all cable is in good shape and that the snatch blocks are of good quality. Anchor the cable with **bow shackles**.

Before using a new cable, or winch, unspool the cable leaving only 4 to 5 wraps on the drum. Then power the cable back on the spool under pressure. Ideally this weight should be around 500 pounds. As you rewrap, make sure the cable goes on smoothly and evenly. This stretches the cable and is used to insure a good wrap around the drum. If you don't do this chore, the outer wraps of cable can draw into the inner wraps, binding and damaging the cable. The winch should have a fairhead roller for easier wrapping and load handling.

Keep the line pull as straight as possible to minimize loading of the cable on one side of the drum and binding. This also insures maximum line pull. Do not winch under load with less than five coils on the drum to prevent the possibility of the cable coming loose. Prevent shock loads when bringing the line taunt by pulsing the switch to take up slack. Monitor the heat of the winch motor when in use by occasionally touching the motor. If the motor becomes hot, shut it off and allow it to cool.

When respooling, an assistant can aid by walking the cable back under pressure. If you are winching alone, use a gloved hand to provide a bit of pressure as you spool to prevent kinks or unevenness.

Follow all **safety rules** when using a winch. A blanket or heavy coat laid over the cable at mid-point can reduce the velocity should a cable break. Do not step over, or allow anyone else to step over a cable under load. Keep any bystanders a distance of at least one and a half times the length of the paid out cable. Always wear heavy-duty leather gloves, safety glasses and helmet any time you're working with cable or winches.

Logs can be loaded on a flat, low trailer using a pair of logs as ramps and a rope harness. Fasten two ropes to the sides of the trailer and lay them out on the ground in front and over the ramp logs. Roll the log in place with a peavey or other means and then grasp the ropes, take them over the log and pull to "roll" the log in place onto the trailer.

MILLING

Sawing the log into **planks or beams**, or milling, is most often done by commercial sawmills and you can transport the log or logs to a mill for the chore. Today, portable and/or one-man mills are also available. For a fee a sawyer will bring a portable bandsaw mill to your property and saw the logs. You can also mill the logs yourself. Both chainsaw and bandsaw mills have grown in popularity with landowners and wood "scroungers."

Sawing with a Chainsaw Mill

Chainsaw mills are the most economical. The Jonsered 600+ Chain Saw Mill is powered by their largest chainsaw, a 94cc 2095 Turbo. The chain is guided on a mill with two 10-foot rail sections, providing an effective cutting length of 17 feet. The mill utilizes a saw carriage that runs on rails at ground level, making it easy to set up the log without heavy lifting. Precision controls let you mill the lumber you want, from siding to thick structural beams.

A portable **chainsaw mill** such as the Logosol M7, one-man portable sawmill is extremely mobile and easy to use. One person can easily transport it to the forest or to your lodge site. The unit is basically a frame with a guide rail that positions a chainsaw to make ripping cuts from a log. You will need a good, heavy-duty chainsaw and Logosol

A portable chainsaw mill, such as the Logosol milling machine can be used to mill logs into various log shapes for log-home building.

recommends either a Stihl MS660 or Husqvarna 3l85XP gas, or E5000 electric chainsaw. You will also need a special **ripping chain** for the saw. One of the main advantages is you can take the mill directly to the log. This means you don't have to drag the log over the ground to a sawing site which often causes dirt, sand and rocks to become embedded in the bark and the log.

Simply set up the frame, making sure all four legs are placed firmly on the ground, preferably on a flat spot. The mill is designed to allow you to roll logs directly from a log table onto the machine's log bed. This provides an easy working height. Then the fun begins. Simply roll the log onto the log bed and crank it up to a working height. Start the chainsaw and saw off the first outer slab, followed by the first non-edged board. Turn the log over and repeat for the opposite side. Raise the log on edge and saw out planks and boards (cutting parallel to the log center.) Turn the log one last time and saw off the outer slab. Then stand the surface boards up and cut the wane or uneven bark edges off.

Portable Bandsaw Mills

Portable bandsaw mills, such as the TimberKing models have also become increasingly popular. These mills can be towed to the logging site, and are much safer and easier to use than circular mills. Rather than a huge spinning **circular saw blade,** these machines utilize a heavy-duty **bandsaw blade.** The thin bandsaw blade doesn't waste as much materials and if you're cutting for rough projects, the surface is smooth enough for use without further working. The smallest of the TimberKing

USING A PORTABLE BANDSAW MILL

1. *A portable bandsaw mill, such as the TimberKing shown here, can not only cut logs into squares, or dimension lumber, but into molding and trim sizes as well.*

2. *Make the first cut.*

3. *The log is rolled to make succeeding cuts to cut the log into a "cant" with four straight sides.*

4. *Cut the "cant" into sizes needed.*

Planks, cants and dimension lumber should be dried or cured. Air-drying will suffice for most building construction . The ends are coated with boiled linseed oil and stacked in a dry place with wooden stickers between the boards to allow for air flow.

Milling Logs

Logs are cut into **lumber** in one of two ways, plain-sawn or quarter sawn. **Plain sawn** is the most common and utilizes less waste. **Quarter sawn** lumber produces beautiful and unusual patterns, but takes more time and wastes more wood. Quarter-sawn lumber resists cupping more, it also wears more evenly and is a reason the method is often used to cut oak flooring.

The best grades and clearest lumber are found immediately inside the bark. In most instances the logs are turned to create a **"cant"** with four straight sides. The log is dogged down and the first cut made. The log is then turned one-quarter turn and another cut made. The log is quarter turned again and another cut made. The log is turned a final quarter turn and the log cut square into a "cant." Then the cant is cut into the thickness desired. As you cut valuable wood such as walnut, you can vary the turning and cuts to garner the most wood. For instance, you may wish to make an initial cut. Turn the log once and make a couple of planks, leaving the bark on one side to garner the most of the center wood. With this tactic you can vary the thickness of the wood needed from as little as one-quarter inch for panels to large blocks for turnings. Don't throw away slabs, these can be used for building slab furniture, or cut into short lengths, they make great firewood.

Curing or Drying

If the wood is to be used in rough-sawn projects, construction beams, planking or fencing, it is sometimes air-dried for a month or two, or even

models is their 1220. It will handle logs up to 12-feet long and up to 29-inches in diameter. With a 15-horsepower electric-start Kohler engine and the transport package, the price for the mill is a little over $6,000. Although this may sound expensive, a few choice logs can more than make up the price. If you have the logs on your property, you can probably pay for the machine. Or, if you don't wish to purchase such a machine, check the local area for someone who does custom band-saw milling to mill your trees.

used immediately. Wood that has cured down to about 25 percent moisture content is the best choice in most instances of planks. One example of a good wood that must be used immediately is **sycamore**. It is light weight, works easily, but twists and curls unless fastened down immediately.

Wood used for fine furniture, house trim, and other precise projects must first be cured or dried. Most woods must be dried down to 6 percent moisture. As with sawmillers, **commercial kilns** may also kiln-dry woods for you. The simplest drying method, although the most time-consuming method, is to **air-dry wood**. This is an ages-old, traditional method. I have air-dried many board feet of lumber in the loft of our barn. All that's required is a dry area with plenty of ventilation. It does, however, take quite a bit of time. Soft woods, such as cedar or pine can air-dry in a couple of years. The hardwoods, such as oak or walnut may require from four to ten years, depending on the thickness and species. Air-dried wood should be "conditioned" for several months in your home or shop.

The first step in drying is to coat all ends with **paraffin** or **boiled linseed oil**. Then stack the wood on a perfectly flat surface with "stickers," or ½ x 2-inch flat pieces of wood placed between the planks. This prevents the planks from twisting or warping, and allows air to circulate and gently dry the wood cells.

Small quantities of wood can also be cured and dried at home with **small kilns**, including solar models. A number of small kiln designs are available on the web from the Department of Forest Products, Virginia Polytechnic Institute and State University Extension. A good deal of this information is linked through www.woodweb.com. Most of these kilns will dry woods such as walnut or oak in two to three months.

You will also need a **moisture meter** to determine the moisture percentage. The Lee Valley Tools Timber Check meter is an excellent economical choice, although there are more sophisticated and expensive models on the market.

Planing and Finishing

Once the wood has been properly cured and dried, it must be kept stored in a dry area and stacked perfectly flat. It can then be planed to the correct thickness and sawed to the widths needed. You can even create your own molding for inside and outside trim.

MANUFACTURED CONSTRUCTION MATERIALS

A 2 x 4 is a 2 x 4, is a 2 x 4. Right? Not necessarily so. The "wood" choices today are innumerable. Lumber is sold as natural wood, pressure-treated wood or manufactured wood products. Natural wood is graded according to the number and types of defects it contains. Manufactured wood products are graded and sold according to their uses. It's important to choose the correct wood for the different constructions and projects.

Natural Wood

Natural woods may be either softwoods or hardwoods. **Softwoods** are made up of the conifers, evergreen

If using purchased wood products for construction, these days a wide range of products is available. This includes traditional dimension materials for framing.

COMMON SOFTWOOD LUMBER GRADES

- **No. 1 (Construction):** Moderate-sized tight knots; Paints well; Siding, cornice, shelving, paneling

- **No. 2 (Standard):** Knots larger and more numerous; Accepts paints adequately; Uses, similar to No.1

- **No. 3 (Utility):** Splits and knotholes present; Takes paint poorly; Sheathing, subflooring

- **No. 4 (Economy):** Numerous splits and knotholes; Large waste areas; Takes paint poorly; Sheathing, subflooring, concrete forms

- **No. 5 (Economy):** Coarse defects and significant waste areas; cannot be painted; Applications similar to No. 4

and cone-bearing trees. The most commonly available softwoods are cedar, fir, hemlock, pine, redwood and spruce. These species are most commonly used as structural lumber, but may also be used for furniture and cabinetry projects. **Hardwoods** comprise the deciduous trees that have broad leaves, produce a fruit or nut and generally go dormant in the winter.

Natural wood can be used **green or air-dried**, but is most commonly sold as **kiln dried**. Construction grade softwoods are commonly dried down to 15 percent, while hardwoods used for furniture and cabinetry are normally dried to 6 percent.

In addition to the general softwood and hardwood classifications, there are also a number of wood species. Some are commonly used, some are less common. Each species has its own characteristics and most common uses.

Standard, **softwood**, **kiln-dried dimension lumber** is the most common for building construction and is readily available and easy to work with. Several species are available including white pine, yellow pine, spruce, fir, Western red cedar and California redwood. According to the Southern Pine Council, southern pine lumber has been used since colonial times. Favorable growing conditions and wise forest management have assured a continuous supply of southern pine products.

Softwood dimension lumber also comes in several different grades. Before selecting the wood, know how you will use it. Each piece of lumber should be grade marked by an agency accredited by the American Lumber Standard Com-

mittee and manufactured in accordance with Product Standards by the U.S. Department of Commerce. Wood products should be identified by **manufactured categories** such as dimension, structural, light framing, decking boards, ceiling and siding. The product should include the pattern name and number assigned by the rules writing agency. This correctly identifies the product and ensures it conforms to standard. Understanding the grades is important but difficult. A number of associations or wood trade organizations all have different grading systems. The grade systems for just one association or organization may entail a number of pages. Other products with their own grades include timbers, mechanically graded lumber, glued lumber, scaffold planks, stadium grade, seawall grades, marine grades, decking, heavy roofing and heavy shiplap boards, and industrial lumber. For a **full grade system**, visit their website. Most building supply dealers will carry only those grades they sell the most of. Your dealer might handle products with a different grading system.

Redwood, with its natural beauty and moisture and insect resistance, is often a choice for quality outdoor projects such as decks, fences and gazebos. The California Redwood Association has its own grading system. Although there are finer grades for interior construction, the garden grades include: deck heart, construction heart, deck common, construction common, merchantable heart and merchantable. These are offered seasoned and unseasoned. They are frequently specified for decks, fences and garden structures where knots or other characteristics have little or no effect. For complete grading information, visit their website.

Western Red Cedar is a wise choice for a number of natural wood projects. It offers dimensional stability, ease-of-use, light weight and its own natural beauty. Western Red Cedar is available in a wide range of products, including siding, decking and dimensional lumber for outdoor use, such as picnic tables and other garden structures. Western Red Cedar siding is available in a wide range of styles and sizes. Patterns include: bevel, the most widely used, is installed horizontally and gives an attractive shadow line; tongue-and-groove can be installed horizontally, vertically or diagonally, and has rough or smooth surfaces; lap house siding is available in a variety of patterns, channel house siding is a popular type of lap siding and can be installed vertically, horizontally and diagonally; board and batten house siding is a vertical design using wide clear or knotty cedar boards, spaced apart with narrower boards.

Softwood moldings are available primed from WindsorONE and Georgia-Pacific's PrimeTrim, making it easy to fabricate intricate exterior molding patterns without the need for priming.

Softwood dimension lumber is sold in standard sizes. A 2 x 4 is actually not 2 x 4 inches, but 1½ x 3½ inches. The table shows the most common nominal sizes and the actual sizes. Softwood lumber is usually measured and sold by the board foot (bdf) or a volume measurement of 144 cubic inches. For instance a nominal one-inch board that is 12-inches long and 12-inches wide is exactly one board foot. Similarly, an 8-foot board that is 2 x 6, measures 2-inches times 6-inches times 8 feet divided by 12 or 8 board feet.

Hardwoods

There is even more variety in choosing hardwoods. A wide range of species is available, many native to the U.S., as well as some exotic imported species. The most commonly used hardwoods include the oaks, birch, walnut, cherry, maple, ash and pecan, but other species are available.

Hardwoods are used for furniture, flooring, cabinetry and interior wood trim. Hardwoods offer the potential for generations of hard use. Their beauty is also not just skin deep. They can live with nicks and scratches and are easily repaired and refinished. Although every board will show the general characteristics of its species, each board also displays a face that is uniquely its own. During the approximately 60 years it takes for a hardwood to mature, each tree develops a one-of-a-kind grain pattern and texture. The grain pattern can also be influenced by the way the tree is sawn at the mill. A **plain-sawn board** is produced by cutting tangentially to the tree's growth rings. It creates the familiar **"flame-shaped" grain pattern**. As this process produces the most lumber, it is the most economical. **Quarter sawn boards** are cut at a 90 degree angle to the growth rings. This method creates some of the most attractive grain patterns in woods such as oak. However, it also yields less wood volume per log, making these boards more expensive. **Rift-sawn boards** are cut at a 30 degree or greater angle to the

CALCULATING BOARD FEET

Multiply the length in feet by the width by the thickness. Divide that amount by 12.

$$\frac{L(ft) \times W(in) \times T(in)}{12} = \text{board feet}$$

Manufactured wood products, such as plywood, or Oriented Strand Board (above) can be used for sheathing, sub floors and other areas.

sells a maple board ¾-inch thick and 5¾ inches wide for around $0.30 per lineal inch, or $3.60 per lineal foot. The exotic woods are sold in random dimensions from 3- to 5-inches wide and 24- to 60-inches long. For instance, a ¾-inch purple heart board runs $10.90 per square foot.

Hardwood lumber is graded according to how many **clear face cuts** can be yielded from a board. These cuts normally range from 2- to 7-feet long. Boards yielding the most face cuts are the highest graded. Many dealers in hardwood lumber handle only the better grades. For more information on hardwood grades, visit their website.

Pressure Treated Lumber

Pressure treated wood has become increasingly popular for many outdoor projects, as well as in some general construction aspects. According to the Southern Pine Council, softwood markets have changed greatly over the past two decades with about 40 percent of all softwood lumber now being produced as pressure treated. Pressure treated wood is available in dimension lumber, radiused lumber for decking and other projects, and as specialized wood products such as posts, deck railing and balusters, as well as plywood.

Arch Wood Protection's Wolmanized Outdoor Treated Wood is treated with a patented **copper-based preservative** and an **organic fungicide**, this product has been proven for more than a decade and across four continents as ideal for applications including decks, play sets, retaining walls, fences, picnic tables, planter boxes, walkways, sill plates and structural members. It comes with a

growth rings. This produces narrow boards with very accentuated vertical or "straight" grain designs that are often chosen when matching grain is important for cabinetry and furniture. Rift sawn lumber is available usually in limited quantities, and is expensive.

Cabinet quality hardwoods are sold in random lengths and widths in order to produce as much material as possible with the least waste. Hardwoods are sold dressed (surfaced) to a specific thickness or in the rough. Standard thickness include 4/4 (one-inch), 5/4 (1¼ inches) and 6/4 (1½ inches), or in larger turning squares and random thicknesses. Hardwoods are naturally more expensive than softwoods. Hardwoods may be sold by the board foot at some local mills or wood dealers. Some of the larger big-box stores may also carry limited amounts of limited species. Hardwoods are available, mail order, but they are not cheap. Many of these boards are sold priced by the linear inch. For instance, Rockler limited lifetime warranty for residential applications, and has earned the Good Housekeeping Seal.

Copper is the active ingredient in the product, protecting against **termites** and most **fungal decay**. Protection against copper-tolerant fungi is provided by an organic azole which has also been used as a fungicide for fruits, peanuts and other crops. The formulation renders wood useless as a food source for termites and fungi while keeping the wood attractive, clean and odorless. Wolmanized Outdoor Wood is a recent addition to the Wolmanized wood family of products. For high grade decking with water repellent added you might consider Thompsonized Wood.

Engineered Wood Products

Engineered wood products have been a main stay in the wood industry for many years, but their uses have become wider as more and more products have been introduced. Engineered wood is a better use of trees, because it uses less wood to make more wood products. **Plywood** is the most common form of engineered wood, as is **oriented strand board (OSB)**. Other common products include **hardboard, flakeboard,** or **particle board** and MDF or **medium density fiberboard**. All have their uses. In addition to the raw materials, specific products have also been introduced, including engineered joists and truss materials, as well as siding and of course paneling. For instance, Weyerhaeuser Trus Joist products include TimberStrand LSL (laminated strand) and Parallam PSL (parallel strand) lumber for framing. These can be used to create straight, flush walls that are criti-

cal for tile application, as well as for kitchen and bath walls that demand ease of countertop installation. Also available are SilentFloor floor joists and TimberStrand rim board, headers, beams and columns. These products create headers that don't shrink and floors that are quieter. Louisiana-Pacific also has engineered I-joists, rim board and laminated veneer lumber (LVL). These offer straighter, stiffer, stronger and more consistent wood products for many construction uses.

Plywood is manufactured from thin "plies" of wood at right angles to each other. This creates a very dimensionally stable product. **Plywood doesn't shrink, warp or swell** like solid woods. And the larger panels allow you to work larger areas without having to glue up or edge-join small pieces. Plywood is commonly used for the larger pieces of cabinets and other built-ins, using solid wood for the facers. Plywood is available as either **softwood or hardwood veneer** faced and for interior or exterior use. It is most commonly sold in 4 x 8-foot sheets, but smaller sheets may be available in hardwood veneers for craft-style projects. The most common thicknesses are ⅛, ¼, ⅓, ½ and ¾ inches. In hardwoods, premium grades will have color-matched faces, so staining and finishing is consistent.

High Density and **Medium Density Overlay** plywood is plywood treated with a resin-impregnated overlay to provide extremely smooth hard surfaces that need no additional finish and have high resistance to chemicals and abrasives. These products are commonly used for highway signs, countertops, cabinets and so forth.

Hardwood plywood consists of inner plies with an exterior hardwood veneer applied. The method the veneer is cut from the log determines the "pattern" and also the cost of the material. **Rotary-cut veneers** are cut from the log like peeling an apple. The continuous slices produce a greatly varying grain pattern. This is the most economical method and is commonly used for birch, oak and ash, or other fairly plentiful woods. **Flat-sliced veneers** are cut from the log, one slice at a time, like slicing cheese. Plywood covered with flat-sliced veneer looks similar to a series of glued-up boards. This material is somewhat more expensive. The method in which the slices are applied to the plywood inner plies is called the "**match**." Random matching is the most economical. Sheets of veneer are randomly chosen, often from different logs and glued in place. This usually results in irregular grain patterns. In slip matching, the slices from one log are butted up against each other in the same manner they are cut from the log. **Book matched veneer** faces are created by turning every other sheet over creating a face that looks like an open book. This is often done with highly figured grain patterns and is the most expensive.

Hardwood plywood may have softwood or a fairly inexpensive hardwood such as poplar for the interior plies. Or the plywood may be combination core utilizing an MDF medium density fiberboard ply between the inner plies and the veneer face. This provides a smoother subsurface for the veneer face, and there isn't as much a problem with tearout when sawing.

The two most commonly used structural panels for building construction are plywood (sheathing) and oriented strand board (OSB). Again, it's important to choose the correct material for the specific job. Because of the construction of plywood with the plies bonded perpendicular, and the majority oriented along its length, plywood is stronger than OSB when applied perpendicular to structural members such as joist and rafters. This makes plywood sheathing a good choice for floors and roofs. OSB panels are manufactured from reconstituted, mechanically oriented wood strands bonded with resins under heat and pressure. OSB is more economical than plywood, does not have any voids and will not **delaminate**. OSB is widely used for roof sheathing, wall sheathing, and as underlayment or subflooring and even as single-layer flooring. OSB, however, is not moisture resistant and once wet it swells and stays that way. Georgia Pacific's Plytaniuim Sturd-I-Floor products protect **subfloors** during construction with a water repellent coating. They also have a smooth, sanded surface that allows you to install floor coverings directly on the subfloor with no additional underlayment. The products also feature APA Quick-Fit tongue-and-groove design to fit panels together. Louisiana-Pacific Corporation's OSB flooring has a patented notch system that quickly drains away surface water.

Flakeboard and **particleboard** are similar in appearance, but are not span or exposure rated and should only be used for interior, non-structural situations. These products also have grades or ratings, according to span and exposure.

One of the most popular newer

materials for many purposes these days is **medium density fiberboard (MDF)**. Consisting of pulverized cellulose fibers, mixed with glues and resins and formed into sheets using heat and pressure, MDF is sanded to an exact thickness. It's a great material for veneered furniture panels and tabletops as well as for painted cabinets. It is relatively inexpensive, extremely stable and available in a variety of standard thicknesses. It is designed only for interior use, is heavier than plywood and when sawn, routed, or otherwise cut, produces a cloud of fine dust. You need a dust mask when working with it. Medium and high density fiberboard is also available as a flooring subfloor.

Hardboard is similar in construction to MDF, but is made of ground wood pulp and resin. Hardboard is available tempered or untempered, smooth on one or both sides. Hardboard is a popular choice for cabinet backing and drawer bottoms. It is also available as a siding material. Hardboard is not moisture resistant, unless treated.

Siding may be natural, or engineered wood. Engineered wood siding may be manufactured as conventional veneered plywood, as a composite or as oriented strand board siding. Both panel and lap sidings are available. Special surface treatments, such as V-groove (such as APA Texture 1-11), brushed, rough sawn and texture embossed (MDO) are available.

Louisiana-Pacific offers a wide range of engineered sidings that offer the look of authentic wood siding without many of the maintenance problems. Three products include: LP's Canexel Sidings for northern markets, a pre-finished high density siding that comes in a variety of profiles and deep rich colors. For traditional markets, LP ABT siding offers one of the widest ranges of lap, panel, soffit and trim products. LP SmartSide siding is another product with a variety of complementing trim, soffit and fascia products. These products are quickly installed and some have hidden nail installation for a blemish-free appearance.

Paneling

Paneling consists of wood products joined in a continuous surface, especially **decorative panels** for interior wall applications. Panels may also consist of natural woods, or manufactured wood products. The latter may consist of plywood or composite panels. APA, the Engineered Wood Association represents most of the nation's wood structural panel manufacturers. A wide range of informative publications are available. For more information on paneling visit the APA website.

Wood is one of the world's truly renewable resources. It's also available in a myriad of forms, and it's important to understand the various wood products and their uses for building construction, garden construction, cabinetry and furniture.

Layout, Foundations, Footings & Slabs

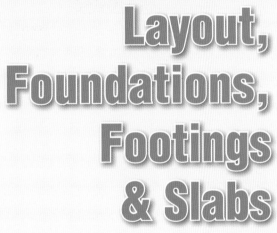

Above: For small pours you can mix the materials on site using Portland Cement, sand, gravel and water.

Properly laying out the building and providing a good solid foundation is extremely important. The complexity of layout, and type of support, depends on the building size, construction type, soil conditions and local codes. Unless you're building in the true wilderness, there will probably be building codes to follow and you will probably have to acquire building permits. Check with local authorities as you plan the construction. I've seen log cabins supported on dry-laid rocks, and some still stand, although they usually develop some sort of "slant." On rock-solid ground and building an economical log structure this can work. In most cases, a standard footing plus foundation or slab is the best choice. If building with logs you'll need plenty of pier support. Unless you're experienced at constructing and pouring concrete and/or block footings and foundations, you may wish to job out this chore to an expert. This is not to say you can't do it. Even a first-timer can work concrete and lay blocks, but it's hard, back-breaking work and proper construction steps must be followed to ensure a safe, long-lasting building support.

FOUNDATION TYPES

Four basic types of foundations are commonly used. The simplest, and most economical, is a **pier footing**. This may consist again of flat rocks, concrete blocks or poured concrete piers. The latter are the best. Make sure you check

FOUR BASIC TYPES OF FOUNDATION

CONCRETE SLAB

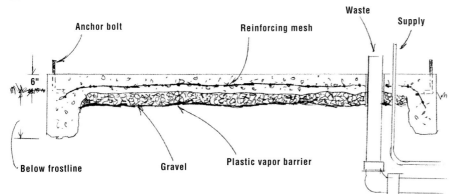

Four basic types of foundation or support can be used on log cabins and hunting lodges, depending on local code rules, soil type, building construction and other factors. They include: piers, poured slab, perimeter foundation (of concrete, concrete block or mortared stone) and a poured basement combined with perimeter foundation.

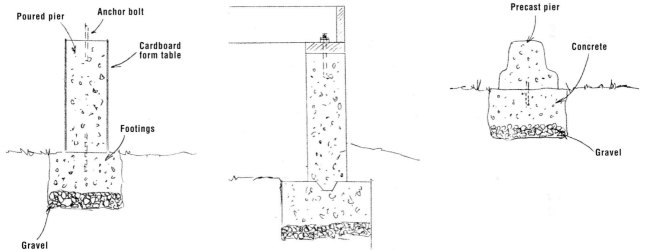

| POURED PIER | PERIMETER FOUNDATION | PRECAST PIER |

with local authorities as to the possible use of piers. In some areas, due to soil conditions, piers are not feasible. **Concrete piers** are normally created by drilling or digging a hole, placing a cardboard form tube in the hole then pouring the footing. Bigfoot Systems, Inc., Bigfoot Tube 8-inch is an 8-inch tapered cone made of recycled HDPE. The innovative interlocking design uses four individual pieces to form a 4-foot long tube. A safety top keeps dirt, rain, kids and pets from falling into the tube prior to pouring the concrete. Piers must be set below the frost line or they will heave in the winter months. Normally piers are formed 2 feet square. The **pier tops** should be established level and at least 18 inches above ground level to provide for good air circulation. Piers may be poured as one piece or as footings with piers on top. The latter provides a wider base, best for heavy construction such as logs. Piers should be spaced around the house perimeter as well as provide support for any **girders**. Check with local codes as to spacing. A **concrete block pier**, constructed on a footing is

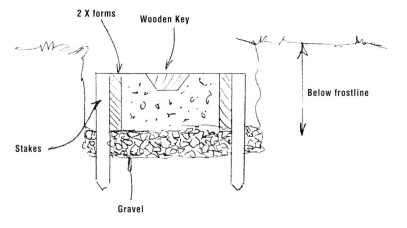

Regardless the foundation, supports must be braced by a footing, constructed according to local code rules.

another option in some areas.

Another extremely common and fairly simple foundation is a **poured slab**. Any utilities such as water, sewer and in some cases electrical outlets must be in place before the slab is poured. Although pouring a slab is hard work, it is not as complicated for the first-timer as some other projects. Slabs consist of a one-piece pour of wall support, concrete floor and a footing that extends below frostline. If log interior walls are to be used a footing should be placed under the wall locations as well.

The third type of foundation is called a **perimeter foundation** and consists of a wall built to support the structure, creating a crawl space beneath. These may be made of poured concrete, concrete blocks or even mortared stone.

A **poured basement**, either full, or in combination with a perimeter foundation is the most complicated, requiring lots of special forms and expertise.

All of the foundations, except the one-piece pier, require a **proper footing**. This must be created at a depth just slightly below the frost

line in your area. Again, check with local authorities. In most instances the footing must be at least 8-inches thick. Some local codes, however, require 12-inch thick footings. If building with logs, the footing and foundation should be wider to support the weight.

LAYING OUT A BUILDING

Properly laying out the building is essential. Take your time and make sure you get it right. Laid out incorrectly, a building can be a nightmare. The most important factor is **getting the building square**; or rather the foundation the building rests on must be square. If the foundation is done correctly, the building construction will be much easier.

The first step is to simply mark the outline of the building with **stakes** at each approximate corner. Drive a stake at one corner, making sure it is solidly in place and can't be knocked over. Then drive a No. 6 nail into the top of the stake. Using a tape measure, measure one long wall, drive a stake and place a nail in its top at the exact wall length.

The next step is to establish the adjoining wall at a true 90 degree angle to the first. Again, measure the wall length and temporarily drive a stake. Run a **string line** between the first two stakes and over to the third stake. Several methods can be used to determine 90 degrees. The first is to measure 9 feet from the nail on one string and mark with an indelible marker. Then measure 12 feet on the adjoining string and mark it. Measure between the two marks. The distance, or hypotenuse of the triangle, should be 15 feet. If not, move the third stake in or out to achieve the proper distance. Layout the remainder of the building corners in the same manner. You can also make up a **wooden triangle** of 1 x 2s. The triangle should have sides of 3, 4 and 5 foot. You can simply lay this triangle against the strings to determine 90 degrees.

Once four corners have been established, measure diagonally between two and then between the other two. The measurements should be the same. If not, adjust stakes until they are equal.

After the corners have been established, **batter boards** are used to create a permanent perimeter mark at all corners. These will stay in place until the footing and foundation has been created. 2 x 4 stakes are driven solidly in place and boards nailed to their outside edges. A batter board is established on both sides of each corner. The batter board tops must also be level with each other. A string line and string level or laser level can be used to make sure all boards are level with each other. Once the boards are level, a string line is established again crossing from the boards directly over the nails in the original stakes. A **plumb bob** is used on the strings to reestablish the corners, driving nails in the batter board tops to tie off the strings. This establishes the outside boundaries of the foundation.

To establish the **footing** and **foundation widths**, measure their widths

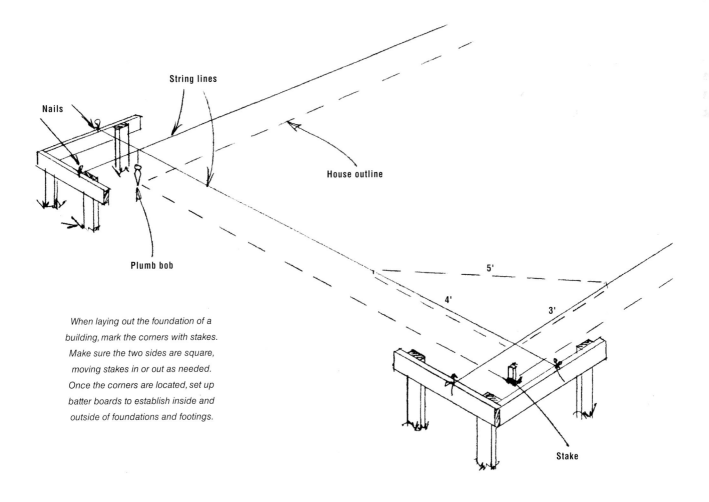

String lines

Nails

House outline

Plumb bob

5'

4'

3'

Stake

When laying out the foundation of a building, mark the corners with stakes. Make sure the two sides are square, moving stakes in or out as needed. Once the corners are located, set up batter boards to establish inside and outside of foundations and footings.

on the batter boards and drive nails for additional string lines. Mark each nail as to its purpose with an indelible marker. Now any **footing excavation** can be done first using a bit of lime to mark the footing outlines following the string lines. Then remove all string lines and excavate the footings. Even if using pier supports, batter boards should be used to hold string lines to locate the piers. Slabs are laid out in the same manner, and in many instances the edges will have a **stiffener footing** poured at the same time as the slab.

WORKING WITH CONCRETE

Concrete is one of the most versatile building materials. It can be used for anything from entire buildings to portions of buildings, sidewalks, patios, post holes, steps and even decorative projects. Concrete work is also easily learned, although it can be back-breaking. Concrete is a mixture of sand, gravel and **Portland cement**. This is not a brand name, but a type. Cement is available in five types, but Type I, which is carried by most building supply dealers, is the most commonly used type for homeowner projects. The materials must be mixed with enough water to form a semi-fluid state which is then poured into a form.

Concrete is heavy and the single key to safe and effective pours is in building sturdy forms. Concrete is available in three ways: **individual bags of cement**, normally packaged in one-cubic foot bags of 94 pounds, which is mixed with separate gravel and sand aggregates; **Quikrete**, which comes in a bag, prepackaged with the required aggregates;

and **ready-mix**, delivered by a truck to the site. Quikrete offers the most convenience for small projects, such as anchoring posts. Merely mix with water according to the package information and pour in place. Mixing your own with cement and aggregates is more economical, but you must have the separate materials on hand and measure them properly. This is also a good choice for small- to medium-size projects.

Mixing with a **powered cement mixer** should be considered for medium-size projects. With this method you can, for instance, pour a wide walk in sections, forming one section, pouring it, allowing it to cure and then pouring another. For strength and performance, concrete pours should be all at one time, unless they're fairly large, in which case they're poured in sections.

The cement, sand, coarse aggregate and water must be mixed in the correct proportions in order to create a durable, long-lasting job. There should be enough **large aggregates (gravel)** to make the mix economical. Yet there should be enough **small aggregates (sand)** to fill in the spaces around the larger aggregates. There should be enough cement to hold all the materials together and the right proportion of water to mix the components and bind them together. The amount of water needed varies with the dampness of the sand. The less water used, the stronger the concrete, but there should be enough water to make the material workable.

A common mixture for foundations and footings is one part cement, three parts small aggregates and four parts large aggregates.

Driveways, garage floors, walks and steps should be mixed one part cement, two parts small aggregates and three parts large aggregate. I like to mix with a **square cement shovel**. Merely count the shovels full of materials. Or you can use a bucket as a measuring device. The amount of water for average work, with slightly damp sand, which is fairly common, is about 6 gallons of water per bag of cement.

Finer pours, for basement walls, walks, garage floors and driveways with the same moderately damp sand would require about 5½ to 5¾ gallons of water. Regardless, thoroughly mix the dry materials together first, then slowly add the water, thoroughly mixing as you go. You may find you don't need quite as much water, or you may need more.

If building a floor, slab, or foundation, the best choice is **ready-mixed delivery**. To order the correct amount of concrete tell the supplier the width, length and thickness of the slab or foundation you intend to pour. They'll help you calculate the quantity needed. On smaller jobs you can figure your own.

Forming

If forming a slab, the first step is to dig up the area and remove all sod and debris. The area should also be recessed to the desired depth. For instance, a four-inch pour might be recessed so that the top is slightly above ground level. The entire area should be well compacted and of a uniform depth. Keep the ground slightly moist as well. The form is then constructed using 2 x 6s. Stakes are driven into the ground on the back (outside) side of the forms every 3

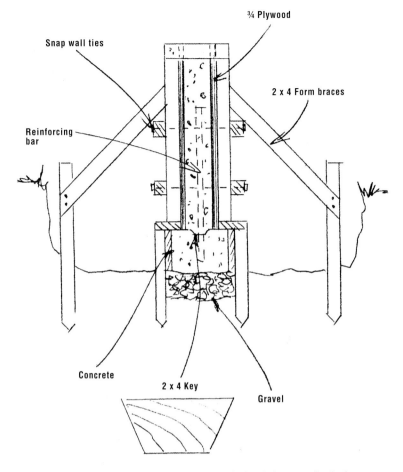

Concrete, poured in wooden forms is often used for foundations as well as footings and slabs. It's important to build strong, correctly sized forms.

to 4 feet apart. The stakes should be driven or cut off flush with the tops of the **form boards**. The stakes are fastened to the form boards using duplex nails, or nails with double heads to they can be pulled out after the concrete sets.

Curved areas can be formed with ¼-inch plywood or hardboard. Make sure the forms are level or of the grade desired. A **carpenter's level** can be used for small projects, a **string level** can be used for long runs, but a **builder's transit** is best for larger pours. A **uniform grade** is then established, using sand or fine gravel 1- or 1½-inches deep. If the slab is large, you will need to divide it into smaller,

WORKING WITH CONCRETE

EXAMPLE OF MARSHALLTOWN'S REQUIREMENTS FOR CUBIC YARDS OF CONCRETE						
Area in Square Feet (width x length)	10	25	50	100	200	300
4-in. thick	0.12	0.31	0.62	1.23	2.47	3.7
5-in. thick	0.15	0.39	0.77	1.54	3.09	4.63
6-in. thick	0.19	0.46	0.93	1.85	3.7	5.56
(Cubic Yards does not allow for losses due to uneven subgrade, spillage, and so forth. Add 5 to 10 percent for such contingencies.)						

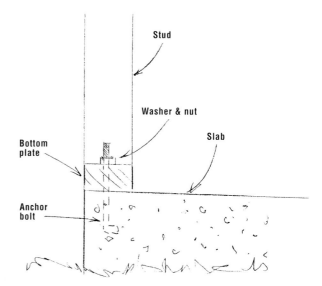

Anchor bolts must be installed in the wet concrete in foundations or slabs to anchor the walls in place.

1. *If a larger pour of concrete is necessary, concrete will be delivered in bulk trucks.*

2. *As the liquid concrete is poured in place, excess material is screeded or dragged off with a 2 x 4.*

3. *The next step is to float the surface to smooth it up. Here a large bull-float is used.*

4. *On slabs, walks and other areas, the surface is troweled smooth. This can be done with hand or power trowels.*

easily worked sections. Driveways and garage floors will need to be re-inforced with **steel rods** or **wire mesh**. Footings and foundations should also be reinforced according to **local code regulations**. Driveways and garage floors are usually poured 4- to 6-inches thick. Sidewalks and other works are usually poured 3- to 4-inches thick. Foundations and foot-ings are poured to code.

Making the Pour

Concrete should not be poured on extremely hot, dry days as the con-crete will dry out before it can cure properly. Concrete should also not be overworked. For this reason the concrete should be spread evenly and quickly once the pour begins. Make sure to overfill the forms slightly. If the pour is overworked, too much water will be floated to the surface, which can cause scaling after the concrete dries.

Once the concrete is well spread over the area and into all corners and crevices, use a **screed board** to drag off the excess. This is a two-man operation and at best is hard work, especially on larger pours. The screed board should extend past the form edges about 3 inches on either side. Beginning on one end of the form, place the screed board over the form boards and then, using a side-to-side mo-tion and at the same time pulling the board, inch it across the form boards to the opposite end. Screed-ing levels the concrete with the tops of the form boards, pulling excess concrete off. Any low spots will be visible and should be immediately filled and the area rescreeded. In standard construction, **anchor bolts**

are needed to anchor the walls to the foundation or slab edges. These can be placed in holders nailed to the form edge, or pushed in place as the pour is made. The first provides the best method as precise loca-tion is established. The anchor bolts must always fall between studs. If you locate one under a stud you've got problems.

The next step is to **float the sur-face** which will take some of the initial roughness off. Do this imme-diately after screeding. Small proj-ects can be floated with a **wooden or magnesium float**. This helps fill any small voids and works the ag-gregate slightly below the surface. On larger pours a **bull float** is used. The float is pushed away from you across the surface with the front edge slightly raised to prevent the blade from digging in. The float is then pulled back at an almost flat angle. The Marshalltown Rota-Leveler **bull float bracket** allows for easy changing of the float level on the push and pull strokes. Floating smoothes the surface and works some water to the surface.

Concrete and Temperature

Freshly mixed concrete is a plastic liquid, the result of a chemical reac-tion that causes the formation of mi-croscopic crystals that bond sand and gravel. The ideal temperature range for pouring concrete is 40° to 80° F. In hot weather, the reaction happens quickly. In cold weather, the reaction slows. Rain and snow melt-water will soak into the con-crete surface, freeze and expand fracturing the crystals that hold the sand and gravel together. In order for concrete to **cure properly**, tem-

SAFETY TIPS FOR WORKING WITH CONCRETE

- Prevent back injuries when lifting heavy concrete bags by squatting and using your legs—not your back.

- Wear goggles to prevent eye injuries from splashing caustic materials.

- Use a dust mask to filter out concrete dust.

- Wear waterproof shoes to protect your feet if standing in concrete.

- Wear chemical resistant rubber gloves to avoid skin irritation.

- Wear knee pads when floating or troweling.

perature minimums and moisture levels must be managed during the curing cycle to ensure that proper 28-day strength characteristics are achieved.

To pour long-lasting concrete in cold weather:

1. **Do not pour concrete on frozen ground.** All items that come in contact with concrete should not be below 32° F. Place tarps over the area and run a heater to raise the ground temperature.
2. **Increase the amount of cement in the mix slightly.** Mix the concrete with hot water or use special Portland cement that develops early strength.
3. **Once the concrete is poured** and finished, spray a liquid curing compound on the surface.
4. **Place insulated blankets** over the concrete for a minimum of four days.
5. **Since the chemical reaction in concrete produces heat,** insulated blankets will keep the heat inside the concrete as long as the edges of the blankets are weighted down.
6. **Do not allow concrete to prematurely dry out.**
7. **Keep ice from forming.**
8. **Use insulation blankets or heaters.** Avoid direct contact with heaters to avoid dusting.
9. **Use extra insulation** at corners and edges of walls.
10. **Remove heat protection** slowly to prevent rapid cooling.
11. **Leave forms in place** long enough to prevent rapid drying.

Finishing

Concrete finishing consists of several steps. Some steps should be done regardless of the desired roughness of the surface. Some concrete finishing results in either a roughened or a smooth surface. Regardless, the first step is to use a pointing or margin trowel to separate the edge of the concrete from the form. Then use an edger around the top edge of the form. This creates a rounded edge that won't chip off when the form is removed. The edger should be held fairly flat, but keep the front tilted up slightly when moving forward and the rear tilted up slightly when moving backward.

Jointing is the next step on projects such as sidewalks and driveways. This prevents cracking of the slabs. Control joints are normally spaced at intervals equal to the width of the pour. It is recommended, however, not to exceed 10-feet in any direction without a joint. The joint should be cut at least one-fourth the depth of the slab. A **jointer tool** is used for this step. Place a straight-edge across the surface and run the jointer along the straight edge to create a nice straight line. As with the edger, hold the front up slightly when pushing forward. After the concrete cures, control joints in large slabs can also be cut using a masonry blade in a circular saw or concrete saw.

A **float** is used next to smooth and level the surface. This will also help remove any marks left by the edger or jointer. For rough or textured surfaces, use a wooden float. For projects requiring a smoother finish, use a magnesium or aluminum float. Hold the float flat on the surface and move it in an arc, overlapping the arcs as you proceed. Don't overwork the surface.

The final finishing step is **troweling**. Small projects can be hand troweled. Marshalltown recommends a 14 x 4 or 16 x 4 trowel for most finishing jobs. The first troweling should be done with the blade held flat down on the surface. Again use the trowel in an arc, overlapping each previous arc by about ½ inch. The surface should be well troweled several times to produce a hard, durable surface. Allow the concrete to set up slightly for the additional troweling. The proper time is when the sheen of water disappears and a footprint leaves less than ¼ inch of an indentation. These trowelings should be done fairly vigorously and with the trowel tilted up slightly, pressing down with the edge. A power trowel, available at most tool rentals, is the best choice for large slabs. Troweling will provide a smooth, hard and slick surface. These surfaces are easy to clean, but can be slippery when wet. Lightly brooming the surface with a shop broom after troweling can provide a rougher, more non-slip surface.

Curing

Keep the concrete damp for five to seven days after pouring. Do not allow it to dry out. Cover it with plastic sheeting and dampen the surface every day or so.

CONCRETE BLOCK FOUNDATIONS

Concrete block **perimeter foundations** can also be established on poured footings. These are somewhat less complicated than poured foundations, and easier for the first-timer. Rather than having to complete the foundation all at one time, you can lay concrete blocks as you get the time and energy. You might wish to mix a batch of mortar and lay a row, quit for the day and start again the next. Blocks are available in several types and can weigh from 25 to 50 pounds, so the work is still hard. **Standard blocks** are normally 8 inches wide, 7⅝ inches high and 15⅝ inches long. This allows you to place a ⅜-inch mortar joint and end up with an 8 x 8 x 16-inch block space. **Interior wall blocks** are commonly 4 inches wide. Check local suppliers as to what types are available. If using log construction, make sure you use heavyweight blocks suitable for the support needed, even on interior walls.

The most important factor is to make sure the footing top is level and smooth. Again, **batter boards** are used to establish the **outside perimeter** of the building, laying the blocks to the string line. Mix only enough **mortar** to do about 30 minutes work. More than that and the mortar may set up too quickly to work easily. You'll have to experiment to discover the amount you'll need.

Mix mortar in a wheelbarrow, mortar tray or with a power mixer. You will probably also need a mortar board to carry the mortar to the area and hold it while you're using it. Use **Type M mortar**, designed for use with foundation walls. This is a mix of 1 part Portland cement, ¼ part hydrated lime and 4½ parts clean sand. Mortar comes in 80 pound bags. Or you can use **premixed mortar** such as Quikrete Mortar. In this case the mix is already established. Regardless of which is to be used, dry mix all the parts well before adding water. Then add just enough water to provide a

A concrete block foundation, while it is hard work, is fairly easy to do as it can be done a little at a time. Begin with the corners and build them up, before filling in between. Use a string line and line level to align and level the rows of blocks.

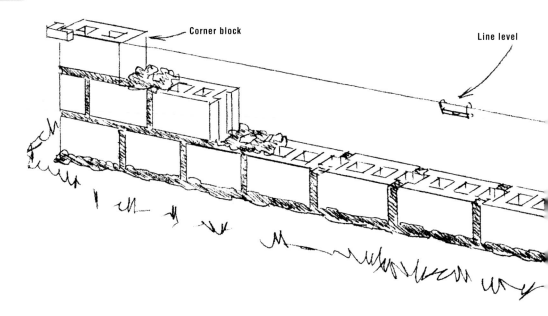

Corner block

Line level

pliable consistency. Add a little water at a time, mixing thoroughly. Properly mixed mortar that is pliable, yet holds its shape and doesn't slump when pulled up with the mixing hoe.

You may wish to lay out the first course dry to determine the course layout of the blocks. Position a block at each end of the building corner. Use the **plumb bob** on the **batter board strings** to make sure the blocks are at the exact corner ends and then dry-lay the blocks between, leaving ⅜- to ½-inch spacing between. Incidentally, if using concrete blocks for the foundation, the best building size is in increments of 16 inches. You can cut blocks in half, but it's almost impossible to cut to any other size unless you have a concrete saw.

Once you have determined the course layout, position the blocks on end and out of the way, but within easy reach. Start the first course by laying a beginning block at a corner. Apply mortar to the footing about 2 inches wider than the block and about 1½ inches thick. Grasping the block on both ends, gently lower it

in place. Make sure it is set properly, again using a plumb bob on the string lines. Go to the opposite corner and set the corner block in the same manner. Using a **mason's string holder** on the corners of each block, position a mason's string between them. Make sure the string is set at the top edge of the block and then use a string level to make sure the blocks are set level. If one is higher, gently tap it downward. If a block is turned in or out from the string line, shift it sideways as needed. Now you can lay the remainder of the blocks, spaced as before, following the string line between the two corner blocks.

To **place the blocks**, turn the block on end, trowel mortar on the edge that goes against the previously set block, grasp each end and smoothly, but quickly, lower the block in place. It takes a bit of practice to keep the mortar from sliding off, but if the mortar is the correct consistency, it eventually becomes fairly easy. Make sure that the outside top corner of the blocks meets the string line and the blocks are set level with

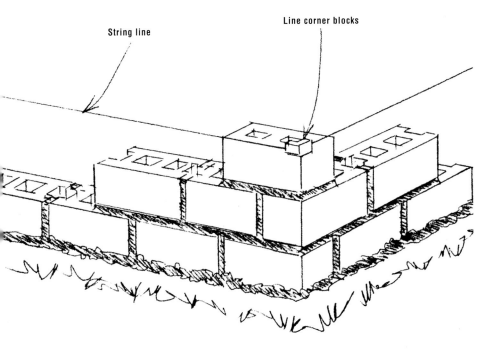

String line

Line corner blocks

each other and level crosswise. Use a small mason's level to determine level. Finish off with a closure block with mortar on each end.

If you need to cut a block, a **concrete saw** can be a great help. You can, however, cut blocks in the center using a **brick chisel** and **short sledge**. Position the block on its side on a smooth, hard surface. Place the chisel over the center slot and tap along the center line. Don't attempt to break it from one side; just "score" that side. Turn the block and tap to score on the opposite side and the block will break in half. Again, this will take some practice.

The next step is to **build up the corners**. This is done by placing a block at the end of the joining wall, positioning the string line between the just laid course and the starter block on the adjoining corner. Then add a few blocks to the new course.

Mortar the top of the corners and set blocks crossing the previously laid blocks. Move the string line up as you start each course, making sure the blocks are laid level with each other and are not canted in or out. Continue to lay blocks at each corner until you can't lay any more without extending the courses.

Be sure to add **steel reinforcing** to the block foundation according to the building codes. In most instances, this means girders placed between courses. Once you reach the top course, add **anchor bolts** in mortar placed in the blocks. Use a **steel lintel bar**, or **one-piece lintel block** to provide support over a crawl space or other opening. As the blocks are laid, use the edge of a trowel to scrape off squeezed-out mortar and flip it back onto the mortar board. Use a jointing tool to compress the mortar between the blocks and finish it off.

Standard Construction

In many instances, standard construction, or stick framing techniques are used for constructing a hunting or fishing camp lodge, storage buildings and outbuildings. Standard house framing is fairly simple and in some cases you can actually purchase a "kit" of materials, including construction plans. Or you may simply purchase the plans. You can, however, design your own fairly easily. Construction methods are fairly standard. Two methods are used, balloon and platform. Balloon is used sometimes with two-story buildings. Platform can be used for either and is the most common. Constructing a single story building is the easiest, a two-story or split-level is harder. Standard platform construction can be done on a slab or on a foundation. The foundation first requires a floor to be constructed. Then the walls are framed on the floor (or slab) and raised in place. Make sure you check with local building authorities as to regulations regarding framing in your area.

Above: Two methods are used in standard house or stick construction — platform or balloon. Platform is the most common on single-story buildings.

PLATFORM CONSTRUCTION

The first step is to "build" the floor on the foundation. **Sill plates** are anchored to the foundation, then the floor joists are fastened to the sill plates and their ends boxed in with joist headers. The headers and outside joists should fit flush with the outside edge of the foundation. **Metal hangers** make installing the joists easier than toe-nailing in place. In many instances of larger buildings, or those with joist spans over 16 feet, a girder is installed to provide support for the floor at midpoint. The **girder** should be supported by piers or foundation and footing. With the flooring framed in, **decking** is added. This is typically ¾-inch plywood or sheathing, or OSB, oriented strand board. In the past, if sawing your own wood, solid ½-inch stock was often used as decking or subflooring. Home-sawn wood has to be cured or it will warp once applied. Solid wood decking is applied diagonally across the joists.

After the deck has been constructed you're ready to construct and erect the walls. The walls consist of **sole plates** nailed to the subflooring, or in the case of a concrete slab, anchored with **anchor bolts**. Studs are nailed to the sole plates and **top plates** are nailed to the studs.

Actually the walls are assembled in one piece, or in the case of long walls, in sections joined together to create the length needed. The first step is to lay a sole plate and top plate side by side and determine any door and window locations. You must know the **rough-opening size** of any doors and windows. Using a **carpenter's square**, mark the rough opening locations. The tongue of the square is 1½-inches wide, the exact width of kiln-dried framing materials. Then mark stud locations. This may be on 16- or 24-inch centers, depending on building design or local codes. Mark both the sole and top plate at the same time. If installing on a **poured concrete floor**, position the sole plate against the **anchors** and mark their locations. Drill holes for the anchors.

Lay the sole and top plates on edge the proper distance of the stud lengths. If you use **pre-cut studs** you can save money and time. A framing nailer can also save time if you

have power at the building site. Several years back my daughter helped frame a building and she had never "swung a hammer." Using a **framing nailer** she had no problems, and we completed the building in a short time. Fasten the studs between the **plates**, positioning their ends in the previously marked locations. You will have to add **headers**, and **double studs** to any doors and headers, double studs and **jack studs** to any windows. The jack studs, fall on the same measurements as the wall studs, 16- or 24-inches on center.

In many instances **hurricane bracing** is added to the walls. These consist of purchased metal strips or 1 x 4s set diagonally across the wall and cut into the outside edges of the 2 x 4s. With the sole plate and top plate nailed into the stud ends, use a tape measure to measure diagonally from corner to corner and then from opposite corner to opposite corner. Shift the wall until the measurements are the same, creating a "square" wall. Lay the hurricane bracing in place, mark the cut locations and use a saw to cut the notches, cleaning out the bottom of the notches with a chisel. Anchor the hurricane bracing in place. If you are not using hurricane bracing, use a temporary diagonal support to keep the wall square as you erect it.

Erecting a wall on a floor decking is fairly easy. Simply slide it in place and stand it up. Temporary stop blocks added to the outside edges of the joists and headers keep the wall from sliding off. If installing on a concrete slab with anchor bolts, you will have to lift the wall up and set it down over the anchor bolts. Regardless, this is at least a two-person chore for even a short wall.

HOW-TO: PLATFORM CONSTRUCTION

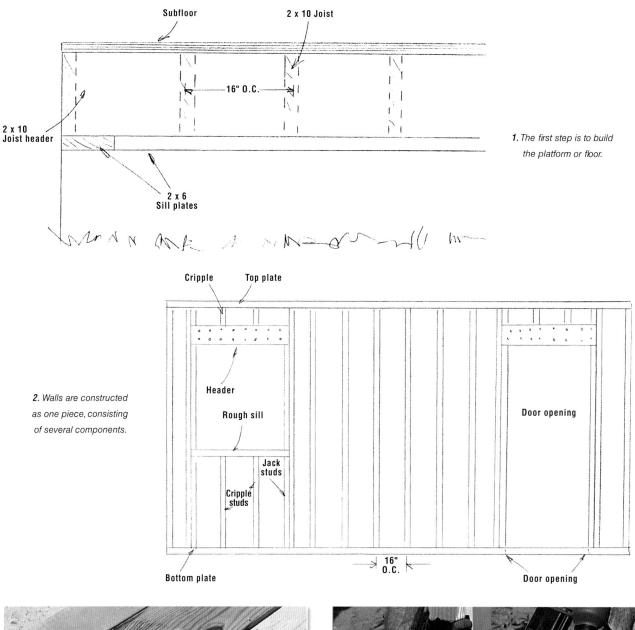

Subfloor

2 x 10 Joist

16" O.C.

2 x 10
Joist header

2 x 6
Sill plates

1. The first step is to build the platform or floor.

Cripple   Top plate

Header

Rough sill

Jack studs

Cripple studs

Door opening

Bottom plate

16" O.C.

Door opening

2. Walls are constructed as one piece, consisting of several components.

3. Lay the sole plate and top plate alongside each other and mark the stud locations, as well as any door and window locations using the narrow blade or tongue of a framing square.

4. An air-framing nailer makes the chore of nailing the wall section together easy.

5. Install hurricane bracing. This can be commercial metal strips or wooden 1 x 4s inlet into the studs. Make sure the wall is square before installing the bracing

6. Erect the wall or wall section, plumb it with a level and brace it in place.

7. If the wall has more than one section, build and erect it. Join the two sections with a second top plate.

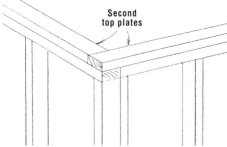

Second top plates

8. Construct and erect the opposite wall and brace it in place. Construct and erect the walls that fit between the two previously erected walls. The corners are anchored with overlapping second top plates (at left). Make sure all walls are square and plumb. If the building is to be finished off inside, you will need to add blocking at the corners (right).

With the wall erected, nail the sole plate to the decking or subfloor or fasten down with nuts and washers on the anchor bolts. Drive 2 x 4 stakes in the ground and provide temporary supports anchored to the wall studs and the **stakes**. Make sure the wall is **plumb** before anchoring the supports in place. If another section is needed, build and erect it in the same manner. In this case the joining ends of the wall sections should join with a stud.

Construct, erect and brace the opposite wall in place in the same manner. Then construct the wall that fits between the two standing walls. This wall is measured to fit between, measuring at the bottom. The ends have a stud, and then the first on-center studs are located, adding the 2 x 4 or 2 x 6 measurement of the first erected walls. Again, headers, double and jack studs and hurricane bracing are installed. The wall is erected between the two adjoining walls, plumbed and then anchored to the outside studs on the two adjoining walls. A **second top plate** is then anchored down over the adjoining walls, crossing them to tie all the walls securely together. Blocking is added at the corners to provide a square corner to fasten interior paneling, wallboard or other wall coverings. Construct and erect any inside walls in the same manner, anchoring them to studs on each end. Ceiling joists are installed, anchoring them to the rafter.

BASIC ROOF FRAMING

Roof framing is one of those carpenter skills that seems quite complicated, and indeed, some roof designs can be a bit difficult. Roofs are basically one of four types: shed, gable, hip or gambrel. Another common design in the Northeast is the "saltbox" which is basically a **gable roof** with one longer side. Today **"cut-ups,"** or roofs with a lot of valleys, dormers and other features are increasingly popular. In many cases of purchased house plans, the details of the roof construction, including **rafter design**, are included.

Pre-constructed trusses have also become increasingly popular. They are made at a factory to match your building and delivered on site. They do require extra manpower and lifting equipment to install. You can also build your own trusses if you have the equipment, or you can rent the equipment to install them. Piece-by-piece rafter/roof construction, however, is still the more common for many buildings. Even if you design and build a roof without plans, simple roofs such as a shed or the **common gable** are fairly easy to construct if you understand the basics and a little geometry.

In order to build any roof (except the shed) type, including trusses, you'll need to first determine a few factors—the span, rise, run and line length. For a shed roof you only need to know the rise, span and line length. **Span** is the measurement across the building from outside supporting wall to outside supporting wall. **Run** is half the distance of the span. **Rise** is the measurement from the centerline of the span to the top of the roof line. **Line length** is the measurement from the outside of the supporting wall line to the centerline of the roof at the top of the rise. Basically you're working with a triangle with two legs and a hypotenuse, the latter the line length.

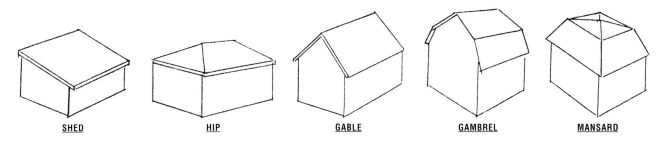

SHED   HIP   GABLE   GAMBREL   MANSARD

Roofs are framed in five basic designs: shed, hip, gable, gambrel and mansard. The gable is the most common, and it can be complicated with multiple roof lines including valleys and dormers.

You will also need to know the desired pitch of the roof. **Pitch** is the slope or angle from the wall plate to the ridge line. Pitch can vary a great deal, from a shallow slope pitch up to a very steep pitch. Pitch for a gable roof, the most common, is generally ¼ or ⅓; which is equal to ¼ or ⅓ the total span of the building, not counting any overhang. Pitch also has its own denotation, determined by the rise in inches in any 12 inches. For instance a 4/12 pitch denotes a roof rising 4 inches for each 12 inches. Having the correct pitch is important. In many instances, a certain pitch may be necessary or even required by local codes. This is in regard to **snow loads**, other weather factors as well as the covering to be applied to the roof. For those in the northern parts of the

Roofs may be framed with individual rafters or with manufactured or preassembled trusses.

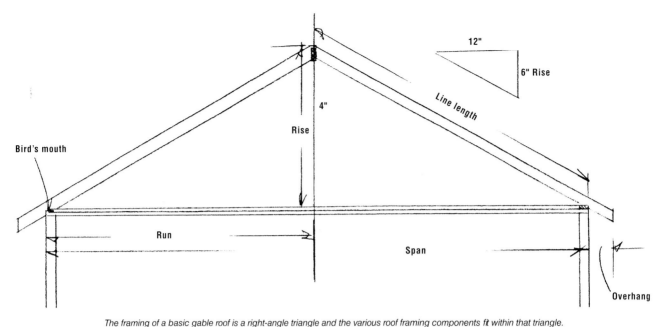

The framing of a basic gable roof is a right-angle triangle and the various roof framing components fit within that triangle.
The rise, or height of the roof at its peak, is the altitude of the triangle; the run or half the building span, is the base of the triangle; and the line length,
measurement from the roof peak to the building wall is the hypotenuse.

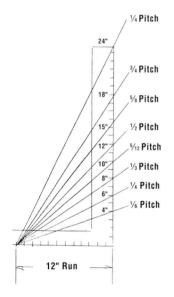

Pitch is the amount of angle or slope of the roof. This is denoted by two ways. By fractions, for instance a ⅓ or ¼ pitch; and in inches, a 6/12 pitch, which means the roof rises 6 inches for each 12 inches of run. A framing square is traditionally used for laying out the roof and determining pitch.

country, an 8/12 pitch is commonly used to keep excessive snow loads off the roof. Those in the southern climates may utilize lower pitches. The minimum pitch, however, that can be used with many **roofing materials** such as asphalt shingles or corrugated metal is 3 in 12. (3/12). For lower pitches, built-up or continuous roll roofing must be applied to keep it waterproof.

Although other types are shown, we will discuss a **gable roof**, without valleys or dormers, as it's the most common and the easiest for a first-time builder to tackle. After you determine the rise, span, run, line length and pitch, the next step is to lay out the rafters or mark the cuts on a **pattern rafter** to create the roof. There are three basic cuts used in creating the rafter, the plumb cut at the top of the rafter where it fits against the **ridge plate**; the tail cut which creates the outside edge of

the **building eaves**; and the bird's mouth which positions the rafter on the top of the wall plate. We will show two methods of laying out rafters; one using a traditional framing (two-foot) square, and the second using the more modern C.H. Hanson Pivot Square.

Hold the **framing square** with the manufacturer's name up—this side is called the "face" of the square and the opposite side is the "back." The long arm of the square is the "blade" and the short arm is the "tongue."

In the example shown here, we'll use a ⅓ pitch. This means a rise of 8 inches for each 12 inches of run (an 8/12 pitch roof). The first step is to lay the square on the end of the rafter board and locate 8 inches on the tongue (the rise), and 12 inches on the blade (the unit of run). Measure from the point on the blade to the point on the tongue. It should be 14⁷⁄₁₆ inches. Multiply this by the run of the building. We're using 10 feet in the example, excluding the overhang. The resulting figure is 144⅜ inches. We add 12 inches for the overhang to get a final figure of 156⅜ inches.

Examine the rafter board to determine if there is any curve or **"crown"** in the board. You should make this first pattern rafter on the straightest board you can find. If there is any curve in the board, layout the rafter so the crown is up. Experience has shown that the weight of the roof will gradually flatten this crown. If the crown were to be positioned down, the roof could eventually sag.

Position the square at the end of the **rafter board**, with the tongue on your left and facing away from you. Position the square with both the 8 inches on the outside edge of the tongue and the 12 inches on the blade on the upper edge of the board. Mark along the backside of the tongue. This is the **plumb cut** for the roof ridge.

Measure from the top of this line down the board to determine the length of the rafter, less ½ the ridge board. This is commonly a 2 x or 1½-inch board, so the measurement is less ¾-inch. Also exclude the overhang at this point. Holding the square in the same position as before, mark down to the side of the tongue. This marks the plumb cut at the inside of the house wall for the **notch (called a bird's mouth)** to seat the rafter on the wall plate. Add the length of the overhang beyond this mark. In the example shown this is 12 inches. Cut the rafter at the ridge line and at the overhang line. Then hold the square on the plumb line that marks the bird's mouth. Mark across the bottom edge of the

blade. Determine the wall thickness or depth of the bird's mouth cut and make a mark. Then move the square to that mark and mark down the bottom side of the tongue to create the horizontal line of the bird's mouth. Cut the notch, first with a **handsaw** or **portable circular saw**, then finish the cut with a handsaw.

Another method of laying out the rafter with the square is called **"stepping off."** Once the plumb cut is marked, simply move the square 12 inches and mark another plumb cut. Continue moving down the rafter and marking plumb cuts, including any odd figures. Some old-timers also like to reverse the square to mark the bird's mouth and tail cuts as shown in the drawings.

Make a **duplicate rafter** from the pattern. Then lay the rafters out on a smooth flat surface, with a 2 x between them at the ridge line and measure to make sure the rise, run and span are correct. You may in fact wish to test these on the building before cutting the rest of the rafters. Once you're sure these two **pattern rafters** are correctly cut, mark them as patterns and mark and cut the necessary number of rafters. Make sure you carefully follow the pattern rafter. A number of years ago I was constructing a two-story office building. One carpenter laid out and began to cut the rafters. He became ill from the extreme heat of the day and another took over for about the last two thirds of the rafters. When the roof framing was completed and decking installed, there was a built-in sag. I don't know if the second carpenter didn't use the pattern rafter, or simply wasn't as precise, but it was a costly mistake.

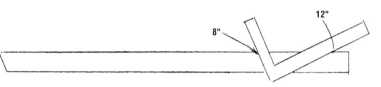

Position the square at the end of the rafter board, with the tongue on your left and facing away from you. Position the square with the 8 inch mark on the outside edge of the tongue and the 12 inch mark on the blade on the upper edge of the board. Mark along the backside of the tongue. This is the plumb cut for the roof ridge.

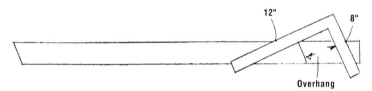

Measure from the top of this line down the board to determine the line length, or length of the rafter, less ½ the ridge board thickness. This commonly is a 2 x or 1 ½ inch board, so the measurement is less ¾ inches. Also exclude the overhang at this point. Holding the square in the same position as before, mark down the side of the tongue. This marks the plumb cut at the inside of the house wall for the notch (called a bird's mouth) to seat the rafter on the wall plate.

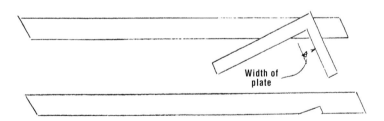

Add the length of the overhang beyond this mark and mark it. Note the square is turned over. In the example shown, this is 12 inches. Cut the rafter at the ridge line and at the overhang line.

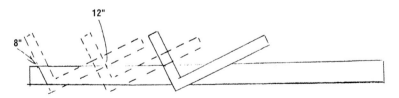

Then hold the square on the plumb line that marks the bird's mouth cut and make a mark. Cut the notch, first with a handsaw or portable circular saw, and then finish the cut with a handsaw.

Another method of laying out rafters with a square is called "stepping off."

The C.H. Hanon Pivot Square makes the chore of laying out a roof quite simple. I sure wish I'd had this tool a number of years and buildings ago. This quality tool is basically a **small "adjustable" square.** It comes with its own heavy-duty belt holder that is also designed to hold a carpenter's pencil and the instruction booklet. The Pivot Square has three edges corresponding to the three sides of a triangle. Degrees and rise are marked on a blade attached to the pivoting arm. With the common rise figures facing you and the raised fence on the right, the bottom represents the base of the triangle (the run) and the right side the altitude (the rise). The long adjustable edge represents the hypotenuse of the triangle, or the line length. The Pivot Square can be set to any whole number pitch from 1/12 to 12/12. Simply adjust the square to the desired pitch and lock in place with the knurled knob. You can then use the square to transfer the angle for the cut to the lumber. Or you can hold the square in place and use it as a sturdy guide for running a portable circular saw. One great feature of the tool is the pitch is also marked on it in degrees of angle. Determine the pitch, then you can set a miter saw or compound miter saw to make cuts in degrees that conform to the desired pitch. The Pivot Square can also be used to lay out pitches steeper than 12/12, as well as lay out **hip-valley rafters.** These figures are determined on the back side of the square. This tool takes a lot of the figuring and guessing out of creating hips and valleys. And, the tool is even more versatile and can be used for other cuts as well.

A series of numbers run along the center of the graduated arc of the adjustable blade on both sides of the tool. Each of these numbers represents the complement of the corresponding angle along the edge. The sum of these two figures always equal 90 degrees. For instance, when you set the square for 20 degrees, the complementary angle of 70 is directly aligned. You can make the 20 degree cut following the set angle, flip the tool over and make the complementary 70 degree cut to create a perfect 90 degrees.

The square also comes with three leveling vials. This makes it easy to measure the pitch of existing structures. **To measure pitch**, position the hypotenuse of the square on the roof, running straight up the pitch. Make sure it not off angle by shingles edges. You may wish to use a four-foot level to set it on for more accurate measurements. The outer end or number 9 on the hypotenuse or adjustable blade should be at the top or upper side of the pitch. Loosen the lock and adjust the square until the level vial on the base reads level, then lock the setting. You can now read the pitch and degrees on the Deg. Common Rise scale of the square.

To lay out a rafter with the Pivot Square first determine the pitch and set the square to the correct pitch on the Deg. Common Rise scale. Position the square with the base or raised edge on top of the rafter board. Mark the plumb line for the ridge line cut near the end of the rafter board. Measure the length of line on the rafter (less the ridge board) and make another plumb line mark parallel to the first. Determine the

rafter overhang and move the square to that position and make another plumb cut mark. To create the bird's mouth cut position the square at the bottom of the middle plumb line with the altitude side against the plumb cut and mark across the board using the square base, and beginning at the bottom of the plumb cut. Once this level line is established, measure and mark the wall thickness, plus about ¼-inch for any slight imperfections along the level line. Then use the square to draw a short plumb line parallel to the others, down from this mark to the bottom edge of the board. This completes the bird's mouth layout.

In many instances these days, wider rafters are used than is suitable for the **fascia,** so the tail of the rafter is also cut to create a narrower, more suitable **fascia board.** This requires laying out a level line on the tail of the rafter. To do this, do not make the tail cut until this has been established. Draw the sub fascia and finish fascia board on the end of the rafter and against the plumb tail cut. Use the bottom edges of these boards to mark the level line cut. Again, once all cuts have been marked, cut the pattern rafters, test and you're ready to erect the roof framing.

Before beginning the framing, determine rafter location on both top plates and mark them using a framing square. The small or tongue side is 1½ inches wide so you can mark the locations of both sides of the rafters. The easiest method of erecting the rafters is to make temporary braces of 2 x materials. These should be the height of the building walls, plus the rise.

USING THE C.H. HANSON PIVOT SQUARE

1. The C.H. Hanson Pivot Square makes it easy to lay out rafters. The tool comes with it's own belt pouch that has dividers for the square, instruction manual and a carpenter's pencil.

2. To begin layout with the ridge board plumb cut, set the adjustable angle-blade to the desired pitch. Position the square in place and mark for the cut.

3. You can also hold the square in place and use it as a portable circular saw guide.

4. Make a second plumb cut the line length measurement on the rafter. Hold the square in place with the base along plumb cut line and mark the level line of the bird's mouth.

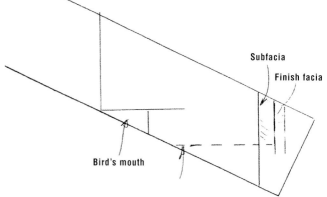

5. Turn the square back in place for the plumb cut to complete the bird's mouth and to mark the tail cut.

6. In some instances the bottom edge of the rafters are also cut with a level line. Lay these out as shown.

Use only enough supports to support the first length of ridge board. Rip the ridge board to the correct width to meet the rafter widths at the ridge. Create a **saddle** at the top that braces the height of the building walls, plus rise, less the width of the **ridge board**. Brace these supports in the centerline of the building. Position a ridge board down in the saddles of the supports. Align the top plumb cut with the ridge board and the heal cut of the bird's mouth with the inside of the wall and nail the rafter in place. As the rafters are installed, add any supports needed or required by code, such as collar ties or center supports. Continue erecting rafters until you reach the end of the first piece of ridge board. Then move the temporary braces for the next ridge board and continue installing rafters.

With the rafters in place, the gable end framing is done. Temporary **collar ties** are used on the gable ends until the end framing is done. Gable-end framing utilizes **vertical studs**, positioned directly over the wall studs and supported by the end top plates. They are notched to fit around the **gable-end rafters**. After the sheathing is installed, hanging or **"fly" rafters** are then installed.

Roof framing doesn't have to be daunting, but if it's your first try, a simple gable roof, say on a small shed is the best bet.

ROOFING

The first step is to install the **decking**. This can be OSB, sheathing, plywood or solid decking. Install with **ring-shank siding** or **coil nails**, staggering the joints on the rafters or trusses. Leave enough overhang for

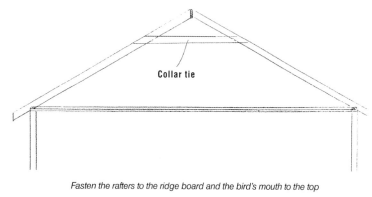

Fasten the rafters to the ridge board and the bird's mouth to the top wall plate, and add collar ties.

the roofing and the fly rafters.

Do-It-Yourself or Pro?
The next step is to determine if you can do the job yourself. Roofing is hard work, and it can be extremely hazardous, especially on a multiple story house and/or a house with steep roof pitches. The latter requires special scaffolding which you will need to rent or purchase. If you're not afraid of heights, or hard work, the techniques needed for roofing are not especially difficult. And, you can save approximately 50 percent of the cost of roofing by doing the job yourself.

Tools
For steep pitches you'll need **scaffolding**, **ladder hooks** or **jacks and ropes**. You should also have tarps to cover the roof in case of inclement weather. Then watch the weather as **shingles** cannot be applied when the weather is too hot or too cold. In addition to a means of nailing down the shingles, you'll need a good utility knife, a heavy sheath, straight edge and chalk line. Always cut from the back side of the shingle as this doesn't dull the blade as does cutting through the granules on the front.

Shingles can be applied with

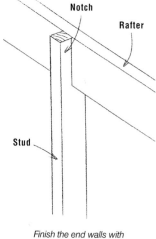

Finish the end walls with blocking studs, notched to fit around the rafters and fastened to the top plate.

ROOFING YOUR HOUSE

1. Decking is fastened down on the rafters.

2. The fascia board is fastened to the ends of the rafters, building felt or asphalt roll roofing is attached to the decking and a drip edge is added all around the roof perimeter.

3. Asphalt or composition shingles are economical, long lasting and easy to install, even by a first-timer. The most common are three-tab — one sheet with slots to create three tabs.

4. Laminated shingles without drain slots (above, left) create a longer lasting roof. In one technique, (above, right) the excess is allowed to hang over the edge of the house and is cut away after the shingles have been laid, (see following page).

roofing nails and a hammer. A pancake type air compressor and a **coil roofing nailer** makes the job easier and quicker, even for a first timer. These tools can often be rented along with the other specialty tools required, but you should figure this cost when determining whether you wish to do the job yourself or contract it.

Selecting Shingles

Composition **asphalt shingles** are used on the majority of houses in the United States. Compared to other products, they are the most practical and are priced reasonably. For the most part they can be expected to last between 20 and 40 years. This information relates primarily to roofing with asphalt shingles. Several considerations should be made when roofing and the first is color. Shingles are available in a wide array of colors. It's a good idea for the shingles to match or harmonize with the exterior color of the home. **Darker colors** are more popular in colder climates, while **lighter colors** are more popular in warm sunny climates. In both instances these colors can result in energy savings. Light colors tend to make a small house look larger, dark colors can make a large house look smaller.

According to the Asphalt Roofing Manufacturers Association (ARMA), the typical roof shingle has undergone some dramatic advances in recent years. A wide variety of shingles can be found with a variety of colors, styles, sizes and incorporate unique performance and architectural features. For instance, the demand for **fire-resistant shingles** has grown dramatically in recent years, especially in the brush fire-prone areas of the West and Southwest. In high-wind and hurricane areas, special **wind-resistant shingles** can provide additional protection for a home's roof, and by extension, its contents. **Impact resistant shingles** may be considered in areas where hail damage is a concern. In the warm, humid areas of the United States, **algae-resistant shingles** can help homeowners protect their roofs against shingle discoloration.

Three-tab shingles are the most common and most economical. The waterline created in their installation can, however, eventually become eroded. One of the more popular shingle styles is the **laminated shingle,** which is manufactured with one or more layers of "tabs" or cutouts laminated to create additional thickness to the shingle, and also a solid surface. With their shadowing effects, laminated shingles give a visual depth and a custom look to a roof. Because there is no waterline, as on three-tab shingles, the laminated shingles also tend to last longer. Local building codes may specify the rating of the shingles that can be used in your area.

Estimating

Shingles are estimated in squares. One **square** of roofing shingles covers 100 square feet of roof. Shingles come in packages to make up one square. The number of packages needed for a square depends on the type of shingle and the number of shingles in the package. Shingles are also measured by their weight, with the heavier and more durable shingles, weighing 235 pounds, common for most roofing applications. This means a square of shin-

ROOFING AND LADDER SAFETY

- Wear shoes with soft, sticky soles, rather than hard, slick soles, to prevent what roofing pros call a "slide for life."
- Keep any cut-off pieces swept up or off the roof.
- Take extra care when using ladders.
- Use only Type-I or Type-II class extension ladders.
- The ladder should be long enough to extend three feet above your home's highest eave.
- Add an additional foot for propping the ladder in place at the proper angle.
- The best ladder position is with the base one-fourth its extended length away from the house.
- Make sure the ladder is resting firmly in place on the ground.
- Never use ladders around power lines.
- Remember, even wooden ladders can conduct electricity when wet.
- Do not allow more than one person on the ladder at a time.
- Use both hands to climb the ladder and keep your hips between the ladder rails.
- Do not attempt to climb a ladder with tools.
- Pull tools up in a bucket.

ADDING SHINGLES TO THE ROOF

Asphalt

⅙ Removed

Starter course

Drip edge

1. First step is to lay a starter course. This may consist of half shingles or whole shingles with the tabs laid facing toward the roof peak.

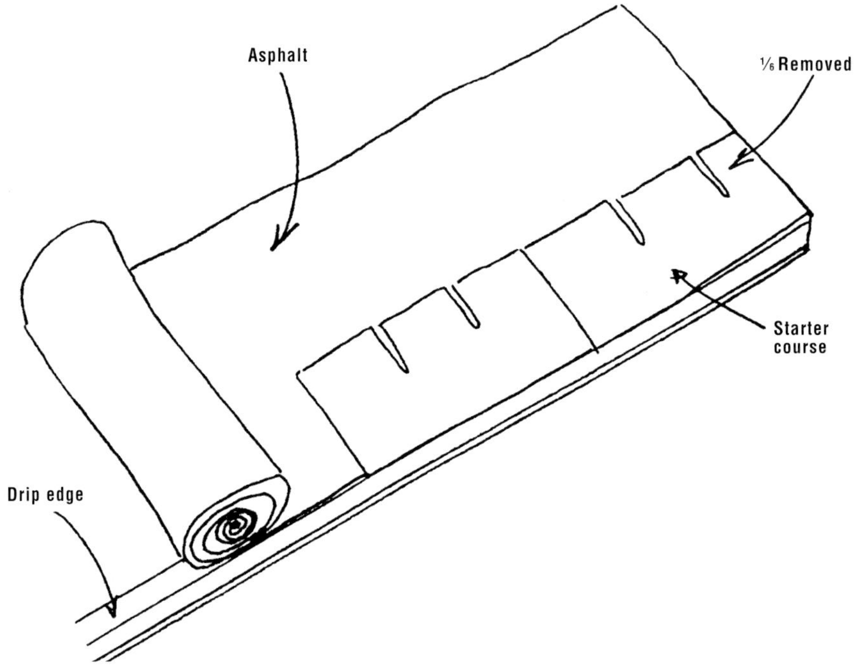

½ Removed

⅓ Removed

⅙ Removed

Full

Full

Starter course

Full shingle

2. Shown at left are two techniques for three-tab shingles. Shingles can be laid in a pattern so no joints overlap the joints below them.

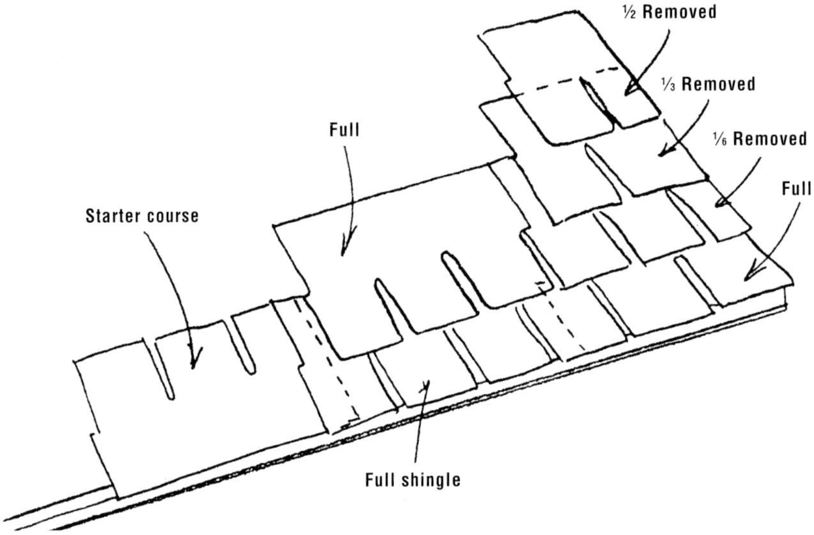

Fifth course – starts all over

Fourth course

Third course

Second course

First course

Starter course – half shingle

3. In the second technique the shingles are allowed to hang over the edge of the roof. The excess is cut away after the pattern is begun.

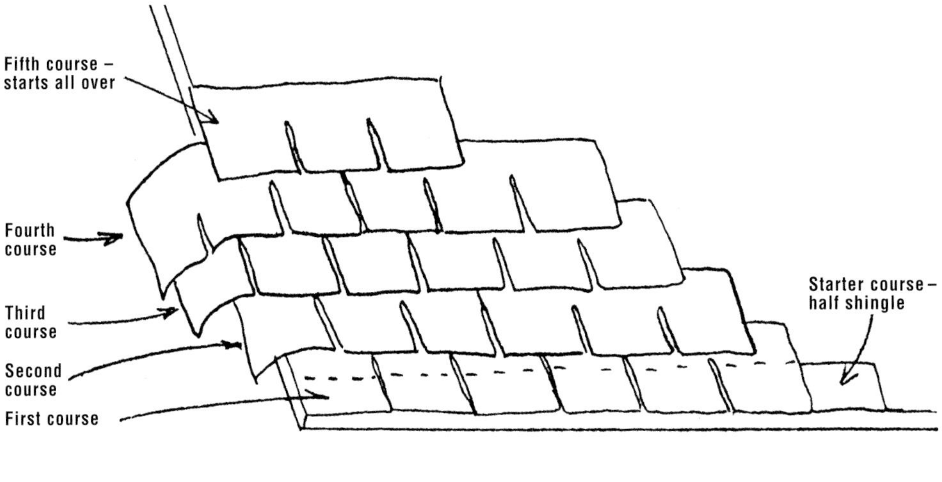

ing sure the nails are driven straight and not angled where they can cut into the shingle.

It's also best to begin the shingling job at the rake that is the most visible and work toward the rake that is less visible.

You can purchase special **ridge cap shingles** or simply cut three-tab shingles in thirds. Laminate shingles require special **ridge cap shingles**. Begin by bending a cap piece over the ridge and along the centerline of the shingle. If the weather is cold, take the pieces inside to warm them. Fasten in place with a nail on each side 5½ inches from the exposed end, and 1 inch up from the shingle edge. The next shingle should overlap to create a 5-inch exposure. Lay the laps away from the prevailing wind direction.

Valleys may be flashed and the shingles cut in a straight line along the valley edge, or the valleys may be laced. Although **lacing** is a bit more complicated, it provides a tighter, sturdier and less leak-prone roof. Lacing is the most common these days, and is the most popular with the experts. To lace a valley the shingles are interlaced as the course go up the valley, creating a solid, shingled surface.

Don't attempt to shingle in extremely cold or extremely hot weather. In cold weather the shingles can break and in hot weather you can mark and scar shingles with your feet.

For more information, check out the ARMA web site at www.asphal-troofing.org.

Doors, Windows & Siding

Above: Windows, doors, siding and soffits finish off and enclose the building. These days a wide range of products provide energy efficient buildings and are fairly easy to install.

Window and door installation is fairly straightforward these days with new products that make it easy even for a first timer. It's important to choose quality, energy efficient doors and windows. They both control the amount of light, air and heat that enters and exits the home. National Association of Home Builders (NAHB) statistics show the average home today has 19 windows, three exterior doors and one patio door—all of which can play a major role in energy use. The first step is selecting reliable windows and doors that reduce energy costs.

The **Energy Star label,** created by the Environmental Protection Agency (EPA), is the easiest way to identify the most energy efficient products on the market. The EPA states that a typical household can save up to 30 percent of their energy bill (approximately $400 per year) by selecting Energy Star qualified home products. In order to be Energy Star qualified, a company must be National Fenestration Rating Council (NFRC) certified. This NFRC certification is conducted by a third-party organization that uses industry accepted standards for evaluating and certifying energy performance. The Energy Star program also takes into account those products most suitable for particular regions and climates. Look for windows with the label

• What is an Energy Star Label?   • What are your window and door insulation options?

• What are the best insulation options for different kinds of construction?

• How do you protect your lodge's siding from the elements?

• How do you install an exterior and interior door as well as a patio door?

that shows it meets Energy Star qualifications for the area you live. Several ratings are available on the label, including the U-Factor. The lower the **U-Factor** — the better the product resists heat transfer. For instance, JELD-WEN suggests Northwest homeowners choose windows and doors with a U-Factor of .35 or below. Another important factor is most remodelers these days replace the older single-pane windows with **dual-pane units** which provide more insulation from both cold and hot weather.

Dual panes involve two pieces of glass with a sealed air space between, resulting in an insulating air pocket. The **U-factor** is approximately double that of single pane windows. The most popular energy saving feature for windows is low emissivity (Low-E) glass, which controls solar heat gain, a major contributor to air-conditioning costs. **Low-E glass filters** out long wave radiation, making it easier to cool your home in the summer. In the winter, Low-E glass keeps your home warmer by reflecting shortwave radiation back into your home. The ultimate in insulating is Low-E glass with the use of Argon gas for the sealed space between the panes. It has a much greater density than air, reducing heat transfer even better. For more information and suggestions about ways to save energy and energy efficient windows, log onto the Energy Star website.

It's extremely important to measure the opening properly for windows and doors and purchase a window or door of the proper size to fit the rough opening. Most window

New construction doors and windows utilize a nailing flange to hold them in place. When installing, fold out the fins and apply a bead of caulk around the inside edge of the nailing fin or to the siding.

and door manufacturers offer pamphlets providing the **rough opening requirements** for their standard window sizes, as well as how to measure for their products. Most manufacturers also provide information on how to install their products. In reality, you should have researched or purchased the window and door units before constructing the building, creating the rough openings during construction to fit the units selected. Some sizes are fairly standard and readily available at major home supply stores. It's best to stick with these sizes.

You should also choose **new-construction style windows.** These feature a full flange on the outside that fits over the sheathing. The windows are installed, then the siding installed over and against the windows. Some windows will come with brick-molding trim; others will require adding exterior trim. In the case of log-home construction, you will have to "box-out" a frame for the windows to fit flush against the logs on the outside. Windows and doors are available as economical vinyl, wood clad with vinyl on the outside and exposed wood on the inside. Some all-wood windows and doors are also available. Most new-construction windows are manufactured flat on the bottom, rather than with an angled sill.

Most manufacturers supply installation instructions. Following is a typical example of a modern new-construction window installation.

INSTALLING WINDOWS

With the opening properly prepared, fold out the nailing fins to a 90 degree

angle to the frame. Apply a full bead of **caulk** around the inside edge of the nailing fin the full perimeter of the window. Lift the window in to place. From the outside use a 2-inch galvanized roofing nail or self-starting exterior screw through the nailing fin to temporarily fasten the window at one upper corner.

On the inside use **shims** and your level held vertically to plumb the jambs. Place shims under the jambs to correct for any out-of-plumb. Back outside, level the window at the head and then anchor at the opposite corner. Back inside, shim the sides equally, making sure you don't over-shim and force them out of alignment. Check diagonally from corner to corner to make sure the window has been installed square and is not twisted. Back outside, fasten the window securely in place by nailing around the exterior of the window through the nailing fin, or fasten using self-starting exterior screws. Further **insulation** and protection from moisture can be created by adding Pella SmartFlash window and **door installation tape** around the outside of the window, over the nailing fin and to the siding. In new construction, the window opening is often sealed by the use of the **vapor barrier** before installation of the window. Most window manufacturers have specific installation instructions on sealing both the interior and exterior. For instance Pella suggests the use of Dow Great Stuff Window and Door Insulation foam for the interior of their vinyl windows.

With the windows installed you're ready to **add insulation, sheetrock and trim** to the inside and exterior.

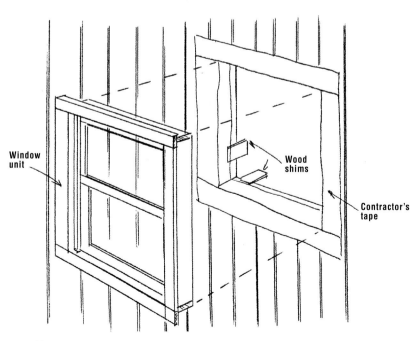

Use tarpaper or contractor's tape as insulation around the window unit. Wood shims, shown above, will let you get the window unit level and square.

Window unit

Wood shims

Contractor's tape

INSTALLING A NEW CONSTRUCTION STYLE WINDOW

Lift the unit in place and use a fastener to temporarily hold it in place at one corner.

Add shims around the unit to level and make sure it is square. Then fasten in place permanently with fasteners through the nailing fin.

Provide further moisture protection with installation tape such as Pella SmartFlash around the flanges. You can also add Dow Great Stuff Window and Door Insulation to the interior.

HANGING A DOOR

An exterior or interior door is also fairly easy to install. They come either as **separate from the frame** or jambs or **prehung**. The latter is the easiest to install, but comes in fairly standard sizes. If you need a size different than standard you will have to build the two separate. With a separate door and jamb you will have to first frame in the jambs. To do this, cut the side jambs to fit the rough opening, leaving about ¼-inch space at the top. Cut ¾-inch wide dadoes ⅜ inch deep and ½ inch from the top edges in the top ends of the side jambs. Cut **dadoes** in the bottom edges of the side jambs for the threshold to fit (for exterior doors). Cut the **top jamb** so it fits into the dadoes of the **side jambs**

and allows about ½-inch spacing between the top of the side jambs and the rough opening. Cut a **threshold** to fit between the side jambs. Fasten the top jamb and threshold into the dadoes in the side jambs with glue and finish nails or screws in predrilled holes. Make sure the assembly is square. Use a diagonal brace to hold the assembly square and allow the glue to set. Once the frame has set you can either hang the door, creating your own "prehung" unit or install the frame and hang the door to it.

If creating a **prehung unit**, you may wish to precut the hinge mortises in the side jamb for the door hinges before assembling the frame. A router and **hinge mortise** attachment makes this easy or you can cut them by

When installing the side and head jambs in a door frame (below), use wooden shims to level and square the jambs. Select a jamb width (below left), that matches the thickness of the frame and wall covering.

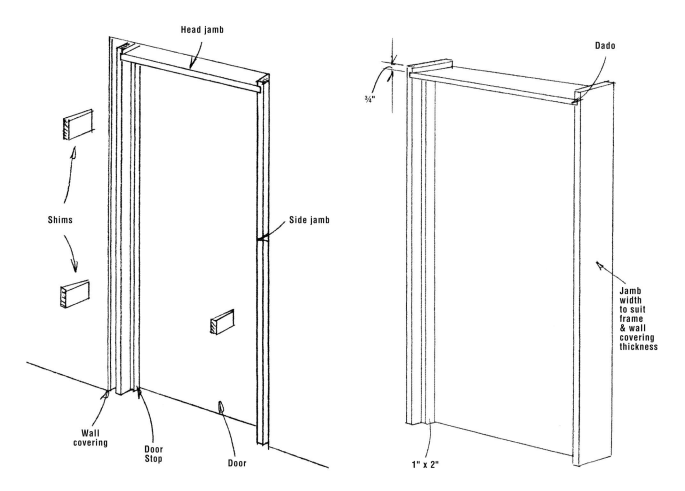

hand. To hang, first measure the inside of the frame and deduct ⅛ inch from the sides and top. Cut the door to this measurement. The door bottom should just contact the threshold. Determine the hinge locations on the door side and cut the hinge mortises in the door. Stand the frame upright and install the door in the frame driving the **hinge pins** in place to secure the door. Temporarily hold the lock side of the door in place with a piece of wood and staples, a thin wooden wedge or heavy-duty tape.

Set the prehung unit in place and plumb and square it. Use wooden shims on the sides, top and if necessary bottom to assure a square and plumb installation. Do not overdrive the shims or you will bow the side jambs making it hard to operate the door. Once the door is square and plumb, drive No. 8 finish nails through the jambs, shims and into the rough-opening framing. These should be in the location where the door stops will be located. In the case of an exterior door, use self-starting exterior wood screws countersunk in the jambs.

A purchased **prehung unit** is installed in the same manner. Remove the temporary holding pieces so the door will swing free. Mark the locations for the door lock and bore the lock holes in the door and jamb. Follow the lock instructions for installation. Once the lock has been installed, cut the door stops and fasten in place to the inside of the door jambs and against the door using No. 8 finish nails. An interior door is now ready for trim.

For exterior doors the spaces between the jambs and opening framing should be filled with **fiberglass**

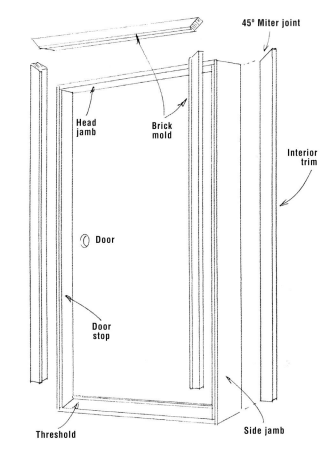

Typical exterior door with exterior and interior trim.

insulation. Again, do not overfill or you can bow the jambs. **Low-expansion foam** can also be used for this step. The exterior door is now ready for both interior and exterior trim.

To install the units separately, create the jamb and install it. Position the door in place, mark for the hinges and cut hinge mortises in both door and side jamb. Hang the door in place with the hinge pins.

INSTALLING A PATIO DOOR

Installing a patio door is also fairly easy, but because of the weight at least two people are required. You'll also need cedar or other types of **impervious shims or spacers**, closed cell foam backer rod, about 30 feet. Pella

Installing a patio door is like installing a very large window. Level, shim, caulk, attach through the flange and seal with tape in the same manner as installing a window.

INSTALLING A PATIO DOOR

Tools
- Hammer
- Tape measure
- Four-foot level
- Carpenter's square
- Drill/impact driver
- Hammer
- Staple gun
- Screwdrivers
- Utility knife

Materials
- Patio door
- Weather-resistant wood shims or spacers
- Flexible, closed-cell joint backing filler
- Window & door flashing tape
- Exterior grade silicone caulking
- 2-inch galvanized roof nails or self-starting deck screws

SmartFlash foil-backed butyl window and door flashing tape and high quality exterior grade silicone sealant will also be needed. You'll need 2-inch galvanized roof nails or self-starting deck screws. For tools you'll need a tape measure, 4-foot level, square, hammer, stapler, utility knife, screwdrivers and a drill. For screws an impact driver can be helpful.

Doors come with complete instructions, and the following is typical of a **standard installation**. First step is to measure the rough opening to make sure the door will fit. The opening should be ¾-inch larger than the door in width and ½-inch larger in height. Measure the height at both corners and in the center. Ideally, a **weather barrier or house wrap** should have been installed before window and door installation. For a good weather seal, cut the barrier and fold the side flaps into the opening, stapling to the inside wall. Fold the top flap and temporarily fasten it in place to the exterior wall. Apply the flashing tape at the sill. The tape

should be cut 12-inches longer than the width of the opening and extending up each side. The corners should be cut with tabs so the tape will install evenly and smoothly. The tape should not extend past the interior framing faces. Patio doors are heavy and should be well supported, including the door sill with an aluminum sill support or wood blocking.

You will need at least two people for the following steps. Remove any packing and wrap from the door as well as the shipping spacers. In the case of a sliding door, the venting or moving panel should also be removed by lifting it out of the bottom and tilting away from the frame. Then lower the panel out of the top track and remove.

Fold out the **fins**, making sure they are at 90 degrees. If the fins are not at 90 degrees, the door won't line up with the interior. Place three ⅜-inch **sealant beads** on the sill tape. The first bead should be about ¾-inch from the exterior rough opening, the second about 2½-inches in from the first bead. The third bead should be applied in the groove of the sill support or ¼-inch from the exterior edge of any wooden blocking used for support.

From the outside, pick up the door and place it into the opening. Do not slide the door into place as this will ruin the sealant beads. The best method is to place the bottom edge of the door on the bottom of the rough opening, then tilt the top into place. Make sure the door is centered in the rough opening with clearance on both sides for proper shimming. Use one roofing nail or screw in the first hole from the corner on each end of the top nailing fin. These are used to hold the door in place while shimming it plumb and square. Using a level and a square, plumb and square the door. Use shims on each side, but do not overshim or you can make the door hard to operate. Begin 6 inches from the bottom on each side. Inside, make sure the measurement from the interior face of the door to the interior wall face is equal all around the door. If these measurements are not equal, check to make sure the fins are all at 90 degrees.

Check again to make sure the door is plumb and square. Fasten the door in the opening by driving two-inch galvanized roofing nails through each hole in the fin, or use self-starting deck screws. Follow specific directions for anchoring your particular door in place. Apply the **flashing tape** over the nailing fins and to the weather barrier. The tape should extend 2-inches above and below the door. Cut and apply the top flashing tape; it should extend at least 1-inch past the side tapes on both sides. Apply this over the ends of the side tapes. This prevents water from running in behind the side tapes. Fold down the weather barrier and tape it in place.

Carefully lift up and reinstall the **sliding panel**. Insert from the exterior of the building. Tilt the top of the panel toward the door frame and insert the top of the door panel into the top track. Move the bottom of the panel in toward the door frame until it is vertical, and then gently set the panel down in the bottom track.

Loosely fill any spaces between the door and the rough opening with **fiberglass insulation** to within 1-inch of the interior door frame. Don't pack too tightly or you can bow the door sides. Insert the closed cell foam sealing

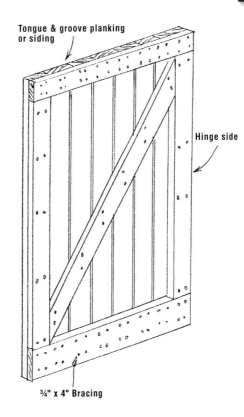

Tongue & groove planking or siding

Hinge side

¾" x 4" Bracing

In the case of a primitive cabin in the woods, you may prefer to make up your own windows and doors in the traditional manner.

rod into the space to within ½-inch of the interior of the door frame, or you can use **expanding foam** as an insulation and sealant. Make sure it is a low-expansion product and carefully follow manufacturer's instructions. Check to make sure the door works properly. Seal off any exterior joints according to manufacturers' instructions and the type of **wall cladding**. Now you're ready for siding.

HOME-BUILT DOORS AND WINDOWS

In the case of a primitive cabin in the woods, you may prefer to make your own doors from materials on hand. The most common type of door is made of solid wood with Z-framing inside and out. It's important to make sure the door is constructed to tightly fit the opening, overlapping and shutting securely to keep out the critters. A variety of hand-latches can be used for a building such as a **trapper's line cabin**. This allows others to enter and take refuge if needed. You can also construct primitive windows and install them in place as well.

SIDING INSTALLATION

Siding for a **framed lodge** can be as varied as for a house or other building. In most instances, however, sheathing should be applied first. This can be insulation board, OSB, or plywood. Adding a **house wrap** such as Dupont Tyvek can provide protection against air infiltration, making it easier to cool in the summer and easier to heat in the winter. It's one of the most economical but beneficial steps you can take. Dupont Tyvek DrainWrap is an excellent weather resistant barrier. The product offers the unique combination of a drainage system and a weather resistant barrier in a single product and promotes water drainage behind siding such as primed cedar by channeling moisture safely to the outside. The inherent water-resistance properties of Dupont Tyvek are enhanced with vertical grooves on the surface to help channel bulk water safely outside to help manage water that penetrates through claddings. In addition, the breathable structure allows moisture vapor to pass through to promote drying in wall systems and help prevent the formation of mold and mildew. And of course the product also reduces energy costs.

Tyvek DrainWrap is installed to the outside of the insulation cavity,

INSTALLING HOUSE WRAP

Before any siding is installed a house wrap should be installed. Shown is Dupont Tyvek DrainWrap. Fasten in place with plastic washer-head nails or staples.

Apply Tyvek tape to all joints and edges.

All joints and around windows and doors should be well caulked using a sealant such as Dap Side Winder Siding and Window Sealant.

preferably over an approved exterior sheathing board. Stand the roll vertically against a wall one foot from the corner and unroll, fastening as you go. Keep the roll level and continue around the building, covering all openings, including windows and doors. Fasten it to the structural material (plywood or studs) with plastic washer-headed or broad nails, or staples. Fasteners should be applied approximately every 12- to 18-inches on the vertical stud line, with additional fasteners around each opening to be cut. DrainWrap should be overlapped at the corners of the building by a minimum of 12 inches. Overlap vertical seams by a minimum of 6 inches.

In new construction, without windows and doors already installed at each opening, cut a modified "I" in the material by cutting across the top of the opening, down the center and at a diagonal to each bottom corner. Pull the side and bottom flaps to the inside and secure to the inside of the rough opening. Install the windows and doors, sealing the edges of the DrainWrap to the window flange with Tyvek Tape. If the windows and doors are already installed, trim Tyvek DrainWrap as closely as possible to the edges and seal all edges and seams with tape.

SIDING TYPES

Siding can be **panels,** such as hardboard or plywood or other engineered products, metal, vinyl or solid wood siding. The latter can be purchased and installed in numerous patterns, or can be as simple as home-sawn, rough-sawn lumber nailed in place with battens.

Panel Siding

The quickest and easiest to install is a panel siding such as Louisiana Pacific SmartSiding. The 4 x 8-foot sheets come primed and if using a **coil air gun** and **compressor** they can be installed very quickly. They do require a helper to lift, position and fasten in place. It's extremely important to install the first sheet flush with the building corner edge and plumb. The bottom edge should extend about ½-inch below the slab or foundation top edge. You can make **window and door cut-outs** in two methods. The first is to measure and make the cut-outs before installing the siding.

A quicker and easier way is to install the siding, then drill locator holes in the corners of the openings and against the rough opening studs. Use these and a straight edge to mark the openings, then cut out with a reciprocating saw, circular saw or saber saw. The siding can be fastened in place in two methods, using a hammer and No. 8d non-corrosive siding or casing nails. Space them 6 inches on center on panel edges and 12 inches on center on the intermediate studs. An easier way is to use a coil air nailer and non-corrosive siding nails.

Solid Wood Siding

Solid wood siding is installed in a variety of patterns including the **common horizontal, bevel lap**. It can also be installed vertically with **board and batten.** An upscale lodge can benefit greatly from the use of a natural-finished siding such all-natural Western Red Cedar. Siding defines the mood and character of the lodge's exterior and reflects the image desired by its

A VARIETY OF WOOD SIDING INSTALLATIONS

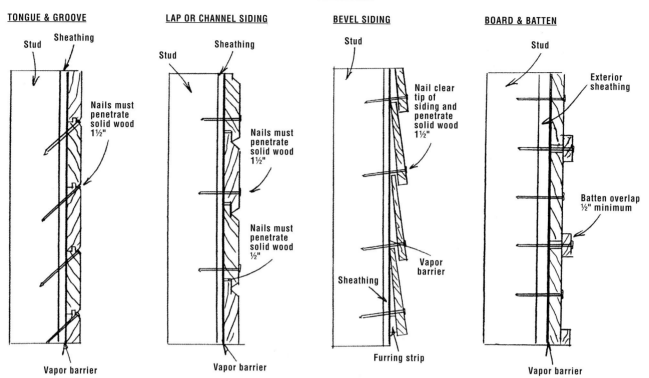

TONGUE & GROOVE

Stud

Sheathing

Nails must penetrate solid wood 1½"

Vapor barrier

LAP OR CHANNEL SIDING

Stud

Sheathing

Nails must penetrate solid wood 1½"

Nails must penetrate solid wood ½"

Vapor barrier

BEVEL SIDING

Stud

Nail clear tip of siding and penetrate solid wood 1½"

Vapor barrier

Sheathing

Furring strip

BOARD & BATTEN

Stud

Exterior sheathing

Batten overlap ½" minimum

Vapor barrier

LAP SIDINGS

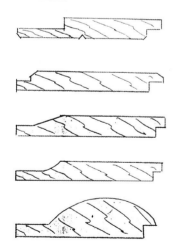

Other solid wood types include bevel lap, tongue and groove and lap, the latter of which are several profiles.

owners. All-natural Western cedar is the perfect choice for those wishing to create natural warmth and add character to an exterior that will last for years. Composite or plastic materials just can't compete when compared to the beauty and feel of all-natural cedar.

Western red cedar has outstanding physical characteristics that make it a great siding choice. These include rich color, smooth grain and a natural resistance to deterioration by insects and weather. Cedar fibers contain natural compounds called **"thujaplicins"** that act as natural preservatives making the wood last extremely long. Free of the pitch and resin found in other softwoods, Western red cedar will take a **wide range of finishes** from lightly toned clear to two-coat solid colors. **Dimensional stability** also makes the mate-

rial a premier choice for siding. It lies flat and straight and is less likely to swell, warp, cup and twist than other soft and hard woods. And, the low density also improves insulation by transporting less heat through exterior wall siding than brick, stone, vinyl or gypsum drywall. Conversely, it helps keep interiors warmer in cold weather. Low density also makes the product a great **acoustical barrier**.

One of the great features of Western red cedar, however, is it's easy to cut, saw, nail and glue. **Do-it-yourself cedar siding** is easy to do for those reasons, plus you're installing one relatively small piece at a time, rather than large, bulky sheets that are awkward to handle and install. Western red cedar siding is available in a variety of styles. Matching **trim boards** are also available. To make sure you get quality Western red cedar siding, make sure you specify cedar siding manufactured by members of the Western Red Cedar Lumber Association. For more information visit their websites. It's important to install cedar siding according to the Western Red Cedar Siding Association guidelines. Proper acclimation and storage of the cedar siding products before installation is important. Although one of the most stable softwoods, cedar will still respond to the environment. It can **swell or shrink** as it reaches equilibrium before it is installed. Keep the wood dry and stack it on the job site covered and at least 6 inches off the ground If storing on damp ground or new concrete, first place a **moisture barrier** down. Knotty cedar that is dried to less than 19 percent should be stacked with vertically aligned stickers. This also goes for trim pieces as well. **Air or kiln dried siding** that

has been kept dry can be installed immediately. **Damp siding** should be allowed to **acclimatize** from three to five days, **dry knotty cedar siding** for seven to ten days and **green siding** for a minimum of 30 days.

After the cedar has acclimatized, and before it is installed, it should be coated on all surfaces, including the ends. The **prime coat** depends on the final coat. Natural and semi-transparent stains serve as their own "primer." Cedar that is to have solid color stains or paint coatings should be primed with an alkyd oil stain-blocking primer. Or you can use a **clear water repellent** on the back of the siding and the primer on face and edges. These primers protect the wood from water penetration, increasing the life of top coats and help prevent staining from mildew and other materials.

Although naturally resistant to

Siding can be panels such as Louisiana Pacific SmartSiding. Fasten panels in place, making sure the panels are plumb and match the stud spacing. Then cut out windows and doors.

Any number of wood products can be used for siding, ranging from plywood and hardwood to rough-sawn from your own trees (above).

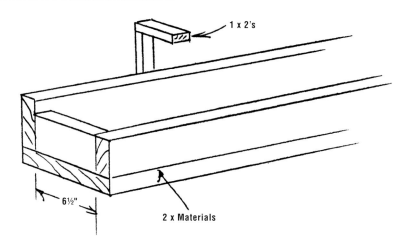

Use a dipping trough (diagram above) to coat Western red cedar with a transparent protective sealant such as Thompson's PLUS Clear Wood Protector (below).

decay and weathering, cedar siding should be protected with a **clear sealant** such as Thompson's Waterproofer PLUS Clear Wood Protector. These clear sealers can be applied with brush, roller or spray. Immersion is a recommended procedure, and is much faster than other types of applications. A **dipping trough** of 2x materials was created for the purpose. The trough is assembled with Titebond III waterproof glue and the pieces clamped solidly together. While clamped, Phillips 3-inch decking screws are used to further strengthen the joints. After the glue has set, all joints are caulked with a good grade of acrylic caulk. The trough rests on sawhorses, making sure it is level in all directions. The siding is immersed in the coating, and then removed to holders above the tank to allow excess material to run off. After the excess material has drained, the treated siding pieces are placed on sawhorses to further dry. They should be left to dry for 48 hours before installation.

Corrosion resistant fasteners should be used to install Western red cedar siding. This includes: hot-dipped galvanized, aluminum and stainless steel. Stainless steel nails, such as those from McFeely's, are the best choice as they are uniform throughout, unlike coated and galvanized nails that can degrade once the surface coating is damaged. Stainless steel nails are also extremely strong, about 20 percent stronger than ordinary steel nails. Ring-shank nails are the most popular because they offer greater resistance to withdrawal. The length of the nails depends on the size and thickness of the siding and sheathing.

INSTALLING INDIVIDUAL SOLID SIDING BOARDS

The nails should penetrate at least 1½ inches into solid wood or 1¼ inch if ring-shank nails are used.

Western Red Cedar siding comes in several different patterns including the most popular, **bevel**. It is also available as **tongue-and-groove** and **board-and-batten**. Lap siding is extremely popular with several varieties of lap siding available. The materials also come in several grades.

The surface should be prepared properly before trim and siding installation. Apply the **vapor barrier** and any **flashings** as necessary. Flashings should be made of corrosion resistant aluminum or galvanized steel. They must be installed at any location a horizontal break occurs in the siding. This includes transitions from cedar to other materials such as brick, at the junction of dormer windows and roof surfaces and over the heads of windows and doors. At any locations where the ends of the siding contact openings or trim, the area should be well caulked. It's important the caulk be a **non-hardening, flexible caulk** such as DAP Side Winder siding and window sealant.

Solid siding is extremely easy to install as individual boards are fastened in place. You can add a few boards as you get time. Inset shows how boards are fastened in place with ring-shank, stainless steel fasteners into the studs.

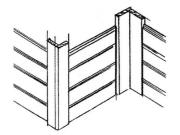

*Inside and outside corners
can be treated in
several ways.*

*Window and door trim is
installed, in some cases
over the siding and in
some cases, before the
siding is installed.*

Using the proper **nailing pattern** for the different siding styles is important. Regardless of the style, the siding must be kept at least 6-inches off the ground. For horizontal patterns, start with the bottom course. On bevel siding, use a **furring strip** to bring the bottom edge out the proper distance. Make sure the first course is level. Each succeeding course overlaps the one below. For bevel siding this is a minimum of 1-inch. On **rabbeted bevel siding**, leave a ⅛-inch expansion clearance. Fasten bevel siding in place using one nail per bearing or stud, spaced a maximum of 24-inches on center. Place the nail just above the overlap. Do not nail through the overlap of the two pieces. All butt joints should be staggered, and the butt joints as well as where the siding meets trim should fit snugly.

Tongue-and-groove siding can be installed vertically or horizontally. Start with the bottom course with the tongue facing up. Six-inch siding is blind nailed with one siding nail per bearing, toe-nailed through the base of each tongue. Wider siding is face nailed using two nails per bearing. For **vertical installations**, start at one corner with the groove edge toward the adjacent wall. Make sure the first course is started plumb.

Lap sidings are installed beginning with the bottom course and working up. Allow a ⅛-inch expansion gap between the pieces if the siding is air or kiln dried. A small jig using a piece of ⅛-inch thick material makes this chore easy. Do not nail through the overlaps. For siding up to 6-inches wide use one nail 1 inch up from the overlap per bearing or stud. For wider sidings use two nails. For vertical installations, nail to horizontal furring strips.

Board-and-batten siding can be installed horizontally or vertically. Wide boards with thinner battens make the most attractive siding patterns. One good choice is 1 x 10 boards and 1 x 3 battens. Battens must overlap a minimum of ½ inch on each board. Vertical siding must be nailed to blocking lines or furring strips.

Inside and outside corners may be handled in one of two ways. Some horizontal siding can be mitered at the corners. Another method is to use trim boards at inside and outside corners.

Soffits

A soffit is the underside of a roof overhang — the finished surface that extends from the inside top of an exterior wall and siding to the outer edge of the roof (fascia). The width of the soffit from wall to fascia can vary from a few inches to a yard depending on the style of construction. Numerous soffit products ranging from solid and ventilated aluminum or vinyl paneling to high-impact resin and engineered wood are all available on the builder's supply market.

Soffits can be either horizontal or sloping. In the case of a sloping soffit, attach the soffit boards or panels directly to the bottom of the rafters, butting the edges tightly against the fascia board and siding. To construct horizontal soffits, the process involves attaching a series of "look outs" (2x4s nailed to the side of each rafter that extend horizontally from the bottom of the rafter back to the siding), as attachments for the soffit board.

CONSTRUCTING THE PROPER SOFFIT

OPEN SOFFIT   **CLOSED SOFFIT**

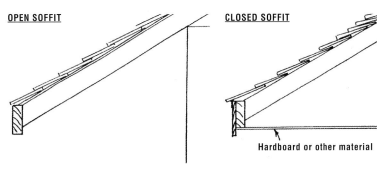

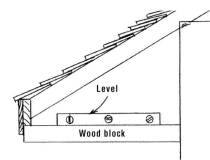

Hardboard or other material

Level

Wood block

Soffits may be open or closed.

Use a block of wood and a level to determine the location of the receiving channel on the house call at each end of the run. Then snap a chalk line.

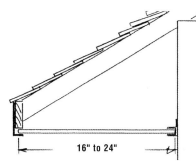

16" to 24"

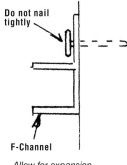

Do not nail tightly

F-Channel

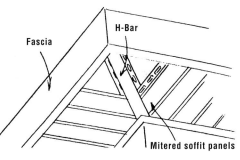

Fascia

H-Bar

Mitered soffit panels

Installation of vinyl soffit depends on the type of construction, open or closed eave and whether the fascia cap is to be applied.

Allow for expansion and contraction when nailing in place. Don't drive nails tight.

Corners are formed by using an H-bar and mitering the panels into the bar.

Constructing the proper soffit is important. A ventilated soffit will permit air circulation and prevent wood rot in the eave spaces.

Vinyl soffit material is measured using a square and can be cut with a portable circular saw with a reversed fine-toothed blade.

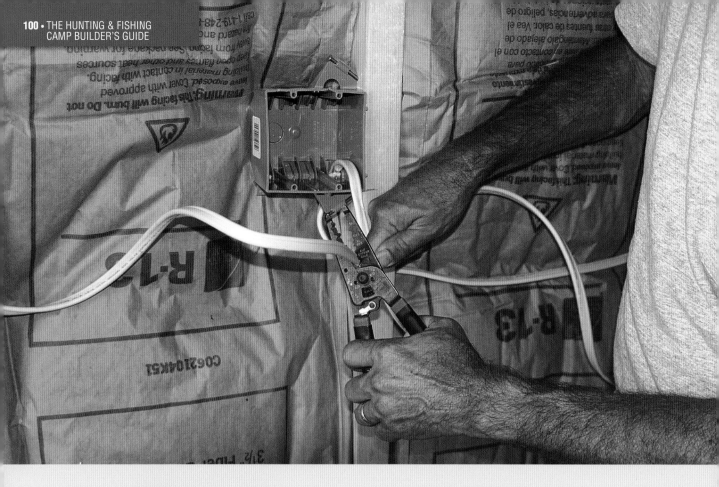

Wiring, Plumbing & Insulation

Above: Three essentials of many lodges and other buildings are wiring, plumbing and insulation. Depending on local code rulings, your skills and other factors, you may be able to do some or all of these chores.

The three essentials in most house construction are wiring, plumbing and insulation. Again, this may vary according to the type of construction, whether log, standard, or post and beam, and they may also vary according to your desires for the lodge. If only used for a week's deer season hunt, you may cut out some of these "essentials." For instance if you don't wish to install running water, an "outhouse" may be necessary. Chapter 14 illustrates how to build a classic outhouse. A weekend cabin can be lighted with oil lamps. In many cases, however, you will want to add electricity, plumbing and insulation.

Wiring and plumbing require technical skills and tools. Some local codes may prevent you from doing these chores yourself, and require experts to be hired. If you are allowed to do the chores, and have the inclination, both plumbing and wiring are not particularly difficult, but you must follow all safety rules. **Wiring rules** are found in the **National Electrical Code Book**. You can usually get a copy at your local library. Both plumbing and wiring is done before insulation is installed. We can't fully cover all the details of both wiring and plumbing, as each would take a full book. Following are the basics. If you are not sure of your capabilities, the best choice is to have the work done professionally.

- How do you properly "ground" your lodge's electrical system?

- What is the National Electrical Code Book? • How do you prepare a wiring plan?

- What are your water supply choices?

- What kind of insulation is necessary for an attic in a log house?

WIRING

Electrical wiring consists of several components including the **service mast** that brings power into the house, a **meter** supplied by the utility company, a **service panel** located inside the building, and the branch circuits. Electricity is supplied to the service panel as high voltage, either 120 or 240, with 240 more typical today. The service panel routes the electricity into a number of **branch circuits.** The service panel is equipped with either **fuses or breakers**, with the latter more common. The service panel includes a main breaker or fuse and a breaker or fuse for each of the circuits. The circuits may be either 120 or 240.

Another component is a ground. All electrical systems must be properly grounded, beginning at the service box. Grounding is actually making a connection of the system to the earth or **"ground"** and is a safety method designed to help prevent shocks and fires. The type of grounding system depends on local **code rulings**. Make sure you check with local codes and ground accordingly. In most cases a ground wire is run to a metal rod placed outside the building and in the earth, or to an appropriate water-supply pipe. The **ground wire** must be attached to the neutral **busbar** of the service entrance box, and additionally the neutral busbar must be grounded to the service entrance box according to the box manufacturer. The entire electrical system must be grounded. System ground and equipment ground are the two grounding methods. In a system ground all neutral incoming wire is grounded and all neutral wires in each circuit are grounded. Use a three-wire conduc-

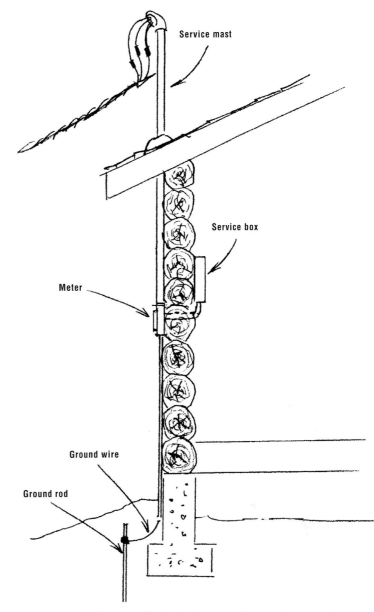

Wiring a cabin from an outside electrical source requires several components.

tor with a ground cable and connect all ground cables to the incoming ground. With an equipment ground, all metal parts of the system are grounded. In metal or conduit raceways, and with metal boxes, the metal is used as the ground. If you use **plastic boxes** and **non-metallic, plastic-sheathed cable**, only the system is grounded. You must ground each box, fixture and receptacle. If you use three-wire cable

It's important to properly plan the routing of all wiring for safety and convenience, with outlets, lights and switches located properly.

with a ground cable and also ground all boxes, you have both a system and an equipment ground. All bathroom, outdoor or receptacles that may be subject to moisture must be equipped with a **ground-fault circuit interrupter (GFCI)**. This device immediately shuts off the current flow should there be a fault in the ground to the fixture.

The **red and black wires** coming in the back of the service panel are "hot" wires and the white wire is called the "neutral." The **white wire** is always installed on the return side of the circuits but current flows through it as well as the other two wires. The

building owner is responsible for installing the service mast and panel. The utility company installs the meter. Even if you shut off the power at the service panel the wires coming in will be hot, except if the meter is shut off or removed by the utility company.

The main safety rule in working with electricity is to **shut off the circuit** you will be working on at the service panel and **make sure it is the correct circuit**. If in doubt, shut off the **main breaker**. Even then it's a good idea to test the circuit with a small tester to make sure the circuit doesn't have power. The second safety rule is that **only wires of the same color should be connected together**. This means you must always connect black to black and white to white, although there are some exceptions. The white wire must never be broken for a connection as it must be continuous to provide the ground. Again this can be broken in some instances, but the connection must be marked as such. By connecting the black wire of the circuit to the incoming black wire side of the panel and the white to the **neutral side**, you create a 120-volt circuit. If you connect the black and red wire to a branch (which requires a 240-volt breaker with two connectors) and the white to the neutral, you create a 240-volt circuit. Service panels and the circuits, and the resulting **wattage** they can supply vary. You should check with local electrical component suppliers as to the requirements you will need for your building.

The **wiring system** should be planned for the entire building with outlets, switches, lights and so forth as well as a **wiring diagram** made on a floor-plan sketch. In the case of purchased plans, this diagram may

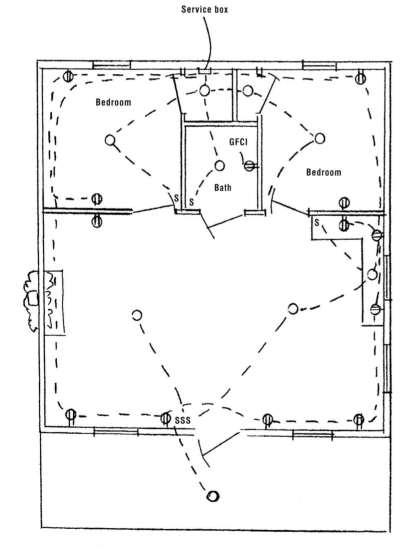

Service box

Bedroom

GFCI

Bath

Bedroom

SSS

TYPICAL CIRCUIT CONNECTIONS

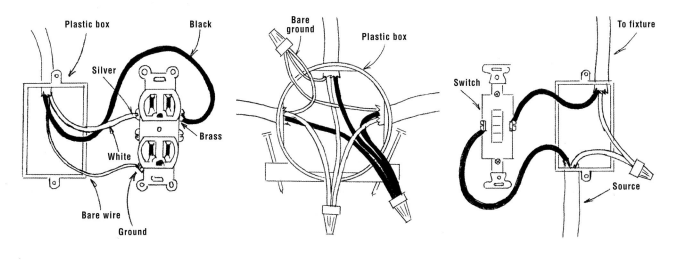

be included. It's important to have an adequate number of circuits. For instance you shouldn't have all lights in the building on one circuit. **Wall outlets** should be spaced no further than 6 feet apart along the walls. You will also need outlets for kitchen and bath counterspace and at least one outdoor outlet. After you determine your electrical needs you will also need to determine the service entrance size necessary to cover the system. Typically you should have at least a 20-amp general-purpose electrical circuit for each 500 square feet of building space. This is a minimum and more circuits are better. You will also need two separate 20-amp circuits for kitchen and laundry areas. And, you'll need **240 circuits** for a dryer, electric stove, water heater, and so forth.

All electrical wiring, including materials, system designs and methods of installing are covered by rules and regulations. The National Electrical Code Book is periodically revised to include the latest materials and information and is available at libraries or on the web. **Local codes** must also be followed, as they can vary from state-to-state and from municipality to municipality.

Wiring is typically done in two stages, the **rough-in** and the **connection** stages. During the rough-in stage, the service mast and panel are installed. Outlet, switch and fixture boxes are installed during framing, by fastening them to framing members. Holes are bored through the framing and the cable run between the boxes, leaving plenty of cable at the boxes for connection. A temporary electrical box can supply electricity to the job site.

Two types of **plastic-covered cable** are available — NM and NMC. NM can be used only in dry locations. It consists of individual wires covered with insulation. Each wire is also spiral-wrapped with paper. Type NMC is dual purpose and can be used for either wet or dry conditions. The individual wires are completely encased in solid plastic insulation. **Armored cable** is encased in a spiral-wound steel cable and is required in some locales. Again, be prepared to follow code rules, including local codes as to the type of

For log homes you may prefer exposed wiring which is easier to install.

materials for boxes, cable, receptacles, switches and lighting allowed. For log homes you may prefer to use **exposed wiring**. It is simple and fast to install. Today **remote control wiring** may be the best choice for log homes.

Once the building is framed-in, sided and in most instances wall coverings applied, the connecting phase is done, although some prefer to do the connecting phase before wall coverings. A variety of **connector combinations** are used for the various switch and light circuits. Make all connections in the circuit, and then connect to the entrance box and breaker, with the entrance box main breaker turned off or unconnected. Then turn on the power. It's extremely important to properly test each completed circuit to make sure it is properly connected. This can be done with a purchased **circuit tester**.

Photovoltaic Systems

Small Photovoltaic (PV) systems can provide a cost-effective power supply in remote locations. PV systems use both direct and scattered sunlight to create electricity and are suitable for use across the United States. The amount of power generated by a solar system at a particular site, however, depends on how much solar energy reaches it. PV elements will produce electricity on cloudy days, but not as much as on a sunny day.

PV electrical systems **convert sunlight to electricity** using semiconductor devices called solar cells. The most common technology is **single-crystal PV cells**, which use linked silicon wafers. **Thin-film PV** uses silicon and other chemicals on a substrate of glass or flexible stainless steel. PV panels produce direct current (rather than alternating current), which is easily stored in batteries. An inverter de-

These multi-module solar arrays are positioned to take maximum advantage of available sunlight.

vice is used to convert direct current to alternating current. Reliable — and somewhat expensive —batteries are needed to store electricity.

PV modules range in output from 10 to 300 watts. If more power is needed, several modules can be linked and installed in an aluminum frame or **"array."** About 10–20 PV racks can provide enough power for a household. In order to capture the most sunlight during the day, **arrays should be mounted at a fixed angle facing south**.

A number of manufacturers offer packaged solar remote location kits. These systems can be installed by professional installers or by the cabin owner. If you choose to do-it-yourself, you'll need basic electrician's skills and have a good understanding of how a solar electric system works and the basic function of all components. Do your research and make sure that you know what you are doing.

Here are the basic elements of an independent solar electricity system. **Solar panels** can be supported by **roof mounted solar arrays (or racks)**. The size of the panel and type of solar cells will determine the maximum wattage it will put out. For example, a 50-watt panel will measure about two square feet, while a 190-watt panel will measure about eight. An alternative to a roof rack is a **pole mount**.

An independent solar energy system uses a **stand-alone inverter** which converts **direct current (DC)** — the type of current stored in and discharged from a battery — into more usable **alternating current (AC)** — the standard form of electricity provided by a wall socket. Be sure to check with your retailer or installer to understand how to operate the inverter. Inverters

ROOF AREA NEEDED IN SQUARE FEET							
		PV Capacity Rating (Watts)					
		100	250	500	1,000	2,000	4,000	10,000
PV Module Efficiency (%)*	4	30	75	150	300	600	1,20	3,000
	8	15	38	75	150	300	600	1,500
	12	10	25	50	100	200	400	1,000
	16	8	20	40	80	160	320	800

* Although the efficiency (percentage of sunlight converted to electrical energy) varies with different types of PV Modules available today, higher efficiency modules typically cost more. So, a less efficient system is not necessarily lest cost-effective.

should be self-charging and have an **automatic on/off feature** (sleep, stand-by or power saver mode). Also make sure that your inverter has **surge capacity** and is capable of providing the surge of energy required by various appliances.

Most solar energy systems store electricity for later use in **lead-acid deep cycle batteries**. These batteries are designed to allow for continuous charging and discharging when sunshine varies from day to day. Lead-acid deep cycle batteries last longer. Always make certain that your batteries are properly sized to the system.

Other electrical elements include: **A main DC disconnect (large breaker)** between the batteries and the inverter to allow easy shut off when switching to battery power, a charge controller, linked between the solar module and battery to prevent the battery bank from being overcharged and a rectifier to change AC to DC.

Solar systems use the same AC breaker panel that you would find in any household. You will also need a system meter to measure electrical usage, the charge in your batteries and how much electricity the solar panels are producing. You may also choose to install a **backup generator** for emergencies and for long periods without sunshine.

PLUMBING

Plumbing has become increasingly easier due to the increased use and allowance of plastic materials. Again, **local codes** may vary. Make sure you understand and follow all code rulings. Waste plumbing systems are all plastic in most areas. Water supply lines may be flared copper tubing or soldered copper tubing or plastic with some galvanized or black steel piping. Plastic is easy, even for a first timer. Plumbing, both **waste discharge** and **supply line systems** are also governed by specific rules and codes. Make sure you understand the code rules on what materials and what types of installation are allowed in your area.

It's extremely important to also make a working diagram of the intended **plumbing layout**. Indicate all appliances, tubs, sinks and so forth, the system will have. This allows you to determine the exact location of any openings in the house framing for running plumbing lines. Again, if you have **a blueprint**, this is usually included. With a plan you can then make up a supply list of the materials needed. The best plumbing layout for most lodges is a central supply. This means you place **waste and drain lines** and supply lines for the bathroom and kitchen in a central core area, or backed up together. This is especially so in a log home where it is important to locate plumbing in the interior of the building so you don't run lines through the log walls. **Central plumbing** also has less freezing problems. Although all cabins without automatic heating will require shutting off all plumbing during freezing weather. A **drain-back system** must be installed in an unheated lodge or cabin.

As with wiring, plumbing is usually done in two stages, the **rough-in** which is done during framing or house construction, and **finishing or installation of fixtures**. Once you've made a plan, mark the hole locations for the pipes using a felt-tip pen. During rough-in, all pipes are installed and threaded through walls, as needed. The **discharge system** is somewhat more complicated than the supply system and is usually laid-out and installed first. You will have to vent the discharge system, usually through the building roof. Once you have the discharge system installed and connected to the house drain, block off

As with electrical wiring, plumbing systems, such as the one in the diagram below, should be carefully planned for efficient flow and drainage and for easy access in the event repairs become necessary.

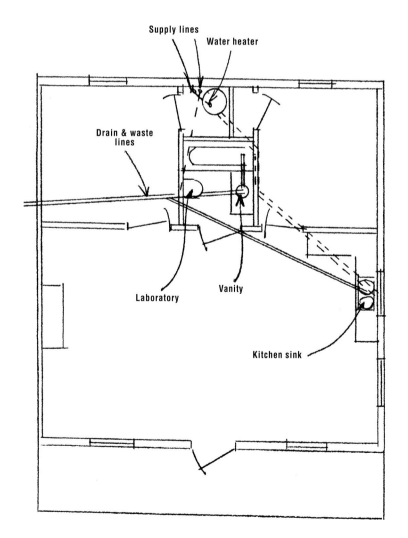

Supply lines

Water heater

Drain & waste lines

Laboratory

Vanity

Kitchen sink

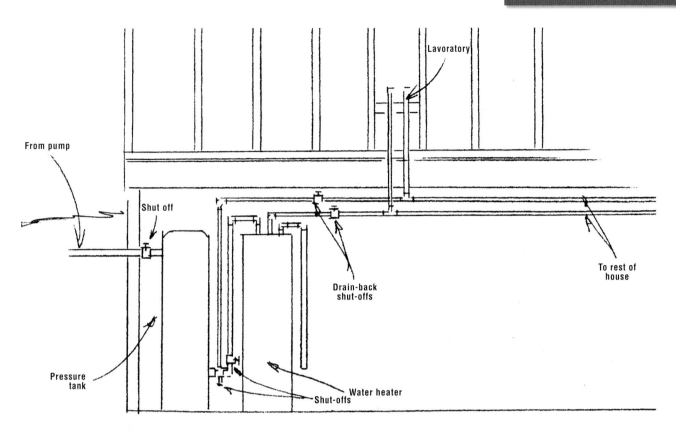

the openings to prevent debris and critics from getting into the system and to keep out **noxious sewer gases** until you can connect the fixtures. With the discharge system installed, you can install the supply line system to mate properly with it.

For **horizontal runs** in both supply and waste lines you will need to cut the studs for the pipes. Make these cuts carefully so you don't over-weaken the studs. The pipes should be well supported and those running through studs should have their faces covered with metal strips to prevent someone from driving a nail through them after they are covered.

Installing Plastic Pipe

Plastic pipe is easy to install. Cut with a handsaw, hacksaw, plumber's pipe cutter, or reciprocating saw. Remove all burrs with a file or knife

and lightly sand the outside edge smooth. **Dry fit the fittings and line** to make sure everything fits properly and then use a felt-tip pen to mark both the pipe and fittings so you can realign them easily. Wipe the pipe with a clean rag and cement cleaner. Then brush the **solvent cement** quickly on the pipe and fitting. Coat the pipe end liberally, but do not put as much in the **fitting socket**. Push the pipe into the fitting socket with a slight twisting motion.

Water Supply

In all but extremely remote locations you will need a safe and adequate water supply for your lodge. This can be any number of things from a developed **spring** to a **dug well**, **cistern** or **deep well**. If using a spring or existing well you should have it tested. This can be done by your

The diagram above shows a water intake and basic hot and cold water system for a lodge or cabin supplied by a well or spring. In this case the pressure tank and water heater are located in a basement or cellar.

local **County Extension Office**. Or you can add a water purification system. In many remote areas, developing a spring may be a choice. This is a simple matter of digging out the spring and lining it with concrete, metal well casing or mortar and stone. We have such an old spring on our place that was dug and lined around the turn of the century and still produces. The spring must also be covered to keep out critters. If the spring is located above your site, you may be able to create a simple **gravity flow**, but you will not have any water pressure. And, it's important to know if the spring runs year round and the volume. Many springs are **wet-weather**, and won't run during the summer months. A **pond or lake** can also be a water source, but again it must be fed through a water purification system.

A **cistern**, collecting runoff rainwater from the roof can also be a possible water source. My parents had such a water system for many years. But it is dependent on availability of rainfall. Cisterns are typically hand dug and concrete lined. In most instances, unless extremely tightly sealed, you will need to use a water purification system with them as well.

A dug well can be a water source, if groundwater is fairly close to the surface. These wells should be at least 10 feet deep or to the source of ground water. Anything deeper than 20 feet can be fairly hard to dig. In all instances, but especially in some clay and porous soils, hand digging a well can be hazardous due to cave-ins. My family also had such an old well, lined with stone and mortar with a well house, rope and bucket above. It provided water for everything from

cooking to the livestock, all hauled by bucket from the well. Sounds romantic, but it can get mighty bothersome and can be really hard work. A dug well typically utilizes a **pump** housed in a well house above the well, with the piping run down into the well. The pump then forces the water to a **pressure tank**. In northern climates the well house will have to be insulated and in many instances a heat lamp or heat tape supplying additional heat to prevent freeze-up.

The most dependable water system is a **drilled deep well** with **submersible pump** located in the well. The pump forces water to a **pressure tank** located in the building. In both instances of either dug or deep well, the water supply line from the well to the building must be located below **frostline**. Drilled deep wells are drilled with big drilling machines and are expensive. The cost is by the foot for drilling and the amount of metal casing needed to line the well. The amount of casing is determined by the soil substrate. For instance our drilled well here in the Ozarks is 280 foot deep, but only 20 feet of casing was needed because the rest of the well is drilled through solid rock. You should check with neighbors as to the average depth needed to obtain adequate water. State geologists can also provide advice.

Other considerations in the water supply system are to include **shut-offs** and make the entire system drainable. This is especially important if the lodge is used only seasonally and left uninhabited through the winter months. A slope of ½-inch per foot of run is a good idea. **Drain-back valves** must be located at each low point. Do not run water lines through

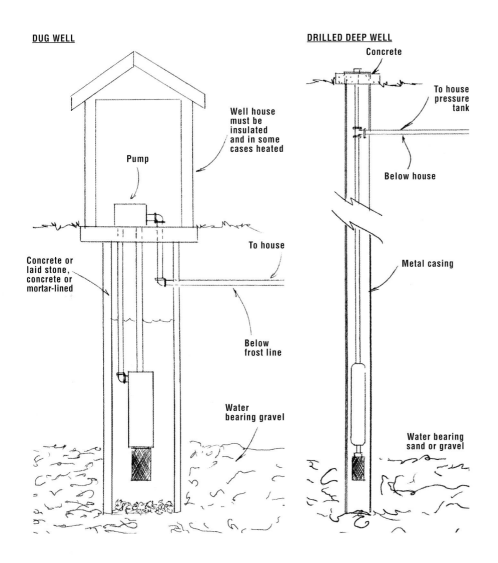

DUG WELL

Well house must be insulated and in some cases heated

Pump

Concrete or laid stone, concrete or mortar-lined

To house

Below frost line

Water bearing gravel

DRILLED DEEP WELL

Concrete

To house pressure tank

Below house

Metal casing

Water bearing sand or gravel

A simple dug well, shown at far left, requires an above ground pump protected by a well house or shelter. Drilled deep wells utilize a submersible pump located below the water table. Both supply water to pressure tanks located in the cabin or lodge.

outside walls as they may also freeze and break. Shut-offs should be installed at the beginning of the water system entryway, at the pressure tank, hot water heater, at each fixture (such as sinks), lavatories and stools. This allows you to shut off specific areas or fixtures to work on them without shutting down the entire system. Make sure you check with local code rules regarding materials and methods.

Water Purification Systems

A wide range of water purification systems are available for structures lacking access to **municipal water supplies**. These systems are designed to provide **safe drinking water** from springs, ponds, lakes, rivers and other sources with varying degrees of purification, sterilization and water output. You should be aware that most of these systems are intended to treat cold water only. Another caution is that no home purification system is absolutely foolproof. If you choose to install any of these systems, it is a good idea to regularly have your water tested.

Point-of-entry water purification units consist of a series of filtration and purification canisters attached to the main water intake. These units use a system of sediment pre-filter, micro and carbon block filter cartridges to reduce or eliminate chemical and microbiological agents. Many incorporate a process called **reverse osmosis**, "ultrafiltration," filters which force water through membranes with microscopic pores. These pores filter out larger compounds such as microorganisms, metals and other chemical contaminants but allow water molecules to pass through. These membrane systems are attached to the structure's main water intake and require careful maintenance, cleaning and periodic replacement of filter and carbon cartridges. The water output depends on the size of the unit. Larger, whole-house filtration units are available for structures that have a pressurized water supply.

Filtration/ultraviolet water purification-sterilizer systems, both portable and point-of-entry, make use of a set of filters that features a 3-stage filtration process. This begins with pre-filter to screen sediment and other large particles that might clog the pipes and filters. This is followed by a ceramic or reverse osmosis filter and finally a **carbon block.** In a final process the water is further disinfected by exposure to high levels of ultraviolet light. The sterilization process removes and kills bacteria, microorganisms and viruses along with heavy metals, pesticides and other chemical contaminants. Filtration/ultraviolet water purification-sterilizer systems are also available as gravity fed counter-top models with battery powered UV light units.

Portable multi-stage water purification units are designed to purify all types of unsafe water in remote areas or in structures that lack water intake plumbing. These portable units combine **multi-stage filtration** using sediment and carbon block filters followed by ultraviolet treatment. Most require a portable generator and electric pump but will provide a relatively large volume of clean water. They require periodic cleaning and replacement of filter cartridges.

Portable gravity water filters are portable, **canister-type** countertop filtration units that reduce water-born diseases and most chemical contaminants, but produce relatively small amounts of potable water per day. Most use ceramic or carbon filters. They are larger versions of the backpacking filters sold to campers and hikers. Always check with the manufacturers' instructions to find out what contaminants are eliminated or reduced by the filters, many commercial units may not remove all biological agents.

Demand Water Heater Systems

Demand water heaters are an alternative to traditional tank water heaters. These units heat water only as it is required, using a **non-tank unit** with a **demand-initiated heat exchanger** that is activated by the flow of water when a hot water valve is opened. Once activated, the heater delivers a constant supply of hot water that is limited only by the output of the heating element. When the water source tap is closed, the heater automatically shuts off until hot water is demanded again.

Demand water heaters are available powered by propane (LP), natural gas, or electricity in a variety of sizes suitable for all kinds of applications. Generally, gas-fired models have a higher hot water output than electric models. Most gas powered tankless water heaters provide 2 to 3 gallons of hot water per minute. Demand water heaters can be located centrally or at the point of use, depending on the amount of hot water needed. These range from **whole-house units** to **small, electric "plug-in" models** that provide hot water to a sink or shower. "Single appliance units" are also available powered by LP. Demand water heaters can be used as a booster for solar or wood-fired hot water systems.

Solar Water-heating Systems

In all types of solar water-heating systems sunlight heats an absorbing surface within a **solar collector** or storage tank. A **heat-transfer fluid** or the **potable water** itself is heated as it flows through tubes in the absorber. Systems with separate **heat transfer-fluid loops** heat potable water in a heat exchanger. The heated water is stored in a separate preheat tank or a conventional water heater tank until needed. There are five types of solar hot water systems.

Thermosiphon systems require no pumps and heat water or antifreeze fluid causing the fluid to rise by natural convection from collectors to a storage tank, which is placed at a higher level. In thermosiphon systems, heat transfer increases with temperature making these systems most efficient in areas with high levels of solar radiation. **Direct-circulation systems** pump water from storage to collectors during sunny periods. Units are freeze-protected by re-circulating hot water from the storage tank, or flushing the collectors. Since recirculation increases energy use and flushing reduces time of operation, direct-circulation systems are used only in warmer climates. **Drain-down systems** are indirect systems where untreated water is circulated through a closed loop, transferring heat to potable water via a heat exchanger. In **indirect water-heating systems**, antifreeze-protected fluid circulates through a closed loop transferring heat to potable water through a heat exchanger with 80 to 90 percent efficiency. In **air-solar systems**, air, heated by the collector, is blown through an air-to-water heat exchange system providing about 50-percent water heating efficiency range.

For most of North America, indirect air and water systems are the most efficient. While air-solar systems are not as efficient as water systems, they require less maintenance since they will not leak or burst.

Sewage Disposal

Two types of sewage disposal are used, and in most instances these are also governed by local code rules. This may be a **lagoon,** or **septic tank** with lateral **drain field**. Most areas will specify which can be used and exactly how they must be constructed or installed. Much of this is due to the different types of soil conditions.

Alternative Outdoor Toilets

For remote areas that lack access to public sewage lines and disposal you may select some style of **outhouse or "waterless" toilet**. These can be as simple as an old-fashioned

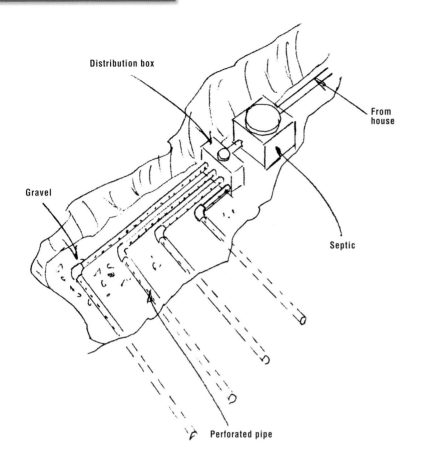

Distribution box

From house

Gravel

Septic

Perforated pipe

Two types of sewage systems are common, a septic tank with a lateral field, or a lagoon, depending on soil conditions and local code rules.

"one-holer" in a shed poised over a pit or an ultramodern, high-tech **composting toilet**. Here are some alternate choices.

The **basic pit toilet** is also called a privy or outhouse. For directions on how to construct a traditional outhouse, see Chapter 14.

A **drum privy** consists of a toilet seat and shelter placed over a removable metal or plastic drum or portable fiberglass container or **"vault."** Ideally, the **waste containers** in drum privies are sealed and self-contained and reduce the chance of ground water contamination. In the most primitive cases "honey buckets," five-gallon sealable **plastic buckets** used for shipping paint, cleaners and solvents, could be used in situations where the container can be fre-

quently removed for proper disposal. Unlike locating a pit privy, the selection of a privy site for a drum privy is not restricted by soil type or the depth of ground water.

When filled, the drum or vault must be removed and transported to a proper **sewage disposal site**. Therefore the location where the drum privy will be used must be accessible to vehicles or at least ATVs. Sewage drained from drums will have to be disposed of at a **sewage treatment facility** or other locally approved location. When selecting a drum privy, always consult with local authorities to find out about **sewage disposal regulations**.

Containers can be switched out and stored on site until they are transported for disposal. Since the containers may be subject to somewhat rough handling during transportation, they should be regularly inspected for cracks and leaks. **Drums and vaults** should also be cleaned periodically for basic sanitation. A drum privy might be a good choice for a camp with seasonal or part-time use where the "pressure" on the privy is not excessive. If the site is accessible to larger vehicles, waste from the drum or vault can be stored in above- or in-ground storage tanks and removed by a contracted **"honey wagon"** or pump truck.

As with all receptacle privies, a drum privy must be **ventilated** by some kind of **vertical pipe** or enclosed **moisture-proof vent duct** that extends from the privy vault to a point well above the roof peak to reduce odor and prevent the buildup of **explosive gasses**. The outlet should be screened and capped to divert precipitation. The seat and lid should be tight-fitting to exclude vermin and insects from the vault interior.

Chemical toilets are for temporary use where there is no onsite waste disposal. They are suitable only for situations where waste can be transported from the site and dumped at an approved disposal facility so a chemical toilet would work well for a hunting camp that is in use for relatively short periods at a time. These units use a **chemically treated reservoir** located directly below the toilet seat.

Generally identified with RVs, aircraft and **"porta-potties,"** chemical toilets are readily identified by the **blue-colored dye, "Anotec,"** in the water. The disinfecting solution is usually **formaldehyde** or a similar chemical or an enzyme hybrid that performs partial disinfection of the waste. **Re-circulating toilets** use a more complicated design that separates solid waste into an internal holding tank and re-circulates the chemical liquid through the toilet tank.

All chemical toilets have limited storage capacity and, in nearly all jurisdictions, waste must be pumped by or disposed of with a licensed septic company or facility in the same way as **chemical waste** removed from an RV or construction site portable toilet.

Small, portable "camping" toilets, consisting of a seat over a container of water treated with disinfecting chemicals.

A **composting toilet** is any system that converts human waste into **organic compost** by the natural breakdown through aerobic process of organic matter into its basic chemical components. Human waste is broken down into compost in a digester

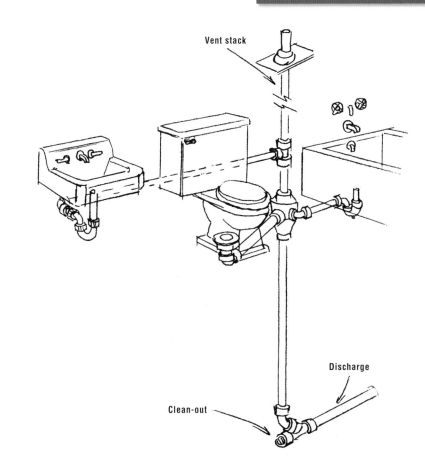

tank or **"basement."** Composting toilets require a **carbon source**, preferably wood chips (hardwood bark chips work very well), to mix with feces to maintain the decomposition process. One scoop is added per use. As with drum and pit privies, the composting unit must be fitted with a vent. To reduce odor, a liquid waste disposal method for urine should be incorporated in the tank to separate urine and feces. This can draw liquid waste to a subsurface leach line, holding tank, or evaporation trays. Odor can also be managed by adding sufficient high-carbon soak material to absorb excess liquid.

More elaborate systems flush waste to a **remote composting unit** below the toilet and require a source of electricity to power heating units

The diagram above shows plumbing for a conventional wastewater and sewage discharge system that would be connected to municipal sewage lines or a septic tank or lagoon.

Vent stack

Discharge

Clean-out

DRUM PRIVY

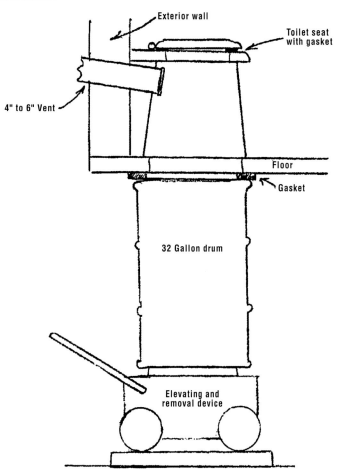

A drum privy uses a toilet seat and some kind of removable "drum" or container. In the diagram above, a 32-gallon steel oil drum is placed under the privy and raised to seal with a gasket around the bottom of the waste opening.

(to destroy pathogens) and exhaust fans to encourage microbial activity and prevent the compost from becoming **anaerobic**, which retards composting and causes unpleasant odor. The waste collecting tanks or "basement" must be insulated in colder areas.

An alternate process is to the so-called **"batch-bin" method** where solid waste is removed to separate **composting tanks**. These can be large commercial plastic agricultural bins where the wastes are thoroughly mixed with additional hardwood bark and recycled compost to soak up excess liquid. The "compost run" lasts four to six weeks, depending

on air temperature. The compost is then removed to a storage platform to decompose and dry further for six months to a year. Most of these systems require skilled management and time in order to function successfully.

Small, **self-contained composting toilets** complete the composting process in-place and are generally fitted with some mechanism to allow the user to periodically rotate a drum or stir the contents within the composting toilet to encourage aerobic breakdown of waste. These models are available commercially and are easily installed with simple tools. Most require access to electrical power to operate. They come in different sizes and are rated based on the number of persons using the toilet on a regular basis. Regular maintenance is required and, in smaller systems, solids may need to be removed several times a year. Properly designed in relation to expected use, self-contained composting toilets should require neither power nor water, and will reduce solids to 1 to 2 percent of the deposited organic materials (feces and toilet paper).

The ideal is that **fully composted waste** can be simply spread across the forest floor. Be aware, however, that disposal of composted material is generally governed by local, state or federal regulations, so be prepared to check with local authorities before installing such a unit. In many locations even completely composted human waste must be disposed of as sewage. While composting toilets may be a good choice for a remote lodge, ultimately the practicality of a composting toilet depends a great deal on the interest, skill and energy of the operator.

COMPOSTING PRIVY

SELF-CONTAINED COMPOSTING PRIVY

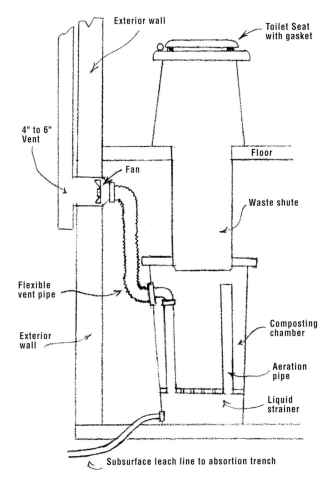

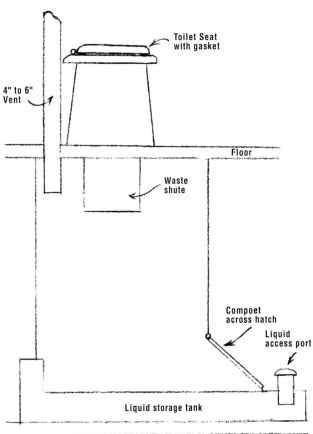

INSULATION

In most instances whole log construction does not require extra insulation, other than that applied during construction. **Caulking** and **sealing**, however, is important. If you have a standard constructed ceiling or attic in a log building, it should be properly insulated. With standard construction it's important to insulate the walls, crawl space and ceiling or attic. Insulation includes **insulation board sheathing**, which is installed during construction, as well as **flange batts** which include a **vapor barrier** on one side and a **Kraft paper wrap** on the opposite. These are commonly used in crawl spaces. **Foil-face or paper-faced batts** have one side covered with those materials and both can be used in walls, attics and sidewalls. **Unfaced fiberglass batts** do not have a covering and are more economical, but don't provide moisture control. Other types include **loose or blown-in insulation** and **expanding foam** which are usually professionally installed. Loose or blown attic insulation, however, can be applied using a machine rented from building suppliers such as Lowe's. *Cocoon Blow-In Attic Insulation* costs less than other types, is **itch-free** and easy to apply. All you do is haul a hose into your attic. There is no cutting, stuffing or fitting. Simply place the ma-

The composting toilet, above left, uses electric fans and heaters to accelerate the composting process. The self-contained unit above requires frequent removal of composted waste and liquid. Many modern self-contained units are more compact.

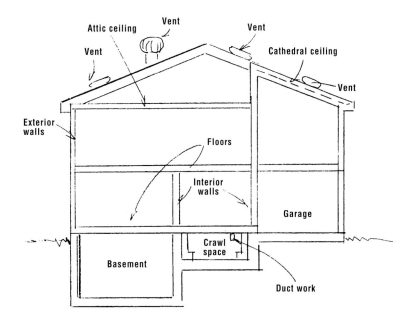

Vent

Attic ceiling

Vent

Vent

Cathedral ceiling

Vent

Exterior walls

Floors

Interior walls

Garage

Basement

Crawl space

Duct work

A combination of efficient insulation and effective ventilation are vital. The diagram above shows key areas that require insulation and primary vent locations.

chine outside and run the hose into the attic. This is a two-person job, with one person in the attic applying the insulation and a second person outside feeding the Cocoon material into the machine. **Soffit baffles** should be used in the soffits and proper ventilation provided in the eaves. **Fixture barriers** should also be placed around heat producing electrical or HVAC components.

Vapor barriers should always be installed facing the warm side of the room. In an unheated attic the vapor barrier is installed down toward the room below. In a heated and finished attic, un-faced batts are commonly used with faced batts between the rafters, again vapor barrier down.

These days insulation products are designed for all portions of a building construction. This includes insulation for foundation walls, slabs, floors, walls and attic. For the most energy-efficiency, all the products should be used, creating a total insulating sys-

tem. The **Owens Corning Insulation System** consists of many products, all working together throughout the building to deliver year-round energy savings and comfort. This includes products for insulating the foundation walls, **crawlspace** (underfloor), a heated crawlspace, under a slab, basement walls, floors, heating and cooling HVAC ducts, exterior walls, interior walls (for **noise control**), attics, finished or unfinished and cathedral ceilings. The system reduces heating and cooling costs, reduces air infiltration and **controls moisture**. Just normal everyday living can put from 5 to 10 pounds of moisture into the home per day. In the winter months this moisture can accumulate and condense on the cold inner sides of exterior surfaces. This can cause paint to blister, form stains on drywall ceilings and walls, even damage the buildings structure. Vapor barriers can help control the amount of moisture passing through insulation and collecting inside exterior walls, ceilings and floors.

All insulation products are based on **R-values or resistance**. Insulation with higher R-Values provides more insulation. Check with your local building supplier as to the R-Values needed for your area and home. Or check out the Owens Corning website.

Batt insulation installation during new-construction is a fairly easy do-it-yourself project. The first step is purchasing the correct insulation. The walls may be framed with 2 x 4 or 2 x 6 studs. 2 x 6 studs allow for more insulation because of their extra depth. Depending on local codes or the desired R-value for the wall, Owens Corning suggests using 5½-inch thick R-21. R-19 fiberglass batt insulation (6¼-inches thick) can also be used, but compressing it into a 2 x 6 cavity lowers the R-value to R-18. For 2 x 4 stud walls, the choices are R-15 or R-13, both of which are 3½-inches thick.

For standard wall heights, use **pre-cut batts** rather than continuous rolls. Each piece of insulation is manufactured to the size of the most typical framing, which is usually built either 16 or 24 inches on center and about 92 inches high. These **cut-to-size batts** will make the job go faster and easier.

The insulation should fit snug against the studs and completely fill the cavity to the top and bottom plates. Cut batt insulation to fit snugly around obstructions such as electrical boxes, plumbing and plumbing vent lines.

When using **Kraft-faced batts** with flanges, staple the flanges every 8 to 12 inches. The flanges can be stapled to the front or inside of the stud. Drywall installers prefer the face to be stapled on the inside of the studs. Owens Corning Fastbatt insulation does not have stapling flanges.

Note: Never leave faced insulation exposed. The facings on **Kraft-and-foil insulation** will burn and must be installed with substantial contact with an approved ceiling, wall or construction material to help prevent the spread of fire in the wall, ceiling or floor cavities. **Unfaced fiberglass** is non-combustible.

You can add even more energy efficiency by adding an **exterior insulating sheathing** such as Foamular rigid foam insulation. It has an R-value of R-5 per inch of product thickness. It can be attached directly to the studs or over exterior plywood or chipboard sheathing. To achieve an R-19 wall system, add the Foamular R-5, plus a 2 x 4 wall cavity filled with R-13 fiberglass insulation. Exterior siding and drywall typically add an R-value of R-1. Apply the rigid foam insulation vertically (parallel to the studs), attaching to studs with collar-head nails. These are nails with large plastic washers already attached to the nail. **Nail length** must be sufficient so that the nails will penetrate studs by 1 inch. Space nails every 8 inches on each stud covered. The material is easily cut to fit around windows and doors and other construction obstacles, but measure carefully in order to avoid leaving uninsulated spaces.

Once the installation is complete, seal all joints with Owens Corning Bil-R-Tape **construction tape** to prevent air infiltration. Note: since Foamular is a non-structural material, it must be installed over adequately braced framing in accordance with local building codes.

Foamular rigid foam insulation can also be added to your foundation walls, basement walls and even under a slab. Before insulating a basement or foundation check for water leakage and fix the problem. All leaks should be sealed on the exterior surface. The band joists should be caulked and sealed to prevent air infiltration at the construction joints and around all penetrations such as plumbing, electrical and HVAC and dryer vents.

Three different methods can be used. (1) You can construct stud frames at the interior of the foundation walls and fill the cavities with fiberglass insulation; (2) you can install Owens Corning Insulpink foam insulation board or Basement Blanket; or (3) you can use Owens Corning Basement Finishing System, which requires no additional paneling or drywall.

BASIC TYPES OF INSULATION

- Insulation board sheathing
- Batt insulation (unfaced fiberglass)
- Batt insulation with vapor barriers
- Loose or blown-in insulation
- Expanding foam insulation
- Fixture barriers
- Exterior sheathing

Attic Insulation

Properly insulating the attic is extremely important. In case the attic is unfinished, lay **walk boards** across the joists and provide a temporary light. **Batt or loose fill insulation** can be used to fill the voids between the **ceiling joists**. The attic insulation does not have to be fastened in place as gravity will keep it down. If the batts have a **vapor barrier**, it should be placed **face-down** toward the heated rooms below. Leave the batts in the package wrapper until you get the package into the attic. When you open the package the batts will expand a great deal. Place the batts down between the ceiling joists leaving a bit of space at the outer walls for air flow. Make all the long runs first, and then cut the shorter pieces. Where pieces are to be joined, butt them together tightly and tape the vapor barrier joints with **foil-faced construction tape**.

Carefully fit around **electrical wiring**, making sure you don't disturb or loosen the wiring. All insulation must be kept at least 3 inches away from recessed light fixtures unless they are indicated with a mark (IC) or insulated ceiling. Fill any spaces between a **chimney** and the wood framing with **noncombustible insulating materials** such as batts without facings. Insulation should also not be placed directly around a flue, but again leaving at least 3 inches all around the flue. You will not need insulation installed between the rafters, if the ceiling is insulated. The exception is in cathedral ceilings and in some cases of attics that are finished off with knee walls.

Proper insulation, such as the vapor barrier batting shown below, can conserve energy and provide a more comfortable structure, even in a humble cabin.

Do not unroll or remove the insulation from the package until you get into the attic. Then unroll and place down between the ceiling joists.

Working with Fiberglass Insulation

Fiberglass insulation consists of tiny strands of fiber glass and some of the particles will come off and drift through the air as the material is installed. This can cause a **serious irritation**. Years ago I worked as a laborer for a construction company building commercial buildings. We constructed a low-roofed, long motel and one of my jobs was to insulate the attic portion. The batts had to be pulled some distance through the attic and installation was tight. I ended up with a serious irritation under my arms and knees that required an emergency room visit. Always wear long pants, a long-sleeve shirt that can be fastened tightly at the wrists and collar. A plastic rain coat, or these days a Tyvek overall is the best bet. Wear safety glasses, gloves, a tight-fitting cap and a respirator. Work for only 10 to 15 minutes, and then get back out into the fresh air for a few minutes.

VENTILATION

Proper ventilation is extremely important. Ventilating creates a positive air flow that allows the house to breathe and prevents the build-up of moisture. The attic should have **eave vents** along with gable and/or **roof vents**. At least two vents are required to create an air-flow, in one and out the other. Owens Corning suggests 1 square foot of free vent area per 300 square feet of attic floor when a **vapor retarder** is used. In situations where no vapor retarder is used, 1 square foot of free vent area should be provided for each 150 square feet of attic floor area. You will also need at least two **crawlspace vents** to create a positive air flow. One square foot of free vent area is recommended for every 1500 square feet of floor area covered with a **polyethylene vapor retarder** (every 150 square feet if there is no vapor retarder). In crawlspaces that are unheated and/or have a dirt floor, it is also recommended the floor be covered with a polyethylene vapor retarder. All vents should be screened to keep out insects.

Finishing

Above: The amount and type of interior finishing depends on the building, the type of construction and how "fancy" you wish to go.

Interior finishing is where the fun begins and the work slows down. The amount of interior finishing needed depends on the construction type and your desires. It can be as simple as a coat of clear finish on a log interior, or the full treatment of sheetrock painted or papered. Again, you may prefer to subcontract some of this work. But you can also do all of it yourself, depending on time, how much money you wish to save and your skills and tools.

INSTALLING DRYWALL

Drywall (also known as sheetrock or gypsum board) is an excellent interior wall treatment. It installs quickly and lends itself well to a variety of wall finishes. It can be spray textured and painted (by far the most popular treatment), finished smooth and painted, wall papered or paneled.

Drywall is made of gypsum, which is hydrous calcium sulphate, one of the most common minerals found in the earth. It contains two molecules of water bonded with calcium sulphate. In a fire, the water evaporates and retards the spread of flames, as does the chalky substance left after the water leaves. The gypsum is covered on both sides with heavy treated paper.

Drywall comes in a variety of thicknesses, lengths and widths. The most popular size for residential construction is ½- or ⅝-inch thick, 8- to 12-foot lengths and 4-feet wide. Special water-resistant sheets are also available.

Good framing techniques are necessary for proper drywall installation. **Stud walls** should be constructed to give a flat, even surface for fastening. Maintaining 16- or 24-inches on center framing for walls and ceilings will make sure the joints can be properly fastened to framing members with a minimum of drywall cutting. **Battens** can be installed in some instances to create a nailing framework. If you use **non-kiln-dried materials**, the rooms to be drywalled should be closed-in from the weather and heated to 55-65 degrees F. for 72 hours first. This will season the wood to prevent nail popping and joint cracks resulting from the "drying out" of unseasoned lumber.

Rough wiring, plumbing, telephone and TV jacks, any special intercom or stereo hookups, and insulation should all be completed in your walls before they are drywalled. Good workmanship includes cleaning out the room to be drywalled first. Remove all scrap lumber and other debris, sweep the floor and provide temporary lighting.

In addition to the **drywall sheets**, you'll need joint compound, joint tape, metal corners and nails or **drywall screws**. You'll also need a **drywall hammer**, specially crafted to nail and dimple around the nail head, or a drill/driver to drive drywall screws. You will need a utility knife with extra blades, a 6- and 8-inch drywall trowel, a corner trowel, a 4-foot metal T-square, **drywall jacks** (either manufactured or constructed on site) for ceiling installation, two sawhorses for layout and cutting, a **drywall jab saw** or sabre saw and a 2 x 4 or 2 x 6 ten to twelve feet long to support the drywall while cutting.

These days many upscale lodges and homes are log with interior finishing to match.

Drywall, to the right of the exposed logs above, is one of the more popular wall coverings and it's fairly easy — but hard work — to install.

It's extremely important to always measure accurately for all **light boxes**, or other objects requiring irregular shapes to be cut in the drywall sheets. These can be cut with a sabre saw, jab saw, utility knife and so forth. This must be done accurately to give a tight fit so the finish work can be done correctly.

To cut a panel, first measure carefully the area to be covered with the

SHEETROCK & DRYWALL FINISHING

Basic drywall tools include a tape measure, utility knife, drywall hammer, jab saw, mud pan, 6-inch joint knife, 8- and 10-inch taping knives.

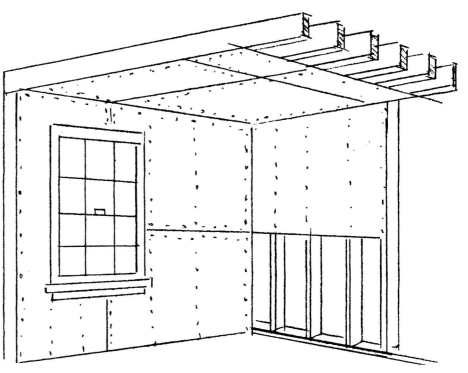

1. *The sheetrock boards are fastened in place with sheetrock screws or nails.*

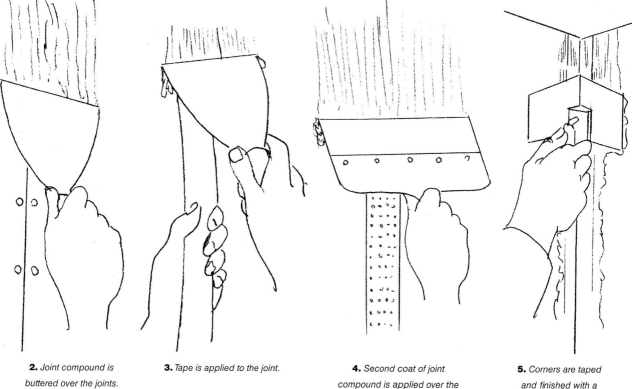

2. *Joint compound is buttered over the joints.*

3. *Tape is applied to the joint.*

4. *Second coat of joint compound is applied over the tape and smoothed out.*

5. *Corners are taped and finished with a corner tool.*

drywall. Lay out the dimensions on the piece to be cut. Check twice before cutting! This should be done on the face side (the smoothest, usually lightest colored side). Now score the drywall along the layout lines with a utility knife. Support the edge of the drywall piece close to the scored line and bend the drywall sheet downward. This will crack the paper and **gypsum core** along the scored line. Cut the remaining paper backing with a utility knife. Edges can be smoothed when necessary with a sanding block.

Ceilings should be installed first. Hold the first panel tightly up against the nailing framework. Use **drywall nails** or screws spaced no greater than 7 inches on center. Nails should be driven straight and driven to hold the drywall tight against the framing members. Be careful during the final strokes of the hammer not to rip the paper—but drive the nail head just below the drywall surface with a dimple (or recess) around the nail head.

Follow the same procedure for the walls, except nails can be 8 inches on-center. **Wall panels** can be installed vertically or horizontally. Drywall sheets installed horizontally, and starting at the top will increase the **diaphragm strength** of the wall, and better support the ceiling drywall sheets. End joints should be staggered for both ceiling and wall installation.

Fill all joints with **joint compound**, then cover them with **joint tape** and finish them off with two separate additional coats of joint compound. The first coat is called a **bedding coat**. Spread it into the joints, lay tape into the compound and smooth the tape into the bedding compound with the 6-inch trowel. Be careful to avoid wrinkles in the tape. A **light skim coat** is then applied and the edges feathered out 2 inches on both sides of the tape. Remember you are applying several thin coats to build up the joint gradually. After the skim coat has dried, lightly sand the joint and apply a second coat. Spread the compound evenly and feather the edges 2 inches beyond the second coat. Nails in areas other than joints should be checked for proper dimpling and then given the same three-coat application of compound. Work just the area around the nail.

Inside and outside corners are handled the same as joints. Fold the tape in the center and press it into the bedding. Then cover with three separate layers of compound like the joints. Outside corners are fitted with **metal corner beads** or **corner angles** and then treated with three coats. Allow all panels to thoroughly dry and then finish the wall and ceiling as desired.

TEXTURED CEILINGS

Any number of materials can be used to apply texture to ceilings. You can even roll it on with special **rollers** and materials, but the finish is not nearly as consistent as a **sprayed surface**. Also a number of materials can be sprayed, ranging from **acoustical**, which consists of tiny beads in a solution to a variety of **"mud" type surfaces** that can be left as is or wiped with a trowel to create a variety of textures. All of these provide a consistent and decorative ceiling and also hide small blemishes in drywall application. Often a textured ceiling can be applied to a drab somewhat sloppy old ceiling to make it more consistent and better looking.

Ceilings are often textured using a texture gun or even troweled.

Regardless of which is chosen, it is messy work. Put on your oldest clothes, cover everything with drop cloths and wear a cap and protective glasses.

Application with the *Goldblatt* **pattern gun** and a **compressor** is basically quite easy and fun. The materials are mixed according to manufacturers instructions and poured in the **hopper**. Position the gun in place and press the trigger. In a short time the ceiling and everything else in the room, including you will be covered with a layer of texture material. If using wiped textures, use the edge of a trowel to create the swirls, but make sure you go in a circulation motion, instead of a straight line. All

that's left is to clean up your mess, stand back and admire your ceiling "sculpture work."

WINDOW AND DOOR TRIM & MOLDING

Window and door trim and molding can set the design of your lodge both inside and out. A wide variety of styles is available, although the big box houses will usually carry only the most common or "popular" styles. Several types are available for **exterior trim**, with more limited species for **interior trim**. If you are replacing a door or window in an existing room or building you will probably need to stay with the style already in place. If you're completely remodeling or building new, the choices are greater. These days a wide range of "designer" windows and doors with matching trim is available. Several traditional styles of both window and door trim, exterior and interior are common.

Window components include the **casings**, which go around the top and sides of the window and the **mullion casings**, which go between divided windows. In the past windows were often trimmed out with stools, a shaped wood trim that goes against the bottom edge of the bottom sash and protrudes into the room. A more modern approach, used with replacement windows as well as for new construction, is a window trimmed without a **stool**. A casing of some sort is then positioned beneath the stool. Today windows are not only available in standard square shape, but a wide variety of arches, rounds and some quite unusual shapes. Exterior window and door trim components may include: **brickmold** or casings. These both provide a thick surface for the siding to butt against. In some instances a drip cap is used on top of the window or door to help keep water from seeping under the siding.

Doors are available **un-hung** or **pre-hung**. Separate doors require constructing a **frame**, which includes the **side jambs, head jamb, threshold** for an exterior door, and door **"stops."** The door is then hung in the frame and the unit installed. Pre-hung doors are much easier and more common. The pre-hung exterior door unit will usually come with exterior casings or brickmold, but you must supply the **interior casings**.

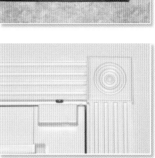

Making Trim

If you have a woodworking shop and the correct power tools, you can make your own window and door trim for both interior and exterior use. The design possibilities are almost unlimited, and you can match species or use more exotic species, such as walnut, cherry, or others if you choose.

Three tools can be used to create door and window molding—a **router, shaper** and a **planer/moulder**. A wide variety of **router bits** are available for creating many of the different casing styles. Some bits can be used hand-held, while others, including bits more commonly used for creating raised panels, can also be used for creating window and door trims, but must be used in a **router table**. In many instances you will need to make more than one pass, usually with different router bits to create a full casing profile.

You can even create your own windows if you desire to use a less commonly available wood species, for instance walnut. Both CMT and Freud offer router-bit sets designed

Window and door trim can set the design of your lodge, both inside and out and again is fairly easy to do, if you take your time.

WINDOW TRIM

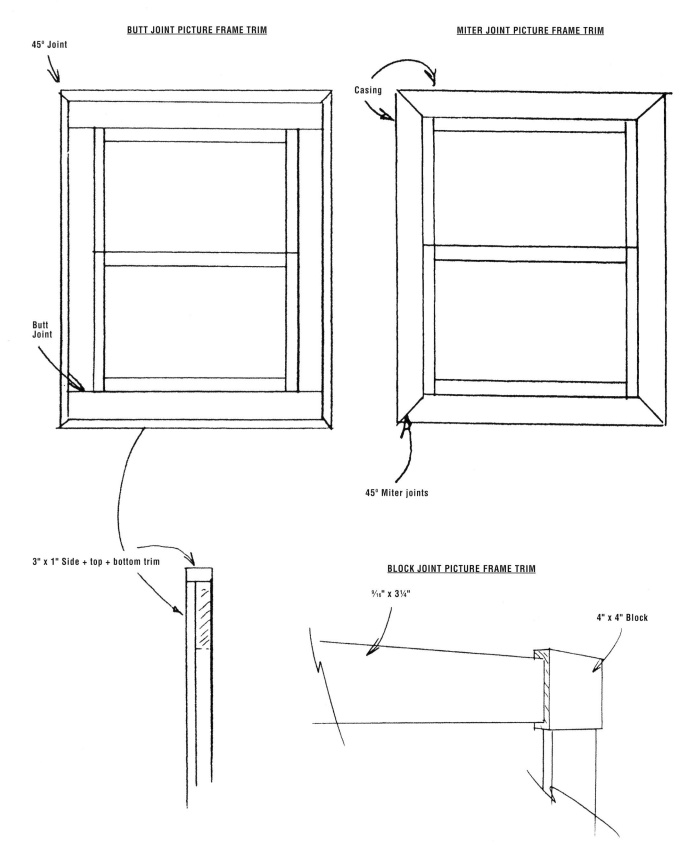

BUTT JOINT PICTURE FRAME TRIM

45º Joint

Butt
Joint

3" x 1" Side + top + bottom trim

MITER JOINT PICTURE FRAME TRIM

Casing

45º Miter joints

BLOCK JOINT PICTURE FRAME TRIM

⁹⁄₁₆" x 3¼"

4" x 4" Block

STANDARD TRIM WITH STOOL

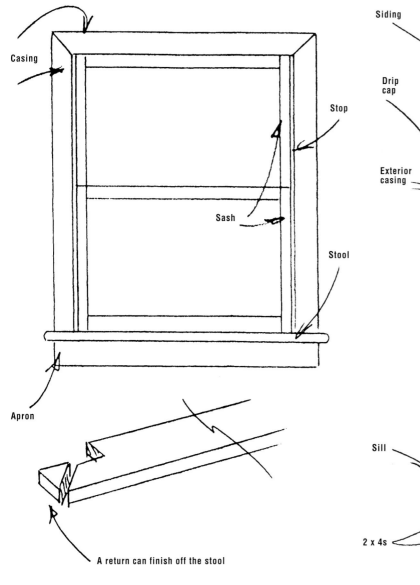

Casing

Stop

Sash

Stool

Sash

Apron

A return can finish off the stool

STANDARD WINDOW TRIM CROSS-SECTION

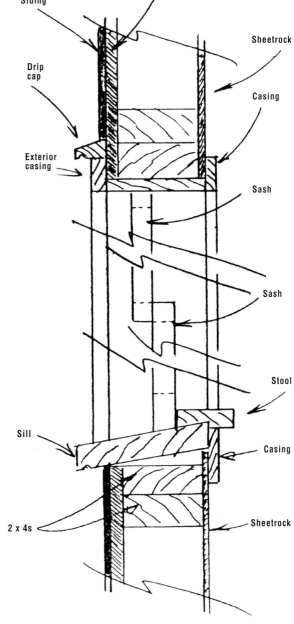

Sheathing

Siding

Drip cap

Sheetrock

Casing

Exterior casing

Sash

Sash

Stool

Sill

Casing

2 x 4s

Sheetrock

TYPES OF TRIM

Window Castings

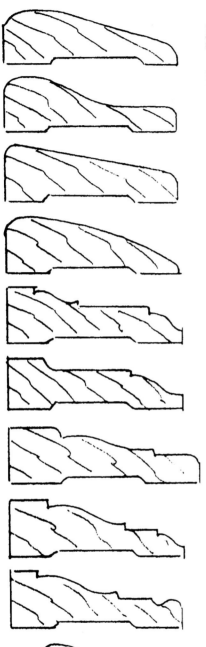

Mullion Castings

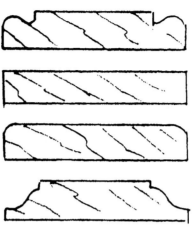

Window Stouls

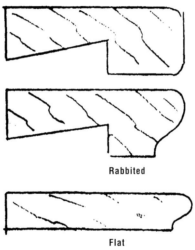

Rabbited

Flat

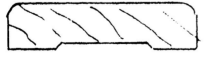

specifically for creating **sashes.** Freud also has an exterior door set as well.

If you intend to do quite a bit of trim, a **spindle shaper** and **shaper cutters** speed up production and is easier to use. The Grizzly 1½ horsepower is a good mid-sized shaper that will handle small shop or home-builder chores. The Shop Fox two-horsepower steps up in size, and has the power for faster cutting of hardwoods. The CMT Shaper cutter heads utilize separate knives, and a wide variety of profiles are available. You can also purchase a **Molding & Profile set** from CMT. The unit features 13 profiles to create almost any decorative molding needed. The cutter head accepts any of the dozens of additional profiles from the company. Freud and Grizzly also carry cutter heads with insert profile knives. A shaper makes the chore fast and easy, but it's important to follow all safety rules when using a spindle shaper. Always make sure the cutter knives are properly and securely fastened in place, and the spindle nut is tight before plugging in the shaper. Feed the work against the rotation and always use the guards supplied with the shaper. Do not make freehand cuts—always use a fence system and pusher blocks.

The ultimate, however, for **shop-created molding** is the Woodmaster 4-in-1 Model 712 Variable Speed 12-inch planer. The unit is a full-featured **wood planer** with two motors, a variable speed for the feed and a separate motor for the cutter head. Its patented Morse-Taper quick-change head allows you to move from planing to molding in less than 5 minutes. The company has over 500 molding profile knives including a wide variety of casings. These also include "colonial" casings for replicating older home styles. Or you can have knives custom ground to match unusual patterns. Their Molding Profile book shows in full-size all the molding patterns.

In order to change from planing to molding, the planing shaft is removed and the molding shaft with the appropriate molding knives installed. **Guide boards** must also be installed on the planer bed to guide the stock against the cutter heads. This can be made quite easily from a piece of particleboard or plywood with a ½-inch minimum thickness. The board should precisely fit the planer bed. Then cut four strips of hardwood ¾ x 1 x 16¼-inches long. Bevel the ends of two of the strips to prevent the stock hanging up on the outfeed side. Using a straight edge, mark a line running the length of the board, parallel to the guide board sides and positioned ⅛-inch less than the distance from the left planer side to the inside edge of the left parting leg of the knife. Glue and screw one end of an **unbeveled strip** on the infeed end of the guide board with its right edge aligned to the chalk line. Glue and screw one of the **beveled strips** to the outfeed end in the same manner. Place a piece of prepared stock on the guide board, against the two fences you just installed, and position the remaining fences snug against the stock. The fit between the two fences should prevent any side-to-side movement of the stock, but should not be so tight the stock cannot feed through easily. Glue and screw the right side fences in place. Use **paste furniture wax** to wax the board and

fences. Secure the guide board to the planer extension tables with c-clamps or bolts; making sure the board is parallel to the bed. With the hood off and the planer unplugged, check for alignment. Replace the hood and make a light cut to allow the parting knives to barely cut a relief in the bed board. After proper adjustment and a test run, it's merely a matter of running stock through the moulding head.

After years of installing numerous

Stock is fed under the knives of a molding machine braced between guide boards mounted on the planer bed.

The windows and doors of this log house main room are trimmed with rough stripped log "molding" in keeping with the overall design.

window and door trims, I've come up with a few tips and tricks. The first, if installing interior trim that is to be stained and finished separately from the walls, the best tactic is to cut or mould the trim, then rough cut to length. Stain and finish before installation. As you final cut the pieces, use a sponge brush to touch up the cut ends before installation. I also like to cut the pieces overlong, position them in place against the door or window jamb and then mark and cut to fit. This provides a more precise fit than measuring and cutting. I always cut on the outside of the pencil line. This usually means making more than one cut for final fit, but the pieces fit snugly and precisely in place. I installed one piece of door trim a year ago, forgot to nail it in place and it stayed upright until the winter drying in the home caused it to loosen slightly. I used to install all trim by cutting with a miter box and handsaw, nailing in place and then setting the nails below the surface. These days I use a small portable air compressor and brad gun for installation, along with a cordless miter saw for cutting.

Window and door trim can set off your home, and installing it yourself brings even more pleasure. The job is relatively easy and simple if you take your time. And, if you create the trim in your shop, the pleasure is even greater. You can often save money, as well as create unusual or one-of-a-kind décor.

Urethane Millwork

An unusual approach to door and window trim, as well as other decorative millwork is **preformed millwork** of urethane. A vast number of products are available from Fypon, makers of **urethane products** for over 35 years. Urethane millwork is moisture, splinter, and insect resistant, and extremely consistent. The product does not warp or split, requires no sanding or sealing and is simply installed by a special adhesive. Typical window pieces include arch molding, half-round spoked pediment, end cap, molding (casing) and even a lower window panel. **Shutters** are also available to match.

Basic door pieces include a sunburst pediment, door crosshead, fluted pilaster, fluted mull pilaster, and plinth block. Crossheads, pediments, arched trim, pilaster and a keystone are other products. Many pieces are designed to work together and some can be ordered moulded as one piece to further speed installation.

KITCHEN & BATH CABINETS

Kitchen and bath cabinets are available in sections you can easily install and join to create the completed cabinetry. With a few tools and a bit of time you can also build your own kitchen cabinets and bathroom vanities. Both upper and lower cabinets have the same basic construction details. Incidentally, you can construct a **custom kitchen cabinet** to fit any space, rather than the small individual sections joined as with purchased cabinetry. Or you can make up smaller units and join them in the same fashion.

Lower Cabinets

On the lower cabinet, the first step is to cut the two sides. If a side is to be concealed against a wall it can be made of more economical plywood. The exposed side should be cut from a good **hardwood- or smooth softwood-surfaced plywood**. The following is the simplest method of constructing, using glue and finish nails that are then set below the surface and the holes filled with wood putty. Cut a ¼ x ¼ inch rabbet in the inside back edge of each side piece for the cabinet back. The **bottom shelf** is raised above the floor on most cabinets to create a "toespace" or **kick board**. Locate the position of the bottom on the side pieces and mark the kick board cut-out on each cabinet side. Cut using a sabre saw. In most instances the bottom front facer is 1-inch in width, allowing for a ¼-inch lip to protrude down into the toe space. Mark this location and then use a carpenter's square to mark a line for the bottom. Cut the bottom ¼-inch narrower than the sides, and fasten the bottom in place with glue and finish nails, making sure it is aligned with the squared marks. A **nailing-strip** is installed at the top

KITCHEN & BATH CABINETS

Tools
- Sabre saw
- Radial arm saw w/ fine-toothed blade
- Carpenter's square
- Staple gun
- Hammer or air nailer
- Hammer
- Pencil
- Router

Materials
- Hardwood- or smooth softwood-surfaced plywood
- Lip hinges
- Veneer tape
- No. 6 & No. 8 finish nails
- Doweling
- Glue
- Wood putty

In many instances these days, kitchen cabinets and bathroom vanities are purchased as "components" and assembled to create the needed cabinetry, but you can build your own.

TYPICAL CABINET CONSTRUCTION

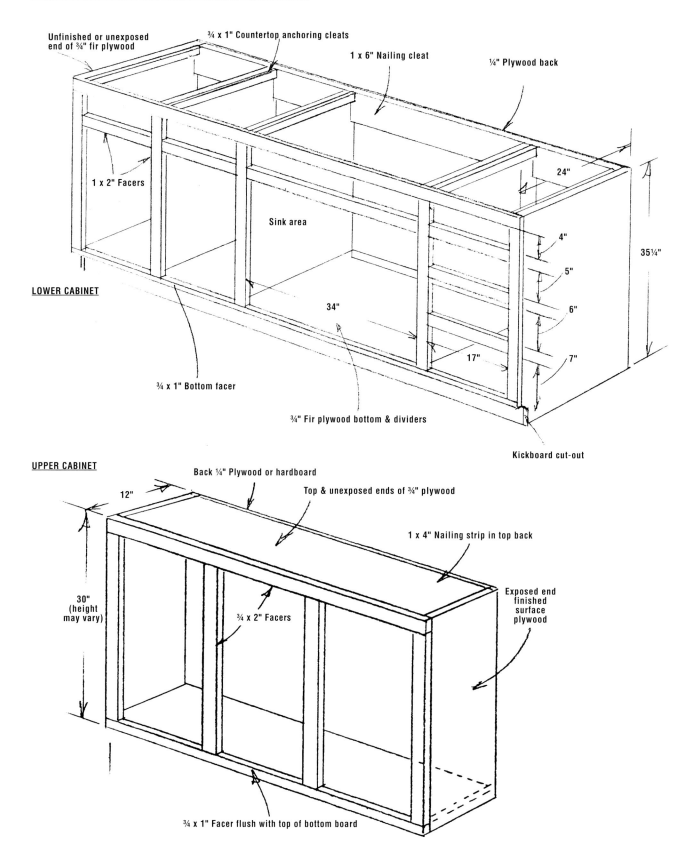

Unfinished or unexposed
end of ¾" fir plywood

¾ x 1" Countertop anchoring cleats

1 x 6" Nailing cleat

¼" Plywood back

1 x 2" Facers

24"

Sink area

35¼"

LOWER CABINET

4"

5"

6"

34"

7"

¾ x 1" Bottom facer

17"

¾" Fir plywood bottom & dividers

Kickboard cut-out

UPPER CABINET

Back ¼" Plywood or hardboard

Top & unexposed ends of ¾" plywood

12"

1 x 4" Nailing strip in top back

30"
(height
may vary)

¾ x 2" Facers

Exposed end
finished
surface
plywood

¾ x 1" Facer flush with top of bottom board

back. Cut this to fit between the two sides and fasten in place with glue and finish nails. Cut the back to the correct size from ¼-inch plywood or hardboard and, with the case lying face down, lay the back in place. Use a carpenter's square to make sure the case is square, and fasten the back in place with ½-inch staples and an air nailer or with ¾-inch coated nails.

Turn the case upright and you're ready to install the **facings**. Cut and install any **dividers** or **shelves**. The simplest method, especially for overlap doors, is to install **veneer tape** over the plywood edges. These edges must first, however, be sanded smooth. A more traditional method is to install individual **facer strips** over the front edges of the case. These normally fit flush with the outside edges of the case, but overlap the inside edges. The two side casings are cut first, fitting them flush with the upper end of the sides and the lower edge of the toe space. These are fastened in place with glue and No. 6 finish nails. Cut the lower facer to fit between the two side facers and the correct width to match the top edge of the bottom shelf and the bottom edges of the toe spaces on the sides. To cut to length, cut one end smooth and square, then hold it in place and use a sharp pencil to mark the length. Cut the pieces square using a fine-toothed blade in a radial arm saw. Glue in place and fasten with No. 6 finish nails into the case-bottom edge. Use No. 8 finish nails through the side facings into the sides to further secure in place. Cut the top facing in the same manner, ripping to width and cutting to length. All facers should have their edges jointed smooth. In this case the top facing is fastened between the two side facings with glue and No. 8 finish nails through the edges of the side facings into the ends of the top facing. If the cabinet has drawers, facers are cut and installed in the same manner. **Door and drawer dividers** are cut to fit between the drawer bottom facer or facers and the upper or lower facer as needed. These can be anchored in place with toenail driven, self-starting wood screws in countersunk holes, with glue and finish nails or with glue blocks from the back side. Wood strips ¾ by 1½-inches are fastened inside the front and back and to the sides at the top for anchoring a countertop in place.

At this point the cabinet bottom is ready to be installed. If plumbing is to be run for a sink, and electrical connections for a disposal are needed, the openings are measured and cut at this time. The cabinet is then placed in position. The cabinet must be leveled in all directions. Use a 4-foot level to determine level and wood shingles as shims to assure a level unit. Studs are located in the wall and the cabinet is fastened in place with screws through the rear top nailing strip. The cabinet back can also be fastened to the wall with screws into the studs. Build or purchase the countertop and install.

Upper Cabinets

Upper cabinets are constructed in the same basic manner, using box or case construction for the sides, bottom and a ¾-inch plywood top. In this case the sides, top and bottom all have ¼ x ¼-inch rabbets ripped in their inside edges for the **plywood**

LAMINATE COUNTERTOPS

Tools
- Sabre saw w/metal-cutting blade
- Handsaw (10-12 point)
- Drill and bit
- Block plane
- Belt sander
- Carpenter's square
- 4-foot level
- Scriber compass
- C-clamps
- Hammer
- Rubber mallet
- Adjustable wrench
- Screwdriver
- Caulking gun
- Roller
- Mill file (fine toothed)
- Brush or trowel
- Router w/laminate trimming bit

Materials
- Plastic laminate — preformed sections or sheet
- Plywood, particleboard or MDF
- Masking tape
- Caulk
- Sandpaper
- Contact cement
- Wood spacer strips or dowel rods

or hardboard back. The **facings** are cut and installed in the same manner. Upper cabinets are anchored to the wall with a **nailer strip** at the top and through the back into the **studs**, as well as with screws through the back into the studs. Home-made cabinet jacks of 2 x 4s with shingle wedges can be used to temporarily hold the upper case in position and help level and plumb it until you can get it fastened solidly in place.

A more intricate form of construction involves creating a **facing frame** of **mortise and tenons joints**. The front facing frame is then anchored to the case sides, top and bottom with glue blocks and countersunk wood screws from the inside or with glue and **biscuit joints**. This totally eliminates the nail holes that must be filled and is the best method for fine furniture cases.

Doors and Drawers

Doors and drawers can be overlap, lip or flush. **Overlap doors and drawers** have the entire front thickness exposed. These are often used on "Euro" style kitchen cabinets and bathroom vanities. Lip doors and drawers normally have a ⅜ x ⅜-inch lip or rabbet around all edges. This allows for using ⅜-inch lip hinges for installing the doors. **Flush doors and drawers** are fitted with their fronts flush with the case facings. These require great care in building and installing. Flush doors don't seal off the cabinet as well as overlap or lip doors.

Door fronts may be made of solid wood or ¾-inch plywood. The outer edges may be left square on overlap doors, but are commonly rounded on lip doors. Drawers are commonly made of solid wood,

sometimes of plywood.

Frame-and-panel doors may be made in several ways. The simplest is to cut **dadoes** in the frame pieces then dowel and glue the frame pieces together, inserting the panel in place as you assemble the frames. Or the frame can be assembled with mortise-and-tenon joints. The best method, however, is to use a router or shaper to create shaped stickings. This creates a shaped joint and provides a larger glue surface, as well as a decorative frame edge.

The **panels** inserted into the frames can be thin plywood panels or solid wood with their edges shaped. The top of the frame and panel can be left straight or an arched panel and top rail may be created on a shaper or with a router.

PLASTIC LAMINATE COUNTERTOPS

Plastic laminate is one of the most durable, beautiful and easy-to-care-for materials for kitchen, bath or bar countertops. Plastic laminate is also fairly easy for do-it-yourselfers to work and the variety of colors and patterns available is almost unbelievable. These include textures that evoke the detail found in handmade paper, woven textiles, brushed watercolor, tooled leather and polished stone.

"Industrial chic" is one of the hottest trends in contemporary design homes. New **metallic laminates** fit well into the "functional" design of a hunting or fishing lodge. **Formica** has five natural aluminum solid metal designs. These include Stainless Aluminum, Soft Abrasion, Satin Aluminum, Herringbone and Vertical Stripes. Three colored metals include: red aluminum, green aluminum and blue aluminum. Formica DecoMetal also includes antique looks including Copper Sargasso, Brushed Bronzetoned Aluminum and Brushed Black Aluminum.

Wilsonart International has introduced METALAMINATES, a line of **foil-faced laminates** that offers limitless design applications. They are laminate and metal all in one, combining the best of both products. The METALAMINATES include the standard metallic looks of titanium, aluminum and stainless steel in addition to glass-block green and champagne. Color options include: Pearl, a matte-finish silver; Champagne, a soft copper color with taupe and silver undertones; Marine, the metallic version of glass-block green; Satin-Brushed Natural; Satin-Brushed Iron; Satin-Brushed Gold; and Stainless. Polished Natural and Polished Gold offer reflective chrome- and bright-brass looks.

Plastic laminate for countertops is available in two ways: as **pre-formed top sections** manufactured to fit a specific area or as **sheet laminate** which is fastened to a support core constructed as desired. Preformed top sections offer a great variety of treatments including molded-in backsplash and a front lipped edge, called **"cove."** In other styles the front edge can be finished with other treatments that include: **square, rounded** or **bullnosed,** finish with a 45-degree angled edge, or even wood edging applied. The front edge can be of the same design or a contrasting pattern for more variety. Preformed top sections must be ordered to fit.

If an L- or U-shaped top is desired, sections are joined together with a 45-degree miter joint.

The **backsplash**, if desired, for countertops with sheet laminates is created separately and fastened to the countertop. The front edge treatment for countertops can be straight laminate edging, wood edging, a combination of the two, or even 45-degree edging.

Preformed Countertops

Preformed countertops require the least work. You'll need a few tools, including a sabre saw, drill and bit, block plane, belt sander, C-clamps, safety glasses, rubber mallet, square, hammer, level, fine-toothed handsaw (10-12 point), masking tape, scriber compass, adjustable wrench, screwdriver, caulking gun and caulk and sandpaper.

The first and most important step is to carefully measure the size of the desired countertop. Make sure to allow for the front and end overhangs since preformed countertops are provided in standard lengths.

In addition to the countertop or sections needed for an L- or even U-shaped top, you'll need fastening bolts (for drawing the miter joints tight); a tube of sealant (such as Formica brand caulk) for caulking joints; end splash and/or end caps (kits are available to match countertop sections); a non-flammable contact adhesive (for fastening the end caps unless the kit has pre-applied adhesive for an "iron-on" method); and woodworking glue for fastening build-up blocks.

If the standard-sized section is too long, it must be cut to the proper measurement. Carefully measure,

You can also install plastic laminate countertops to match your décor.

Preformed tops are available that can simply be fastened in place. Corners are constructed using 45-degree miter cut sections with a sealant, such as Formica brand caulk and fastening bolts.

including the end overhang, which is normally 1 inch. Place a piece of masking tape over the area to be cut and mark the cut line with a sharp pencil. Use the fine-toothed handsaw to make the cut, cutting from the top, through the masking tape to avoid chipping the laminate. Sand and/or file the cut edge smooth.

Turn the countertop upside down on a flat surface. Cut ¾ x ¾-inch build-up wood strips or wood strips of a thickness to match the front build-up strips. Glue the strips on the end or ends using C-clamps to hold until the glue sets. Make sure the end edges are flush with the countertop edge. Sand if necessary.

Follow the instructions with the end cap kit for their installation. For **glue-on kits**, apply contact adhesive to the back side of the end cap and to the wood edge. Carefully position the end cap in place and then tap with a wooden block and lightweight hammer to seat properly. Sand or file the edges smooth.

For **iron-on caps**, set a household iron to medium heat. Using a back-and-forth motion, iron the end cap in place. Allow to set and cool for one minute, then tap the cap carefully with a wooden block and small hammer, or tap with a rubber mallet. Using a fine file, apply pressure only on the up or "in" strokes to smooth the end cap edge.

Sink cutouts can be cut in one of two ways. If the sink comes with a cutout pattern, position the pattern on top of the countertop, making sure there is no blocking beneath to obstruct the sink. Drill a starting hole along one edge, then use a sabre saw with a fine-toothed blade to make the cutout. If the sink doesn't have a pattern, place the sink rim or rangetop rim on the countertop in the desired location. Mark around the edge of the rim, and again make sure there is no blocking beneath the sink. Use a sabre saw to cut a hole ¼- to ¾-inches smaller than the line, or following manufacturer's instructions. Make sure the corners are clean and chip free.

If the sections are to be made into L- or U-shapes, apply a bead of sealant to each precut mitered edge. Tighten the fasteners together just enough to hold the sections in place. Make sure to align all front edges as you tighten the fasteners. Tap the surfaces, using a wood block and lightweight hammer to avoid damaging the surface. Once all sections are properly aligned, tighten the fasteners securely. Remove excess sealant.

Countertops with a **molded-in backsplash** also have provisions for scribing the backsplash to the shape of the wall (to a certain degree). Place the countertop on the cabinet and in the correct position. Use a scriber/compass to mark the top edge of the countertop or backsplash and then belt sand or block plane the line to the contour of the wall.

Place the top back in place, making sure it is in the correct location and level, then secure to the cabinet with wood screws from the underside. Install the sink or stove top as desired.

Working with Sheet Laminate

You can easily create your own countertops for bath or kitchen cabinets, bars or even decorative tables using **sheet laminate** on a constructed surface. In most instances this

CUSTOM LAMINATE COUNTERTOPS

To create a "custom" countertop using sheet laminate, use a brush to apply contact cement adhesive to the support core.

The laminate is glued in place using a roller to prevent air bubbles.

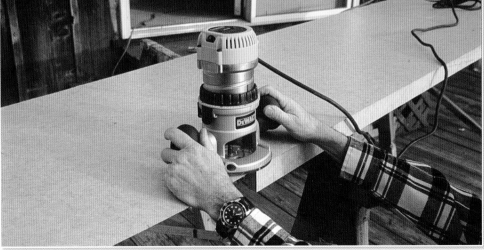

A router with a laminate trimmer is used to trim the edges.

should be **solid one-side plywood, particle board** or **MDF**—materials with a smooth surface for properly gluing the laminate in place. You can also install laminate over existing laminate, provided it has been cleaned, degreased and lightly sanded. You will need a sabre saw with a metal-cutting or fine-toothed cutting blade, safety glasses, a roller, fine-toothed

mill file, brush or trowel (see adhesive can for recommendations), contact cement and spacer strips of thin wood (or dowel rods).

The first step is to construct the **support core**. Cut the wood pieces to size and shape; make sure all cuts are square. If the top is to be a U or L, you can cut separate sections, cover them with laminate and then join the sections using fasteners just as with preformed tops. If the top is not too large and cumbersome, you can join the wood sections first, and then cover them with the laminate. If the top has a backsplash, it is constructed separately, covered, and anchored to the back of the top.

The most common **edge treatment** is with strips of laminate, matching or contrasting with the top surface. In most instances the edge must be built up to create an overhang and add "depth" to the front edge. A ¾ x 1½ inch wood strip is fastened to the front of the wood surface. Glue and clamp, and/or use cement-coated nails and glue to fasten the wood strip in place. In some instances, a ¾ x ¾-inch wood strip may be installed on the underside and flush with the front edge of the support core surface to create this build-up. This is commonly used when a rounded corner is created.

When creating a **rounded corner edge**, do not use a sharp radius; a gentle curve is the best tactic. A piece of plywood or support core board of the same thickness is usually used to create the underside build-up in this case. Glue and clamp the piece in place, and then scribe the radius of the curve and use a sabre saw to cut the glued-up section. A belt sander should then

A stainless steel sink and dishwasher with a laminate countertop in this lodge's compact kitchen blends in well with the rustic interior.

be used to smooth up the cut.

Measure the **support core piece** and the **laminate** carefully. Cut the top laminate piece ⅜ to½-inch larger than the surface to be covered. Then cut the edge strip, again making it 3/8-inch wider and longer than the edge to be covered. The laminate can be cut with a sabre saw using a fine-toothed blade. Make sure the laminate is well supported so it doesn't crack or chip. A table saw or radial arm saw with a fine-toothed blade can also be used, and produces a cleaner and more even cut. I keep an old plywood blade on hand just for this chore. Begin by fastening the edging in place. Apply the **adhesive** to the back of the edging piece with a brush. I like to lay the piece on the top surface, next to the edge. Any excess adhesive brushed past the edge piece will be removed later. Make sure the surface of the edge of the support core piece is free of sanding dust or dirt. Apply two coats of adhesive to the support core edge. Allow all to dry thoroughly, and then bond the edge piece to the support core piece. If it's a long piece, take a hint. Have someone help hold and support the strip as you align and press the strip in place. Use the roller to bond the strip firmly in place.

My dad ran a cabinet shop for many years and I learned several good tricks from him. After gluing the edge strip in place, turn the top upside down and use a belt sander, sanding from the edge inward to smooth the bottom cut edge. Then turn the top over and do the same for the top edge. This removes any glue from the application of the edge piece, smoothes up any joint between the support core and front edge build-up piece and smoothes the laminate edge with the support core top.

The next step is to apply the **top laminate piece**. Lay the laminate piece on the support core, top side down. Apply the adhesive with a roller, brush or trowel, following the adhesive brand recommendations. Allow to dry thoroughly. Set the laminate piece aside. Thoroughly clean the support core surface and apply two coats of adhesive. Be careful not to allow adhesive to run down over the applied edge. One trick is to brush outward toward the edge; this prevents runs.

Allow the adhesive to dry thoroughly, and then place dowel rods or wood strips 6 inches apart on the support core surface. Position the laminate on the strips. Align the laminate with the support core edges. Pull out an end strip and apply pressure with the roller. Continue pulling out strips and applying pressure until the entire laminate piece is solidly secured. Pay special attention to all edges.

Use a laminate trimming bit in a router to cut away the excess laminate and trim the edge. Finally use the mill file with downward and "out" strokes to smooth up all the edges.

Log Home Building

Above: Log homes or lodges can be as elegant and large as any other dwelling.

The romance of building a log home in the wilderness has long been the dream of many sportsmen. A special place, hacked out of the wilds by their own hands in the traditional American pioneering spirit. Granted, much more is involved these days than simply cutting down a few trees and stacking the logs together into a cabin. But, yes, you can build your own log home or hunting or fishing lodge in a variety of ways, depending on the amount of work, time and money you are able to invest.

Today log home patterns and "kits" are available in a wide variety of styles, shapes, sizes and materials and can range from a simple cabin in the woods to an ultra-sophisticated mansion, complete with multi-car garages, basement and all the amenities. Log homes offer a great deal. They are aesthetically beautiful, but also a home that is cooler in the summer and warmer in the winter due to the bulk of the materials. Not only is this more energy efficient, but also a savings on the environment.

Log homes help conserve natural resources as well. It takes less

- Should you buy a log home kit or build it yourself? What is chinking?

- What log cabin plans are available? • How to insure a sturdy, long-life building?

- What are the corner styles used in traditional log construction?

- Why is the Scandinavian scribe one of the more difficult corners to construct?

wood to construct some log homes because there isn't the waste of milling the wood, and the energy needed to mill the wood is also saved. The logs used are often the **"thinning" trees** normally removed to allow better grade trees to grow to saw-log size. One of the main advantages most sportsmen find, however, is the ease of maintenance. Log cabins don't require painting, scraping and all the other hard work involved in the upkeep of a lodge. The biggest advantage most find, regardless of the size of log building being constructed, is the cost. Log homes cost less, sometimes even when custom built by a manufacturer, but if you want to trade your own sweat for dollars, you can really make a savings.

Log buildings can be acquired in several ways. The simplest, and most expensive, is to purchase a **manufactured log home** and have it erected by the log home manufacturer. The logs in these buildings are normally milled to precise shapes to insure tight, secure buildings. Or you may prefer to have a **log crafter** build the lodge. These are usually "one of a kind" homes built to the purchaser's designs. If you desire a small hunting cabin in the woods, but don't have the time, desire or skills to build it yourself, this might be the best choice.

The next step, involving more work but a great deal less cost, is to purchase a **"kit" log home** and erect it yourself. This is essentially a package of "precut" logs. These are also available in a wide variety of types. For instance you can purchase only milled or debarked logs if you wish to cut your own notches, window and door openings. The second

In their advertising, most log building companies show floor plans to help in choosing your log home. On the following pages are some classic old and new log cabins and lodges.

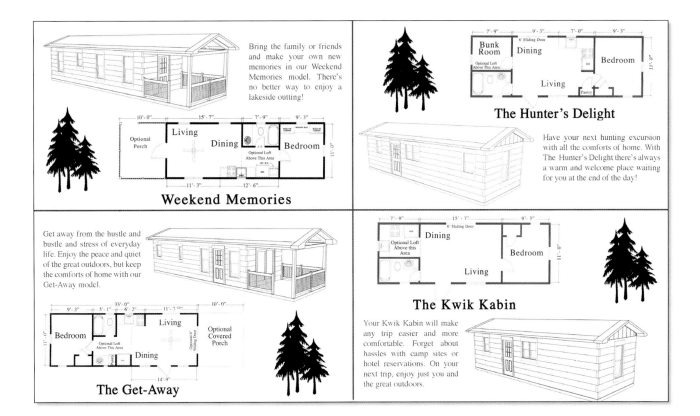

Weekend Memories

Bring the family or friends and make your own new memories in our Weekend Memories model. There's no better way to enjoy a lakeside outing!

The Hunter's Delight

Have your next hunting excursion with all the comforts of home. With The Hunter's Delight there's always a warm and welcome place waiting for you at the end of the day!

The Get-Away

Get away from the hustle and bustle and stress of everyday life. Enjoy the peace and quiet of the great outdoors, but keep the comforts of home with our Get-Away model.

The Kwik Kabin

Your Kwik Kabin will make any trip easier and more comfortable. Forget about hassles with camp sites or hotel reservations. On your next trip, enjoy just you and the great outdoors.

LOG SHAPES

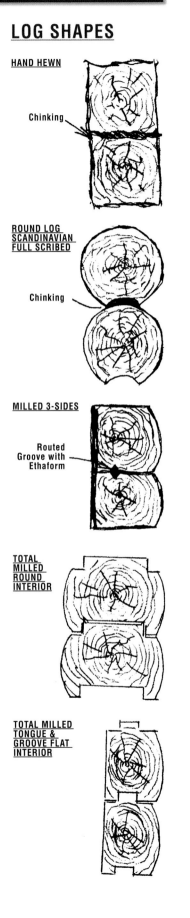

HAND HEWN

Chinking

ROUND LOG SCANDINAVIAN FULL SCRIBED

Chinking

MILLED 3-SIDES

Routed Groove with Ethaform

TOTAL MILLED ROUND INTERIOR

TOTAL MILLED TONGUE & GROOVE FLAT INTERIOR

type consists of the walls only, along with spikes, gaskets and other items needed. The third type is a "shell" which includes the walls, roofing, doors and windows. The last is the complete package and it includes everything mentioned before plus flooring and all the other materials needed to complete the building. When purchasing a manufactured home kit, make absolutely sure you understand exactly what will be furnished and how. In most instances you will be purchasing a building from a drawing and floor plan. The complete shell kit comes with a set of instructions and numbered logs. These take quite a bit of effort in construction, but with patience and a little skill, you can build your own log home.

Of course, the ultimate is to create your own **log lodge** from "scratch". This also offers a lot of advantages, mostly saving money. You're basically trading sweat for dollars. This may also be the only practical method of building a hunting camp in an isolated area where building materials can't easily be trucked in place. Even if you don't have access to logging timber, or the logs, you can often purchase logs. If in an area where logging is done, you can contract with a logger. Or as mentioned earlier, purchase logs from a log home manufacturer and design and build your own cabin. One friend of mine, living near a national forest, purchased "thinning logs" quite economically from the Forest Service.

Log Types

Log buildings are constructed in several ways and the first step is to determine the type of log con-

struction you will be utilizing. This includes **Scandinavian full-scribed, chinked round logs, milled square logs, hand-hewn square logs, rustic slabbed logs** and **milled logs** with rounded exterior and flat interior. Log joints may be scribed, scribed and chinked, hewn and chinked, or with a variety of notched or tongue-and-groove joints. In some of the latter cases the joints are also insulated with foam insulation. Many of the latter types are commonly available from log home manufacturers or log kits. **Chinked** logs require more regular maintenance than chinkless logs. Logs can be milled to a square shape using a saw mill or they can be hewn by hand. The Logosol Log Moulder fitted to their one-man chain saw mill can also be used to mould full profile logs in a number of patterns, such as flattened on top and bottom, milled round edges and others. **"Log siding"** can also be made using the Woodmaster moulding machine and planer. These "half" logs are then attached to the outside of standard stick-framing.

Log Preparation

Using naturally **decay-resistant logs** such as cedar is one step in insuring a sturdy, long-life building. A building can be constructed of green logs, but this creates some problems. As the logs dry they shrink, creating problems around windows, doors and at corner joints. If using green logs, the windows and doors should not be installed until the logs reach equilibrium.

Unpeeled logs with the bark left intact will deteriorate more rapidly than peeled logs. The bark slows down the drying, allowing some decay in the interior before the log becomes fully seasoned. And, the bark harbors and encourages the attack of bark beetles, wood borers and other insects.

Cutting and peeling of the logs should be done during the cold months. This allows for some **drying** to take place before warm weather. It's easiest to peel the bark immediately after logging and this also helps in insect protection. **Peeling** can be done with a **debarking spud**, a sturdy flat-blade tool with the edge ground sharp, an axe and adz or with a big draw knife. The peeled logs should be stored up off the ground and separated with **wood stickers** so air can freely circulate around them. Ideally, the logs should be stored in a open shed or shelter and protected from heavy rains. Tarps can be used, but stickers should be placed on top of the logs to hold the tarp up off the logs and help provide more ventilation. Logs should be air-dried for at least six months.

Many log home manufacturers actually **pressure-treat** their logs for longevity and protection against decay and insects. Creosote or pentachlorophenol preservatives used in the past for some buildings should not be used inside a structure for human habitation because of the health problems they present. A variety of **waterborne preservatives** are available these days that are environmentally friendly, clean and easy to apply. Normally these are applied just after peeling and before curing.

Proper construction details can also make a difference in preventing decay and log deterioration. Good **drainage** around the foundation is important so storm water can't collect around and under the building. The site should be graded so water drains away from the building. Wide eaves, gutters and downspouts can also be used to direct water away from the building. For a single story building, the overhang should project 24 inches and the eaves should extend beyond roof supporting members. A steeper **pitched roof** can also drain away rainwater faster.

Quite often cabin builders take the easy way and lay the bottom logs directly on or close to the ground, hastening decay. Unless properly treated with chemicals, even the most decay-resistant logs in contact with the ground will eventually rot. It's simply good construction techniques to place **bottom logs** or **sills** 12- to 18-inches above the ground on **foundations** that will keep the wood dry. **Ventilation** under the building is also extremely important. Piers or foundation posts provide natural ventilation. The space between them can be filled in with screening or latticework, but the latter should be pressure treated. Solid foundations should also have proper ventilation, with generous openings on all sides, as well as an opening to the crawl space. In extremely damp areas, a layer of polyethylene sheeting placed on the ground below the building can also help prevent dampness.

In some parts of the country **termites** can be a problem with any type of wood construction, including log homes. Ground-based termites can do tremendous damage without visible sign. Make sure the area and building is protected from termite attacks.

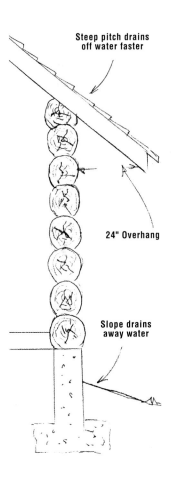

Steep pitch drains off water faster

24" Overhang

Slope drains away water

Using proper construction methods can make a difference in decay and log deterioration. A wide overhang and steep pitched roof can help.

Logs should be peeled to remove bark that can harbor insects and mold. This can be done with a debarking spud.
Or you can use a large draw knife or timber framer's slick.

During construction make sure all **joints** and the **framing** around doors and windows are tight and no crevasses are allowed to catch and hold water. **Caulk** any cracks or openings in these areas. Most logs will check and crack and moisture can enter through these as well. Major cracks in logs should be placed facing down so they don't trap water. The joints between logs are also possible water-trapping areas. Open joints should be chinked or caulked. One of the best and easiest methods of preventing water entry is to cut deep grooves in the top and bottom surfaces of mating logs using a router and insert-

ing a caulked spline. In the case of scribed log construction, the underside of logs is carefully hollowed out to fit the log beneath. Logs should be further protected by the use of a good water preservative on the exterior and around all windows, doors and joints, after construction. These **preservatives,** such as Thompson's Waterproofer PLUS are simply sprayed over the completed structure. The preservative may be clear or a variety of transparent and semi-transparent stains.

Corner Styles
The next step is to determine the type of **log corner design.** Several

SCANDINAVIAN SCRIBED LOG "SADDLE NOTCH"

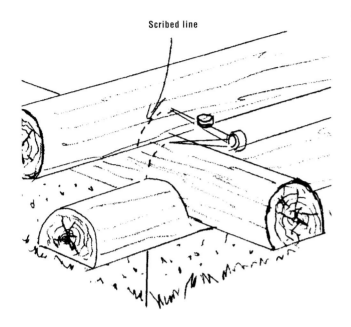

Scribed line

Lay a log across the sill logs and anchor it in place with log dogs. Use a log scriber to scribe the bottom of the log to match the profiles of the logs beneath it.

The Scandinavian Scribed Log, also called a Saddle Notch is one of the sturdiest, but more difficult.

1. Flatten two opposing sill logs and anchor them in position.

2. Cut the notches on the underside of the log.

SCANDINAVIAN SCRIBED LOG "CHINKLESS JOINT"

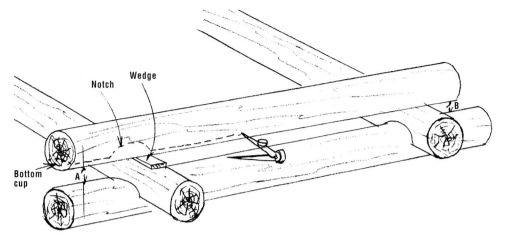

Notch
Wedge
B
Bottom cup
A

In the chinkless Scandinavian style, a cupped groove is cut in the bottom side of each log to fit down over the one below. Make both ends of the log to be cut an equal distance from the log below it, using a wedge if necessary. Then scribe for the cut.

1. *The cut can be started with a chain saw and completed with an adz, or completely cut with a chain saw.*

2. *Place silicone caulk on the bottom edges of the cut, position the log in place and fasten securely with a large spike.*

different construction types can be used. **Scandinavian** scribed log construction typically utilizes interlocking corners. The logs are notched to interlock at the corners with a half-height difference. The Scandinavian scribe is one of the more difficult corners to construct as you must scribe the log bottom and the notch exactly to fit over the log below. These corners do not normally require further fastening. Another common method is the **Swedish cope saddle notch**. In this case the logs are not scribed on

their bottoms, but fit full with milled joints or splines, making it somewhat easier to do. Another fairly simple joint is the **sharp notch**. This is commonly used on full-round logs and is quick and simple. Milled surface logs, or those milled on two or three sides are commonly installed using **butt-and-pass corners**. This style is one of the oldest and the easiest to construct. In this case the logs butt and pass each other, and are anchored in place with spikes. Another style that has become increasingly popular is the **corner post**. This is more commonly used with post and beam and in modern houses where several construction methods and materials are used. This is also the most common method when half-log siding is used. Although a tradition in many parts of the country, the most difficult notch is the **dovetail**. It can be used with round or square logs, but is most commonly used with hewn or milled square logs. Following are the steps in creating the different log joints and corners.

Scandinavian Scribed Log

This chinkless style, also called a **Saddle Notch**, is one of the most difficult, but also one of the sturdiest and with good weather protection. It's extremely popular in the north country. Position two **sill logs** opposite each other in place on the foundation and anchor in place with anchor bolts. Usually this is the two **long-wall logs**. Note the sill logs normally have their bottom edges flattened so they sit properly on the foundation or piers. It's a good idea to apply a thorough coating of caulk along the foundation before installation. Log sill sealants are also available for sealing the sill logs to the foundation. The sill logs must also be notched to allow 2 x floor joists or log floor joists to rest on the foundation.

Flatten the two **right angle sill log bottoms** to the same approximate depth as the previously anchored logs. Position them over the previously anchored logs with their butt ends extending the same distance as the first logs. The butt ends of the upper logs should be opposite the butt ends of the lower logs. Lock them down in place with **log dogs**. You will need a

log scriber with a double bubble level which shows when the points are horizontal or vertical. Set the scriber to half the diameter of the bottom log. Beginning at the bottom edge of one end of one bottom log, **scribe** the shape of the log onto the log end anchored above. Go to the opposite end and repeat. Roll the log over with the bottom side up and again dog it in place. The **notch** can be cut in several ways. A broad axe and adz can be used. Or you can use a rough-cut handsaw to make initial cuts down to the contour lines and then knock the pieces out and clean up with a chisel or adz. You can also use a small chain saw, again cutting down to the **contour lines**, cutting out and smoothing the notch. You may still need to use a chisel to make sure the notch is smooth. Roll the log back in place and check for fit. The notch should be one-half the thickness of the bottom log and should sit firmly down on the foundation sill. Take your time with this first step as you want a good solid, water-tight foundation. Once the **notches** are cut correctly, anchor the log down onto the log ends below and to the foundation.

The next logs are notched in somewhat the same manner, except you also must account for the cupped groove in the bottom. Position the log in place over the previously anchored sill log. Make sure both ends of the log bottom are equal distance from the log below it. If necessary raise one end of the log up on a small wooden wedge to create this equal distance and dog it in place. Set the **scribe** to measure the distance of the largest gap and add about a half-inch. Scribe the full length of the log and as you reach the

PLUMBING THE LOG WALL

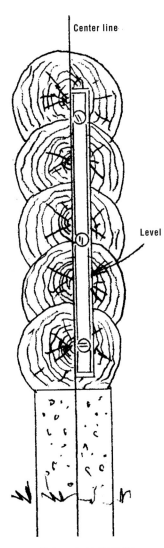

Center line

Level

It's important to keep the log wall as plumb as possible. Mark the centers of each log and use a level to align them properly.

<u>SADDLE NOTCH</u>

*The Swedish cope saddle
notch uses the same
saddle notch, but without
the underside cup.*

<u>SHARP CORNER NOTCH</u>

*A sharp notch is one of
the simplest notches and
quite traditional.
It can be cut with nothing
more than an axe.*

corner continue scribing the **saddle notch** that allows the log to fit over the log ends below it. Roll the log back in place upside down and dog it down. Cut a **cupped groove** in its bottom to fit over the log below it. This can be done with an adz or using a chain saw to cut a V and finishing it with the hand adz. Once you have this cut made, cut the **saddle notches**. Roll the log back in place and try fit. Cutting these notches and the groove to fit the logs below takes practice and time, but it's important to get a good fit. Once you're satisfied with the joinery, place **silicone caulk** on the bottom edges of the upper log, position in place and anchor down. You may also wish to add fiberglass insulation to fill any voids.

The logs should be **positioned crown up** and **alternating butt ends** as you go around the perimeter. It's also important to erect the log walls plumb. You definitely don't want a wall that flares out at the top. Logs are rarely the same size so one method of doing this is to mark the centers on the ends and use a level to make sure the center lines align properly. You can also drive a pair of poles at each end in the approximate center of the wall and run a string line. This will help you align logs as you erect them. It's important to continually check diagonally to make sure you have a "square" or square as possible building. In most instances the logs are erected leaving the ends uneven so you can get the best fit of log-to-log. Then a plumb bob is used to mark a straight line down the logs and a saw used to cut the ends even. Each log should be secured to the one below it with 10- to 12-inch spikes spaced

about 3 feet apart and set in counter-bored holes. Any **electrical wiring cavities** such as wire runs, outlet and light boxes must be cut in the logs before they are erected. When logs must be joined in the wall, a half-lap joint should be cut and used. Make sure you anchor the ends together securely and caulk well.

Swedish Cope Saddle Notch

The Swedish cope logs are left without the bottom cup or groove and joined with splines. The same **Saddle Notch** is used to join the corners.

Double Notch

Another method can also be used, the double notch, with a notch on top and one on the bottom of the crossing logs. This also alleviates the need for cutting the bottom cup or groove, but produces a much weaker corner joint. Again, the Saddle Notch is used for the corners.

Sharp Notch

Another simple notch is the sharp notch. This is quick and easy to build and again no under cup or groove is used. If you're building a simple cabin for only occasional use, it might be a good choice. With this method the joints must be well chinked. The ends of the logs have a sharp knife edge cut on them, and the logs on top have their undersides cut to fit the notch. It doesn't take as much cutting to create the notch and an axe is about all that's needed.

Butt and Pass

This is one of the simplest joineries and typically used with logs that are milled on at least the top and bottom, and sometimes on the inside as well, for a flat interior wall. The first sill logs are laid with log ends protruding past the foundation the desired amount. They can be further trimmed after the walls have been erected. The adjoining logs are cut so their butt ends meet the outside contours of the protruding logs. If the inside faces are round, for a tight joint, the butt ends should be scribed to meet the contour of the adjoining log. As the joints are basically open, they should all be well caulked. This style produces a very symmetrical and attractive interior wall surface, but is not as strong as other joints.

Corner Notch

A corner notch is also fairly simple, but is more commonly used in post-and-beam or when several materials and styles are used in one building. One method of corner notch is to cut a slot in the corner logs and then cut a notch in the end of the joining logs and use a spline.

Dovetail

The **simple dovetail** is a difficult notch to cut, but an extremely beautiful notch that is commonly used with hand-hewn logs. It creates the traditional American log cabin appearance. In addition, because the notch locks the logs together, it's one of the strongest. The **double dovetail** is even stronger. The ends of the logs may protrude slightly, but are more commonly cut flush.

First step is to hew the logs to create a **square log**. Or mill the logs to create four square sides. The traditional method of **hewing** the logs is to use a heavy axe and broadaxe. Position the log up on a couple of short

logs and dog it in place. Snap a **chalk line** on two sides of the top to establish the outside edges of the area to be flattened. Using a heavy axe, chop down to score or cut wedge shaped chips out of the log down to the chalk lines. Then use the **broad-axe** to cut away the material between the previously made cut. A **foot adz** can also be used to remove the material between the axe cuts, and for some it's easier to use than a broad-axe. Yes, it's hard work. You can use a chain saw to make the initial cuts and a broad axe to complete. Or you can mill the logs square with a chain saw or portable bandsaw mill, but the logs won't have the hand-hewn appearance made by the axe cuts. Once you have created one flat surface, turn the log over and use a square to mark the same width cut on the opposite side of the log. Hew this side, then turn the log, dog it down and chop down to the edges of the previously hewn edges. Remove the material between, turn the log and finish with the fourth side.

As with other types of log construction the first step is to lay the front and back **sill logs** in place with their ends set slightly protruding past the foundation edges. Set a bevel gauge to 75 degrees and mark the diagonal cut on the end. With a small hand square, mark a squared line on both the inside and outside of the log, beginning at the previously marked diagonal line on the end. Measure the depth the dovetail will be; this is the width of the log that will rest on top. Again use a square to mark across the top of the log.

Use a hand saw or chain saw to make the back of the **notch cut**, down to the horizontal lines marked

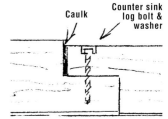

When logs must be joined the best tactic is to use a half-lap anchored with large spikes.

BUTT JOINT

A butt and pass joint is often used with milled logs and is common in kit log homes.

CORNER POST

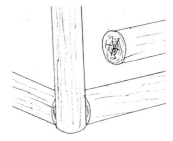

The corner notch is quite often used when several styles of construction are used in a home. It's simple, but one of the weakest.

TRADITIONAL HAND-HEWN DOVETAIL LOGS

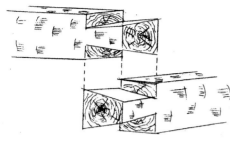

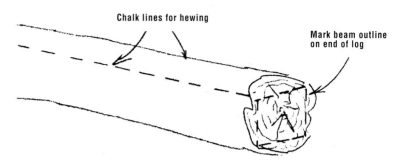

Chalk lines for hewing

Mark beam outline on end of log

The dovetail is a beautiful notch, and extremely strong because it locks the logs together. But it is difficult to cut. The dovetail, however, is traditional with American log cabins.

The first step is to hew the log to a square shape. Mark the log size on the small end of the log and then match the mark on the opposite or larger end. Snap a chalk line between the marks to create lines to hew to.

1. Using an axe or even a chain saw, cut down to the lines.

2. Then using a broad axe, or foot adz, remove the material between the cuts. Turn the log and repeat for each side.

3. First mark the notch cut in the bottom log. Mark a diagonal line using a bevel gauge set to 75 degrees.

4. Then mark a squared line on both the inside and outside of the log, beginning at the previously marked diagonal line on the end.

5. Measure what the depth the dovetail will be; this is the width of the log that will rest on top. Again use a square to mark across the top of the log.

6. Use a handsaw or chain saw to make the back of the notch cut, down to the horizontal lines marked on the inside and outside of the log.

7. A hand rip or chain saw can be used to make the diagonal cut back to the back-of-the-notch cut. Repeat on the opposite end and anchor the log down in place. Repeat for the opposite wall as well.

8. Position the overlapping logs in place and dog them down. Use a small square held against the inside edge of the lower log to mark the inside back cut of the bottom dovetail. Measure the depth of cut and mark it on each side.

9. Position the bevel gauge in place and mark the joining dovetail cut. Repeat on the opposite end. Turn the log over and cut the dovetail notches in each end. This type of log and corner shape does require chinking.

on the inside and outside of the log. A hand rip saw or chain saw can be used to make the diagonal cut back to the back of the notch cut. Another method is to use a large chisel to make the cut. In any case the cut should be well smoothed. Repeat on the opposite end and anchor the sill log in place. Repeat for the opposite sill log.

Lay in place the **overlapping logs** that will adjoin across the two previously **dovetailed logs** and dog them down. Use a small square held against the inside edge of the lower log to mark the inside back cut of the bottom dovetail. Measure the depth of the cut and mark it. Then position the bevel gauge in place and mark the joining dovetail cut. Repeat for the opposite end. Turn the log over and cut the dovetail notches. When you're satisfied with the fit, secure the log in place. You now have the sill logs in place. Cut the top of the **end log dovetail notches** in the same manner as the first. Then cut the adjoining log notches to fit. As you can see, this method is time consuming and it also takes a bit of practice. This type of **corner joint** and hand-hewn log construction does require chinking.

Creating Door and Window Openings

Logs can be laid with window and door openings as you go, but the best method is to **cut the openings** after wall logs are laid up to the upper edges of the proposed frame. You will, of course, need a rough opening for getting in and out of the building during construction. To cut the **window and door openings**, tack-nail **guide boards** for the rough opening sizes to the logs. Make sure they are

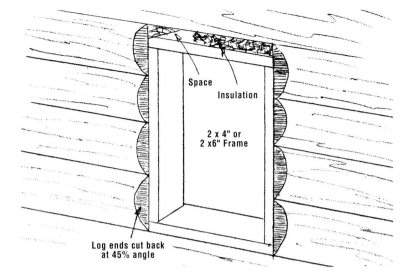

Window and door openings are often installed with a spline and dados in the frame and log ends to allow for settling of the logs.
Leave a space at the top for settling and fill it with insulation.

plumb and square. Use a chain saw to cut along the guide board edges. Window sill cuts should be made at about 10 degrees to allow rainwater to run off. In most instances the window or door frame is not anchored solidly to each log as this can create problems when the logs settle. A **spline and dado** is commonly used to anchor the window and door bucks. Then the **upper frame** is installed and the log above it erected. Leave approximately 2 to 3 inches between the top jamb and the log above it for settling. Fill this with fiberglass insulation. Door jamb widths can be made the same size as the average logs, or you can taper logs to meet the jambs. Make sure you coat all log ends with preservative before installing the jambs and caulk everything with plenty of silicone sealer.

Chinking

In the old days the spaces between the logs were chinked with materials on hand, including moss, mud, grass

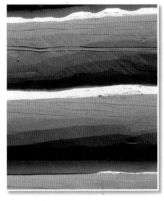

A variety of chinking materials can be used to fill between logs.

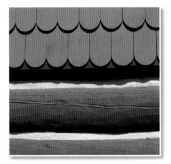

This upscale version from the Big Cedar Lodge on Table Rock Lake in Missouri shows how gable ends can be finished off.

SPLITTING CEDAR SHAKE SHINGLES

Cedar shake shingles are a tradition in many cabins.

You can create your own shake shingles with a few hand tools. The first step is to cut a log into a bolt of 18 to 24 inches. Then split the log into halves, using a wedge and sledge. If it's a large diameter log, split it into quarters.

Position a froe about 3/8 of an inch from the edge of one surface and use a heavy-duty wooden mallet to drive the froe down through the log to split off a shingle.

and even chunks of wood. Modern **chinking**, however, consists of expanded hardware cloth or screen wire stapled between the logs with fiberglass insulation stuffed between the inside and outside wire pieces. **Masonry chinking** or **mortar mix** is then applied over the metal and troweled smooth. These days a wide range of modern chinking materials, such as Log Jam and Chinker's Edge, are available that are easier to use and will even stay flexible.

The **gable ends** can be created using logs, or a more common and easier method is to use some sort of wood siding over the gable ends and down to the top of the wall line. One type of gable end covering that works well with log construction is wooden shakes. **Wood shakes** can also be used on the roof, if you have the time and inclination to do the splitting.

Hand Split Shakes

Wooden shakes have been a **traditional roofing material** for centuries. Shingles are sawn while shakes are split from a length of log called a **"bolt."** With nothing more than a few hand tools, a supply of wood and plenty of time, you can hand-split your own **shingles**. The tools you will need include a splitting maul and wedges, a wooden mallet and a froe.

As for the wood, you will need a supply of straight-grained, easily split wood such as pine, larch, cedar or even white oak. The logs should be cut into bolts as long as you desire, usually ranging from 18 to 24 inches. Often you can acquire **logging slash**, or butts or tops of trees, for these "short" log lengths.

Make sure that the log sections contain no knots or crotches or limbs to contend with. The next thing you'll need is plenty of time. Splitting enough shingles for even a small building is time consuming and hard work, but is definitely an economical way of acquiring shingles and provides the self-satisfaction of doing something in an old-fashioned, long-lasting, self-sufficient way.

The first step in **splitting the shakes** is to split the log or bolt into halves. Then, if it is a large diameter log, split it again into quarters. Position the froe about ⅜ inch from the edge of one surface and drive it down through the log end with a wooden mallet. Once you have the froe almost buried in the log end, pull the handle end sharply downward and sideways to split off the shakes.

In almost all instances the shake will split at an angle, rather than perfectly straight. If you have started right, the split will run from ⅜ to ½ or ⅝ inch in thickness. If you started on the wrong end of the log, however, the split may run from ⅜ inch to nothing. If it does, start the split thicker or turn the log end-for-end. You will have to turn the log end-for-end after splitting off each shake to have the least amount of waste and provide the easiest splitting method. If splitting the quarter from the point, you will have to first remove the **heartwood**.

FLOOR FRAMING

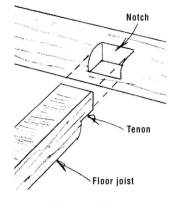

Floors can be hewn boards resting on hewn logs or 2 x framing. Regardless the joists are fit into notches cut in the wall logs.

LOG ROOF FRAMING

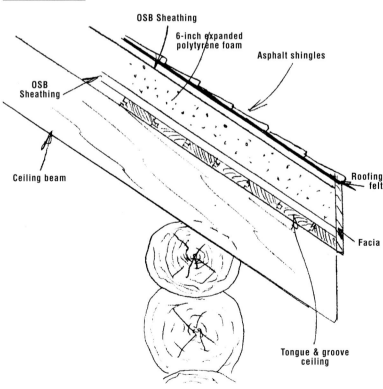

The rafters or beams are then covered with a built-up roof showing an exposed ceiling.

Log homes often utilize an open ceiling with exposed log or beam "rafters."

Raising a log wall can be tricky and dangerous. Having lots of help is a good idea.

The safest method of erecting log walls is with logging equipment designed for lifting and moving logs.

Floors

Floors can be old-fashioned **hewn floors**, sitting on hewn log joists, or modern day OSB or plywood on 2 x **framing.** The latter is quicker and easier. Or you can pour a **concrete slab** and erect the building on the slab. Again, make sure the logs and the floor are well off the ground.

Log Roof Framing

Log homes can have log or beam **ceiling joists** and an attic space between with standard **roof framing.** In many instances, however, log buildings will have an exposed, vaulted ceiling. In this instance log beams are installed along with wall tie logs or beams to keep the walls from spreading. Tongue-and-groove decking is applied as the roof underlayment and inside of the ceiling. Insulation is applied over the decking and the roofing material applied.

Interior Divider Walls

In case you desire to create the interior walls of log, the ends of the interior wall logs must be notched into the exterior wall logs. The **interior log walls** must also be well supported on piers or inside foundation supports.

Safety: Raising a log wall is hard work, sometimes tricky and dangerous. A 20-foot log can weigh more than 600 lbs. If it gets away from you it can quickly injure or even kill you. A **peavey** is often used to roll logs around on the flat ground, but you'll need some means of getting the logs up into position on the walls. A **log ramp** is the simplest method of getting logs into place. Or you can use a **gin-pole** or **tip-up hoist**.

The ramp should be placed on the uphill side of the walls if possible. Always make sure the logs are at least 3 feet longer than the support walls so they don't roll off inside the building. Make sure everyone stays clear of the log as it is rolled up in place and until it can be safely dogged down. Square or hand-hewn logs require a gin pole, or tip-up hoist for erecting them in place on the walls. It's best to have two hoists, one for each end of the log. Replacing your ladder with rented scaffolding on the inside of the building makes it easier and safer to work on the logs.

OTHER BUILDING CONSTRUCTION TYPES

Above: Pole building construction is often used to erect sheds and shelters at camp, but the technique can also be used for lodges as well.

In addition to standard stick and log construction, several other types of construction methods can be used for constructing your hunting or fishing camp lodge.

POLE BUILDING

One of the simplest and fastest types of construction is pole building. And, it's also relatively economical and easy to do, even for the first timer. More than one landowner has constructed a metal covered pole "shed" and lived in it while constructing a home or lodge, then later used the shed to store equipment. A pole structure consists of **poles** or **"posts"** set in the ground. Horizontal members called girts are fastened to the poles, then vertical siding applied to the girts. Siding may be wood or more commonly metal. If horizontal wood siding and a wooden or concrete floor is to be installed, **vertical studs** are installed between the poles. For the most part, pole structures are more economical because they require less wood for framing than stick construction. In many instances **trusses**, rather than rafters are used to support the roof, as this can create a **"free-span" building** without the need for interior supports.

POLE BUILDING CONSTRUCTION

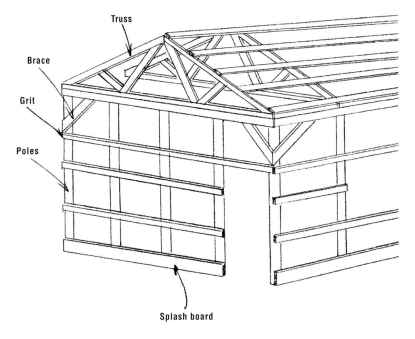

Basic pole building consists of poles, horizontal members called girts, and often a truss roof.

The most important factor in pole construction is to make sure the poles are properly set and plumb.

The first step in creating a pole structure is to check with local authorities on any **rules and regulations** regarding pole structures. You should also check the depths needed for the concrete pole supports. This can vary according to local soil and weather conditions. Regardless, it's important the concrete supports be below frost line in order to properly support the building.

Poles should be **pressure-treated** and must be set in or anchored to **concrete piers** sunk in the ground. Poles may be round or square, although the latter are easier to work with. They should also be equal diameter from top to bottom. Tapered poles can be used, but it's important that their outside edges are plumb, and this can be more difficult than using even-diameter poles. The poles should also be relatively straight or

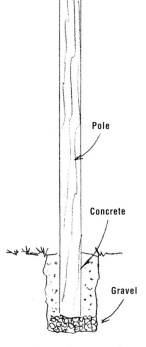

In most instances poles are placed in holes dug in the ground and anchored in place with concrete.

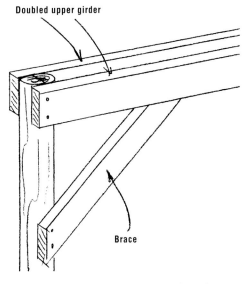

Rafters or trusses are supported on the ends by double girders and braces.

*First step in cutting the mortise and tenon is to lay out the mortise, then use a drill
to cut successive holes.*

Follow with a chisel to smooth up the sides and corners.

you'll have construction problems. Poles or posts can be purchased in 4-, 6- and 8-inch sizes, and it's also important to match the size to the structure. Smaller buildings can utilize 4-inch, while larger barns and sheds should have 6-inch poles. You can also use "home-cut" poles milled on a portable saw mill, treated with preservative and then cured for about 6 months before use.

As with any building it must be laid out correctly as described in Chapter 4. Even a pole structure is easier to build and finish if it is constructed square. Determine the **location of poles, set up batter boards** and **string lines.** Then dig the pier or **concrete support holes** to the proper depth. Reset the string lines and erect the corner poles. Again make sure they are properly located. It's also extremely important they are plumb. Use a 4-foot level, and you can even attach it to a leveling board to get a more precise plumb. Another advantage of pole structures, especially those without a concrete floor is they can be constructed on somewhat unlevel ground. The tops of the poles don't have to be level at this point. Make sure, however all poles, especially those on the lowest ground location are tall enough for the building wall desired. Once the poles are erected and plumbed they must be braced so they will stay in place. Use 2 x 4 stakes and temporary 2 x 4 braces to hold them in place. Then they must be anchored to or in the concrete. In the latter case, which is the most common, **concrete** is mixed and poured around the poles or posts up to about an inch or so above the top of the soil line. Smooth the top down with a trowel.

Once all **corner poles** are set, go back and using the string line, set the poles between, including those around any doors. Allow the concrete to set thoroughly before any other construction.

The **girts or horizontal members** are now installed. These are commonly 2 x 4s. Except for the top girts that must support the roof. These are often 2 x 6s or 2 x 8s. Begin at the top.

Measure up the wall height needed on the poles and using a string line and string level or long straight 2 x 4s and a 4-foot level, determine level height on all poles. Cut all poles off at that height using a portable circular saw or chainsaw. Fasten the top girts in place with pole barn nails or 3½-inch deck screws. The latter are easy to use these days with the cordless impact drivers. Make sure all girts are installed level.

Once the **top girts** are installed, install the **intermediate girts** in the same fashion. Make sure they are also level. The **bottom girts** of many pole structures utilize **pressure-treated splash boards.** At least one 2 x 6 should be used, and in cases where the ground slopes you may need to apply several splash boards to achieve the height needed on the bottom end. Frame around window and door openings using standard stick construction methods. In case of using roof trusses, install **inner girders** to the inside of the side posts.

Erect and anchor the **trusses** in place down on the top girts and inside girders. If using **metal covering, purlins** are used to anchor the metal roofing material. As you erect the trusses, purlins or 2 x 4s on edge are fastened down on the trusses.

If rafters are to be installed a top plate must be fastened down on the top girt. **Joists** must first be installed, then the **rafters** erected in the same manner as for **stick construction**, as shown in Chapter 5.

POST-AND-BEAM

Post-and-beam, or **timber frame construction** is another popular traditional log-building technique. Timber framing is an ancient method of

Use a square to lay out the tenon, and then cut with a handsaw.

construction used in the "old world" and brought to America with the Colonists. Typically, post-and-beam utilizes **squared logs**. They can be milled with a portable bandsaw mill, chainsaw mill or you can **hand-hew** them. In timber-framing the framing of the construction is of timbers, then other types of construction are used to fill in or cover the **framing**. This may be brick, stone, logs, stucco, or various sidings over the timber framing.

POST AND BEAM CONSTRUCTION

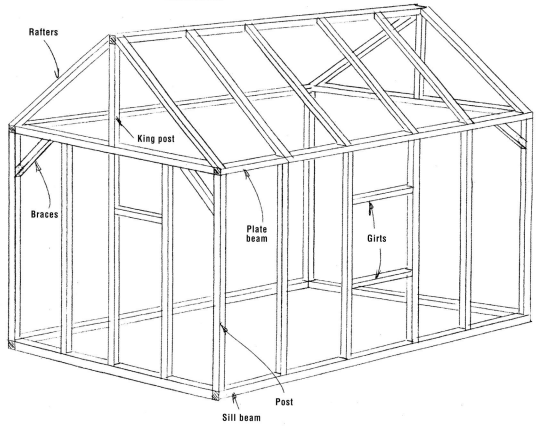

Post and beam, or timber frame construction, above, is an ancient method used in the "old world" and brought to America by the early colonists. Post-and-beam uses squared posts and beams fastened together with hand-cut joints and wooden pins. Shown below and on the facing page are the principal joints used in timber frame construction. Joints are usually strengthened with the use of pins.

SHOULDER MORTISED TENON   **BRACE JOINT**   **POST & SILLPLATE JOINT**

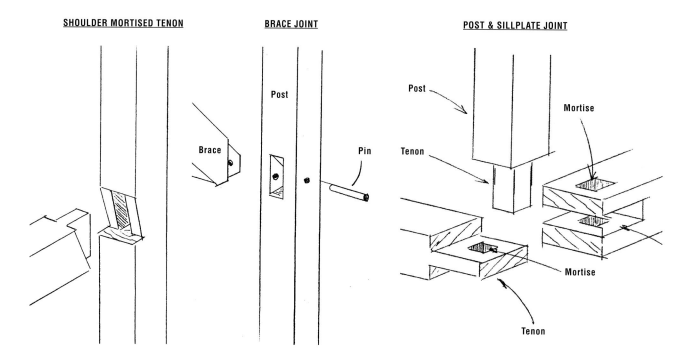

POST & BEAM MORTISE & TENON

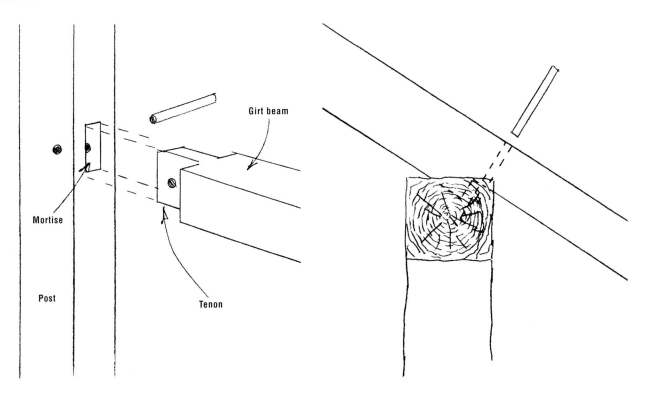

Girt beam

Mortise

Post

Tenon

RAFTER & TOP PLATE

POST & TOP GIRDER

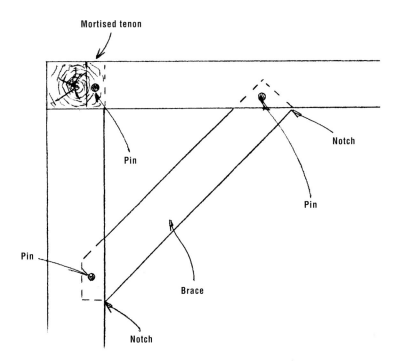

Mortised tenon

Pin

Notch

Pin

Pin

Brace

Notch

RAFTER JOINT

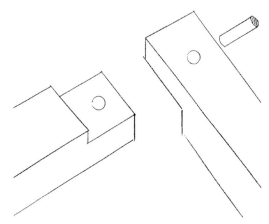

A masterpiece of the timberframer's craft, a massive upright oak post supports equally massive beams or "bents."

The wood species used for timber framing will vary across the country with availability. In many cases the **hardwoods**, such as oak, walnut, beech and others are typically used. Timber framing consists of the **sill logs, support posts and beams**, as well as the **rafter and tie beams**. In timber framing the sills are first installed on the foundation. The walls called **"bents"** are constructed as one piece, similar to stick construction and erected. **Tie beams** called "girts" are used to anchor the walls together, then the rafters installed in pairs in the same manner as for stick

framing, except they are fastened together in a different fashion.

Timber framing timbers are joined with **four principal joints**. These are traditionally cut using hand tools such as hand augers or brace-and-bit, big chisels and hand saws. You can also cut them quicker with modern powered machinery, but purists scoff at the idea.

Adjoining **sill plates** and the **corner posts** are typically joined with a tongue and fork. This is basically a **mortise and tenon** on the ends of the adjoining sill beams and a square hole through the mortise and tenon.

A fork or tenon on the end of the **support posts** fits down in the mortise cut in the two adjoining sills. Intermediate posts set in sills utilize a simple mortise and tenon. The girts are fastened in place with a shouldered tenon and mortise joint. The corners of post and beam are always braced as are the support posts in many instances. A chase mortise and tenon is used for these joints.

All joints are also further strengthened with **wood pins**. A variety of methods is used to hold these pins securely in place. In many instances the holes are slightly offset so the pin is wedged in place. **Square pegs** are also used and when driven in place in a round hole produce a very tight wedge. Pins are also nicked and often installed green. Wedges and pins in pins are also used to keep the pins, and the joints from shifting.

Cutting a Mortise-and-Tenon with Timber Framing Tools

Begin cutting the **joint** by laying out the location of the joint on the sill and post using a small or combination square. The **tenon** always runs parallel to the **beam**. Lay out the **mortise** first. Then use a drill slightly smaller than the size of the finished mortise and bore successive holes the length of the mortise. Use a **stop-guide** such as a wooden block or tape around the bit so you do not drill all the way through the beam for the mortise. Make sure these holes are bored at a 90-degree angle to the beam or the joint won't be straight, resulting in a construction that is out of plumb or square. Use a sharp chisel with a heavy wooden mallet to cut or pare away the wood to the final line. A corner chisel can be a great help in making sharp, even corners.

Carefully measure the mortise and lay out the tenon, again using a small square or combination square. Cut the tenon slightly oversize, using a hand backsaw. Then use a sharp chisel to gradually pare the tenon down so it will fit in the mortise.

The **pins** are typically cut using a drawknife and holding the stock in a shaving horse.

**TIMBER FRAMING
(POST-AND-BEAM)**

Framing Tools
- Framing Chisels
  (1½ & 2")
- Framing Slick
- Framing Mallet
  (32 to 48 oz.)
- Hand Saws
  (crosscut & rip)
- Hand auger or brace-and-bit
- Corner chisel
- Block plane
- Rabbet plane
- Shaving horse
- Drawknife
- Utility knife

Log Working Tools
- Broad axe
- Felling Axe
- Adz
- Barking spud
- Timber saw
- Froe
- Cant hook
- Peavey
- Timberjack

Measuring Tools
- Framing (carpenter's)
  square
- Combination Square
- Protractor or
  compass square
- 25' tape measure

Heating

*Above: You just about can't have a
hunting or fishing camp lodge without
a fireplace, not only for the ambience,
but for heat as well,
and you can even cook with it.*

Fireplaces are a very popular feature of many hunt and camp lodges. The obvious reason is most of these are located in the woods and sometimes don't have electricity or any other form of heating. And, fireplaces simply add "ambience" to any room. Fireplaces are not especially hard to construct, although they do require lots of hard work. Fireplaces may be constructed from stone, or brick, but it's important to follow specific rules for construction in order to create a fireplace that is safe to burn and will draw or burn efficiently. Actually simple fireplaces are fairly inefficient, most of the heat goes up the chimney. Because of their use, the structural and other problems they can present, fireplace construction is usually strictly regulated. Make sure you check with local authorities regarding any rules and regulations, as well as construction methods allowed.

BUILDING A FIREPLACE

A fireplace just goes with lodges and a simple and traditional fireplace can be constructed, often with the materials on hand. It does take hard work, lots of stone, a means of mixing mortar and attention to detail. The fireplaces in old log cabins were usually constructed separately and unattached to the walls. They were also often supported simply with large, **dry-laid stones**. They usually shifted or settled, and constant **chinking** around the fireplace and adjoining walls was required. They were often drafty, smoky and very inefficient. But a log cabin in the woods simply wouldn't be right without a fireplace.

A fireplace, however, may be made more efficient by constructing around a **steel shell** with forced air, or installing a **fireplace insert** or **hearth stove**. The first is to use a **"forced-air" fireplace**, if you have electricity to the site. These consist of a steel form that not only creates a more efficient fireplace, assuring a smoke-free fireplace, but it also simplifies building the fireplace. The steel form has **ductwork** through which electric blowers send cold room air to be heated and discharged back into the room. Thus, the fireplace becomes a genuine space heater.

Fireplaces can be built on an inside wall, with openings in two or three faces; on an outside wall, in the corner of two inside walls (or one inside and one outside wall) or as a free-standing unit. Metal forms are available for all of these styles.

A **chimney** and fireplace can weigh several tons, and it must be well supported. A **concrete support pad**, well below frost line must first be poured and it should be well reinforced with reinforcing rods and steel mesh. The top of the support pad should come level with the house floor, or just below it to allow for firebricks and hearth, depending on whether you desire a raised or flush hearth. The latter is best as it does help prevent sparks out on the floor.

A fireplace can be constructed during the wall construction, or after. In the latter case the wall must be cut out for the fireplace. In this case it's important to support the ceiling

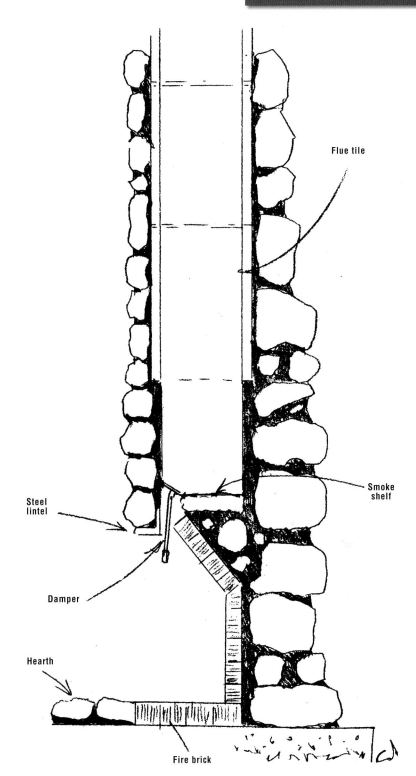

In constructing a fireplace be certain that it is well supported by a sturdy footing and foundation. As indicated in the crossection above, the throat, smokeshelf and damper must be constructed properly so that the fireplace will "draw." A rule of thumb is the narrow throat should be approximately 1/10th the area of the fireplace front.

Simple fireplaces can be constructed of stones found on the property and mortared into shape.

out or **ash pit** is also involved and this is created in the hearth during the pour. A metal door in the hearth and on the outside is used to remove the ashes. The metal form is then completely covered with insulation, adhering the insulation to the form with mortar as per the instructions with the purchased form.

The exterior and interior of the fireplace are then constructed with **masonry**, using stone, or brick. The chimney should be constructed of **flue-tile** and carefully fit and mortared so there are no openings or cracks. The exterior can be faced with stone, brick or you can build a concrete block exterior and face it with **flat stones**. The chimney masonry should be tied to the walls with metal ties. Stainless steel flue liners have become increasingly popular.

The **interior or fireplace face** will create the décor of your home so it should be carefully constructed using well chosen materials. This is where the "artisan" part in construction comes in. My wife Joan constructed our stone fireplace, or rather I hoisted the chosen stone in place and mortared it while she selected the next stone. All the stones in our fireplace were gathered from our fields and woods. If your lodge is in an area with available stones you're in luck, but count on lots of back-breaking lifting, loading, carrying and toting.

Three different types of **stones** are available, **quarried, ashlar or fieldstone**, but you'll probably have to use what you have locally. These days a wide variety of manufactured stone is also available. These are more consistent in coloring and shape and have become increasingly popular. **Quarried stone** is cut to

well until the fireplace is constructed. It's easiest to construct during wall construction, constructing the fireplace first, then building the wall around it and fitting the two together properly. Once the **support pad** and **sub-hearth** has been poured the hearth is set with **firebrick**. This must be done with special **heat-resistant mortar**. When the mortar has set and the bricks are solid, an additional layer of firebrick mortar is troweled over the firebrick and the metal form is positioned in place, leveled and plumbed. In some instances a **clean-**

shape and can have three cut faces and one face left rough. **Ashlar stone** is quarried or cut on all sides and is most often seen in churches and other public buildings. **Fieldstone** is as is and can vary greatly in coloring, shape and size. When selecting stones for fireplace construction, it's best to choose those with flat square sides or at least one or two flat sides. The round "cannonball" types of stones are harder to mortar in place, but are the only ones available in some areas and do have a definite appeal. If purchasing stones, to determine how much stone you'll need, multiply the width times the length times the height. Then divide the cubic feet by 27 to **determine the cubic yards**. Add 10 percent for breaking and waste with cut stone and 50 percent for fieldstone. The latter is because you'll have some stones that simply won't fit anywhere.

You can purchase **pre-mixed mortar** such as Quikrete or you can make you own. In the latter case use one part Portland Cement, ½ part hydrated lime and 4½ parts clean sand. Or you can use **masonry cement**. In this case, mix one part cement with four parts sand. In either case use just enough water to mix properly. Mix in a wheelbarrow or mortar tub and use a hoe or mortar hoe to thoroughly mix the dry materials together. Then pour in a little water, mix, and add water and mix until you have a consistent mix. Don't overwater nor try to use mortar too dry. It should be pliable, but stay up in position when pulled up with the hoe blade. **Masonry color** can also be added for more appeal.

To create the **interior**, select the largest stones you can find and those

with straight edges. These will be used to create the outline around the fireplace opening as well as the corners if you have a square cornered face. Place mortar on the subhearth and position the first course of stones in place. Dry fit or try several stones until you get the one that fits best and then place it firmly down in the mortar. You may have to fit smaller stones between the larger ones, but avoid using very small stones.

Allow the **mortar to set** for about half an hour until it is firm, then brush off any excess from the faces of the

The interior fireplace design and mantle are not only important for proper and safe use, but can add to the décor of the room.

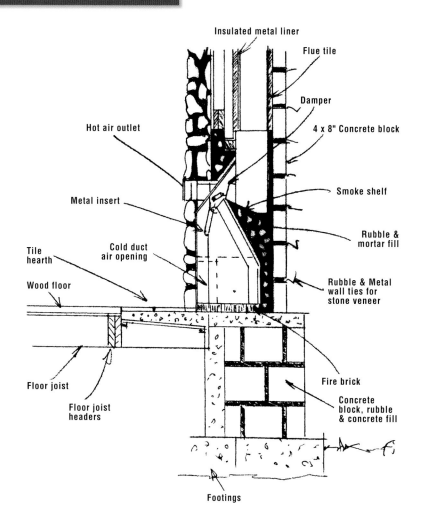

Insulated metal liner

Flue tile

Damper

Hot air outlet

4 x 8" Concrete block

Metal insert

Smoke shelf

Tile hearth

Cold duct air opening

Rubble & mortar fill

Wood floor

Rubble & Metal wall ties for stone veneer

Floor joist

Fire brick

Floor joist headers

Concrete block, rubble & concrete fill

Footings

A force-air fireplace such as the one shown in cross section above, consists of a steel shell that assures a more smoke-free fireplace and a blower that provides circulation of heated air.

This typically is a ⅜ x 4 x 4-inch or larger **steel angle** reaching across the stones to support the stonework above the opening. Make sure this is installed level and allow mortar to set thoroughly. Then you can continue laying **stone courses** up the sides and over the opening. You may wish to stop the courses and add a mantel, or simply take the stone to the building ceiling. The latter is very common in lodges as it provides a great place to display a game trophy.

In most instances the **cold-air outlets** must be boxed and **ductwork** placed in the house walls or floor, or in some cases in the fireplace face. The **hot-air outlet** is usually located just above the face. Mortar a layer of stones in place over the lintel, then place a purchased metal grill in place, level and mortar it in place. In some instances a **"soldier" course** of stones can be layered to create a **"natural" grille**.

Because you'll be toting mortar around and needing a place to hold it, **a mortar board** and **support box** can be very handy. The mortar board is simply a scrap of wood with a "handle" that can be a short piece of closet pole or 2 x 2. A four-sided box makes a handy "holder" so the mortar doesn't slide off when the board is set down between jobs. In instances of flat stones or those that tend to slide off, or with too-soft mortar, a brace can be used to hold the stone securely in place until the mortar sets.

The outside portion of the fireplace should be built along with the inside so both are about the same level of construction at all times. As you build the brick or stone wall around the metal form, the space between the wall and the form is

stones and "joint" the mortar lines. Use a round-head bolt and stiff bristle brush to remove excess mortar between the joints, and smooth them out. This takes a bit of practice. If the mortar is too soft you will brush and pull too much out. If it's too hard you won't be able to easily clean and **"sculpt" the joints**. And don't rush the job, do only one or two courses at a time, allow these to set and then proceed with the next. If you stack too many courses, the whole shebang may slump back down on the floor.

Once the inside walls are level with the top of the fireplace opening you will need to install a **lintel**.

filled with mortar and rubble. When you get level with the throat of the metal form you must build a **smoke shelf**. Note that the bottom of the shelf is below the **throat**. The function of the shelf is to catch drafts of cold air and redirect them upward to join with the rising column of hot air and smoke. If a smoke shelf is not included in the fireplace structure (and it sometimes is not), cold downdrafts will push smoke out into the room through the opening—a typical "smoky" fireplace that does not draw well.

As the fireplace chimney gets higher, it's not a bad idea to rent **scaffolding** to make the job easier and safer. Work slowly and carefully here as you "corbel" the masonry in to create the opening and support the **chimney liner**. As you lay up the clay-tile liner, you want to make sure the mortar in the joints is flush with the inside. To do this, fill a sack with rags or straw—make sure the sack is a snug fit for the flue tile. Slowly pull the sack up as you add the lengths of tile and mortar. The sack will smooth the joints and drag up the excess mortar.

A critical part of the chimney is where it passes through the roof. This area must be well **flashed** to prevent water leaks. Concrete block can be used as the supporting shell with real or manufactured stone on the outside. Or, you can use all stone. The **flue liner** is extended above the chimney 8 to 10 inches and the chimney must be 3 to 5 feet above the peak of the roof for proper draw. Some locales require a special flue-liner rather than flue-tile. This is typically a stainless steel liner with specially formulated insulating

mortar poured down the flue around the liner to seal it off and prevent the problem of flue-fires raging through cracks in the chimney construction.

Plan your fireplace and chimney carefully and take your time. It's a job to be proud of when you're finished, and it must be done right.

ZERO CLEARANCE FIREPLACE

An alternate method is to install a zero-clearance fireplace. Because of the variances of the fireplaces, it is extremely important to install them according to specific manufacturer's instructions.

FIREPLACE INSERTS

You can also increase the efficiency of your fireplace with an insert installed after the fireplace has been constructed. Inserts will greatly improve heat generation over conventional brick or stone fireplaces. Simple fireplaces are only 10 percent efficient at best. As the temper-

You can also increase the efficiency of your fireplace with an insert such as the Vermont Castings WinterWarm fireplace insert shown here.

ature drops outside, the efficiency declines even more. A good insert, however, can operate at 40 percent efficiency if it is fired correctly.

Inserts are available as single wall, double wall and triple wall. The most common is the **double-wall model** or one with two metal boxes, one inside the other. The fire is built in the inside box. The open area between the inside and outside box serves as a heat exchanger. Air is circulated through this space usually with a fan. An **air intake** is usually placed low, near the floor and in front of the insert. A **fan** blows the air around the firebox and then out a vent placed near the top front of the insert. **Single-wall inserts** are less expensive, but less efficient. And they must be connected directly to the chimney. If smoke from a single

wall gets in the fireplace it can be blown into the house. A **triple-wall** is the most expensive, slightly more efficient and the third wall creates a cooler exterior so it has a lower clearance to combustible materials.

In most instances the inserts vent the insert firebox gases directly into the firebox of the fireplace. It's important to have the insert vent as close to the chimney as possible. You will have to remove or wire up the damper.

Make sure you measure your **firebox size** in inches. This includes the height, width of the firebox at the front face as well as at the rear wall. And measure the depth. Most inserts are available in three sizes designed to fit most standard fireplaces. Bigger is not necessarily better. A smaller firebox will often operate with better efficiency, although it takes more filling and work.

WOOD STOVES AND HEARTH STOVES

Wood stoves and hearth stoves are another alternative. The latter are becoming increasingly popular and offer more efficiency than an insert due to the fact you not only get heat from the forced air, but **convection heat** with the unit protruding into the room.

Free Standing Wood Stoves

A wood heating stove or even a wood cook stove can be an invaluable source of economical heat for many hunting and fishing camp lodges, especially if a supply of firewood is readily available. Since nearly 70 percent of a stove's heat comes from **radiation**, it is important that it be made of a metal with a high conductivity rating and have sufficient surface from which the

A wood cookstove, such as the deluxe model shown above, can be a useful source of room heat. Cooking on a wood stove, however, requires special skills.

heat can radiate. Stoves should be **airtight** to aid combustion and lined to retain heat. **Cast iron** and **steel** are good materials for stoves and have nearly identical conductivity ratings, but in general, the thicker the metal, the longer the stove will last.

There are three basic choices in **wood stove construction**: sheet metal, plate steel, cast iron, or combinations of these metals. As a general rule, the heavier the stove, the better the heat-retaining and radiating capabilities. **Sheet metal stoves**, while relatively inexpensive, are made of thin gauge metal and have a shorter life than plate steel or cast iron stoves. They will heat a room quickly, but they also cool rapidly. They should be installed on several inches of dirt or sand in a firebox to prevent burnout by hot coals.

Plate steel stoves (⅛ inch thick or more), hold heat longer than sheet metal stoves. A firebrick lining will provide more uniform heating and protect he metal from warping. Many will be fitted with accessories such as doors and cast iron or firebrick firebox liners that serve to extend the life of the stove.

Cast iron stoves warm up slowly and hold heat well. Cast iron holds up well under heat, has a long life, and generally does not warp. Cast iron stoves should be handled with care and well maintained because cast iron is brittle and cracks easily.

There are three main types of wood stoves: box (radiating), airtight (convection) and pellet-fed. **Box or radiant heat stoves** are not tightly sealed and draw air for combustion through their doors, radiating heat through the firebox to the surrounding air. Radiant heat stoves

PREFABRICATED CHIMNEY

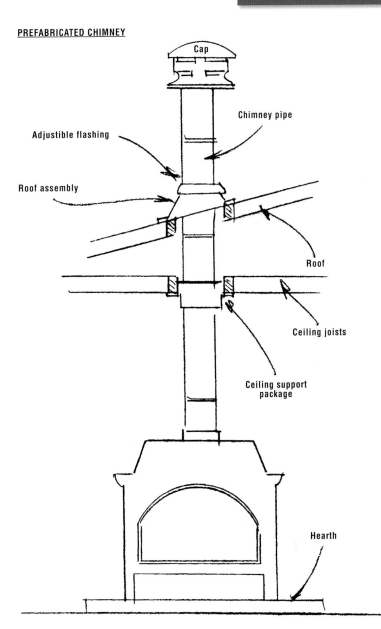

are the most traditional form of wood burning stove, and in the past were manufactured under various names such as pot-bellied, Franklin, parlor and other stoves. Homemade **oil drum stoves** fall under this category. These stoves generally do not have damper controls and permit a large percent of unburned gases to escape up the chimney or stovepipe.

Airtight or convection stoves feature sealed fireboxes and tight fitting

Components of a wood stove, as shown in the diagram above, include a fireproof hearth and a properly installed flue. Care must be taken in insulating the openings where the flue passes through floors and roof to avoid fire hazard.

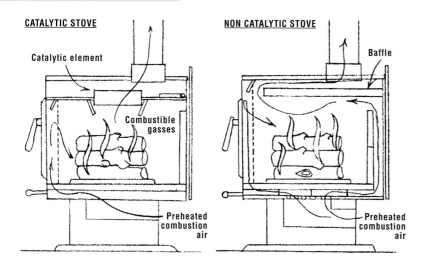

Woodstoves are manufactured in a wide variety of styles and are availavle in traditional box and catalytic models (see the diagrams above).

combustion chamber mechanically. They are fitted with a fuel hopper to store the pellets. Most hoppers hold between 35 and 130 pounds of fuel, which will last a day or more under normal operation. In pellet-fed stoves, a feeder device drops the pellets, a few at a time, into the combustion chamber. The rate at which pellets are fed into the burner determines the heat output. Pellet stoves have the advantage of having a steady and easily managed fuel source, but require an electrical source to power fans, controls and pellet feeders. Many models can be directly vented and do not require a chimney or flue.

Another advanced type of wood burning stove is the **catalytic wood stove**, also known as secondary burn stove. To work best these stoves reach temperatures of 1100°F, hot enough to burn combustible gases before they can exit the chimney. Catalytic wood stoves include a metal channel to heat and feed air into the stove above the fire to help burn volatile gases above the fire without slowing down combustion. The stove's firebox is insulated to reflect heat ensuring that the gases stay hot enough to burn. **Catalytic combustors** should be inspected at least three times every season and replaced according to the manufacturer's recommendations.

If you choose to install a wood burning stove in your hunting or fishing camp, be prepared to do a little research to determine the **appropriate size** for the structure where it will be used. A good rule-of-thumb is that a stove rated at 60,000 BTU can heat a 2,000 square-foot structure, while a stove rated at 42,000 BTU

doors and are fitted with a manually operated or thermostat-controlled air-intake damper to permit air circulation around the firebox and regulate the rate of fuel consumption. Convection heat is more effective at heating a larger area than radiant heat and airtight stoves provide slow-burning heat for long periods with relatively little attention.

Pellet-fed stoves use processed wood pellets that are fed into a can heat a 1,300 square-foot area.

When you go to select a wood stove, bring the measurements of the room and a diagram of where the stove will be located. Note whether air flows freely between rooms and determine how well the room will be insulated. The stove retailer should be able to provide guidance on the size stove you need. You can also consult with a professional stove installer who can help determine the size of the stove you are considering.

Most manufacturers rate their stoves either by the number of cubic feet or the number of rooms the stove will heat. As a general rule, 2.6 square feet of firebox bottom is required for each 1,000 square feet of room area. Without open rooms or a forced air duct/ system, attempting to heat more than one room with a stove may well result in uneven temperatures.

Another consideration is your **fuel source**. Do you plan to cut and gather your own firewood and do you have access to a sufficient supply and will you need to acquire permits from the U.S. Forest Service or state agencies? Consider that **wood-cutting** requires a working knowledge of cutting trees and timber, time and investment in equipment such as axes, saws and splitters. If you choose to purchase firewood, take into account the length of time you need to heat your lodge and the cost and availability of firewood in your geographical area. Remember that orders for purchase and delivery must be placed well in advance of the heating season and you will also need to acquire your wood early enough to give it time to season.

Above all, wood stoves must, however, be properly installed and operated or they can be a **fire hazard**. Two types of chimneys are considered safe for wood stoves. The first is a lined **masonry chimney** and the second a **UL listed "Class A" all-fuel chimney**. Single wall, metal stove-pipe must never be used alone as a chimney. **Single-wall, metal stove pipe**, however, is commonly used to connect the stove to the chimney although double-wall packed pipe is also used. Stoves may be vented into a flue constructed for the stove, or installed in a fireplace to increase its efficiency. A wide range of stoves are available on the market, including direct heat and circulating stoves that use fans to circulate heat.

Even with careful installation, wood stoves can be potential **safety hazards** for any structure. These hazards include excess heat radiating from the stove or stovepipe and flames shooting out of chimney cracks. Other dangers include escape of sparks or hot coals and excess heat radiating from the stovepipe to flammable materials.

With **proper installation**, most of these risks can be avoided and you should be prepared to follow basic safety procedures. Manufacturers nearly always include safety instructions with each product and the Underwriters Laboratory tests and lists stoves that meet standards of the Wood Energy Institute and National Fire Protection Association.

Before installing a wood heating stove, determine **local building code rules** regarding wood stoves. And check with your **insurance company** as to their regulations regarding wood stoves. In some instances local codes or your insurance com-

SELECTING AND INSTALLING A WOOD STOVE

- Check your state and local codes and follow all safety precautions.

- Read and follow instructions provided by the manufacturer for proper installation.

- All wood stoves should have sturdy legs that provide a minimum of 4 inches (preferably 8 to 10 inches), of air space between stove bottom and floor.

- Allow a clearance of at least 36" on all sides of the stove to prevent fire or reduce risk by installing approved radiation shields.

- Any glass windows should be made of thermal shock resistant safety glass.

- Ensure that the stovepipe is well insulated where it passes through a wall or the cabin's roof.

- Extend stove pipes and chimneys about 3 inches above the highest point of the roof.

pany may not accept wood stoves. Then, before you light the first fire, make sure your insurance company representative as well as local building codes or fire department representative check your stove installation and approve of it in writing. If you are installing a stove in an existing chimney, make sure you have the chimney inspected by a local fire inspection official or chimney sweep before using the stove.

The first step in installing a stove in new construction is to **properly locate the stove and chimney**. The stove and chimney should be located in a central location with good air circulation to as many of the building rooms as possible. In new construction, it's best to construct an interior, centrally located, masonry, tile or metal-lined chimney. Interior chimneys not only stay warmer than exterior chimneys, they also do not have as much creosote build-up and will also help heat the building. Make sure you check for all recommended safety clearances for the chimney and stove location. The stove must not block any exits or fire escape routes, nor interfere with daily traffic patterns.

Or you may wish to install a **prefabricated metal chimney**. Two types of metal prefabricated flues are available. The **air-cooled or triple-wall type** has three tubes of stainless steel with air circulating between the tubes. The second type, called **solid pack** consists of two stainless steel walls filled with a solid insulation. These types of chimneys typically come in kit form and are fairly easy to install, even for a first timer. If installing a prefabricated metal chimney make sure it is labeled "UL Class A approved." In order to be la-

beled as such the chimney must be able to withstand the extreme heat produced by a chimney fire. And, it must be installed according to manufacturer's instructions.

The following are some general rules for chimney construction. Chimneys must project at least 3 feet above the highest point they exit through the roof of a building and at least 2 feet higher than any part of the building within 10 feet distance. Do not vent more than one stove into a single flue as this can cause **downdrafting** and is a fire hazard. Two areas must be given particular care in construction—where the chimney goes through the floor or ceiling joists and where the chimney goes through the roof. Make sure there is adequate space. There should be at least 2 inches of clearance between the chimney and floor joists, roofing or other combustible materials. The chimney must be air tight and should have a tight-fitting clean-out door and a cap. The cap not only minimizes downdrafts, but prevents rain and snow from penetrating the chimney.

Make sure you follow the stove manufacturer's instructions for installation. Several types of prefabricated stove pipe are available, including very economical, single-wall construction. Some manufactures may call for packed-solid stove piping.

The stove must sit on a **hearth** of **solid brick, stone or concrete**. The stove should never be installed over carpeting, a wood floor or any other combustible material. The hearth must extend at least 20 inches past the loading side of the stove, or where the wood is loaded and ashes removed. The **pad** should also extend back behind the stove so that the **stovepipe elbow** can't radiate heat onto an unprotected floor. In addition to the stone, brick or masonry hearth, a **fireproof base** should also be installed. With proper installation a stove can be a great addition to your lodge, but it must be properly cleaned and maintained and inspected yearly.

PROPANE & OIL HEATING SYSTEMS

Propane or **liquefied petroleum gas** (LPG or LP) is a relatively inexpensive and efficient heating fuel source suitable for a dwelling that is not connected to an electricity grid or municipal gas system. Your cabin or lodge site will, however, require road access fit for propane delivery vehicles.

Propane is stored in a specially designed tank and flows to the structure through **underground pipes (flexible copper tubing)**. The tubing is connected to an appliance connector, a relatively short flexible tube that carries gas to an appliance. The **LP storage tanks** can be installed above or below ground. **Above ground** is the simplest method, as it does not require excavation, simply level ground and concrete blocks as supports. Generally, a 500-gallon tank will serve an average four-bedroom structure.

The most common propane heating systems are **central forced-air furnace systems** that require a system of ductwork in the cabin. High efficiency, low-profile furnaces are available from various manufacturers that will fit into tight spaces. If your cabin has access to electricity, most propane furnaces will be fitted with electronic ignitions. A stand-alone furnace will require standing pilot lights.

Combo-heater systems are available that incorporate the water heater to provide space heating. Hot water is circulated through a heat exchanger coil in the furnace air handler, and warm air is distributed throughout the cabin by ducts.

Most propane units, furnaces and hot water heaters, can be direct vented vertically or horizontally, eliminating the need for a chimney.

Oil Furnaces and Boilers

Oil-fired furnaces and boilers are popular heating choices in parts of the country with limited access to natural gas, such as the Northeast. **Fuel oil** is a clean-burning fuel and a number of companies now offer heating oil blended with biodiesel. Oil heating systems will require the installation of a furnace and ductwork or a furnace, boiler and radiator units. In addition, your cabin will require an outdoor fuel tank and good enough roads to permit access by fuel delivery trucks.

An above ground propane tank is the easiest system to install. The gas flows to the cabin or lodge through underground tubing.

Decks, Sunroofs & Porches

Decks, porches and sunroofs can add to the enjoyment of your lodge. Even if you don't construct them during your initial building, you should plan for them when building. Decks and porches can be a small extension off a family room, bedroom or dining area; or they can be a spacious "outdoor" room large enough for a party or to hold a group of hunters relaxing after the hunt. You may want to include a front porch as well as a back deck. Porches and decks can be single level or multi-level; they can be some of the simplest "first" projects for a beginner, or elaborate examples of sophisticated craftsmanship. Porches are basically covered decks and can be a simple sunroof design or solid shingles as an extension of the building roof. Porches can also be totally enclosed for insect protection.

Above: Decks, porches and sunroofs are fairly easy to construct and can add to the enjoyment of your lodge.

DECKS

Decks and porches are fairly easy to build, and the first step is planning, design and layout. What will the primary use be? Will it be a place for barbequing or smoking game at the lodge? Do you need to build it in the shade, or do you want some sunlight for relaxing on cool mornings after the turkey hunt. How big do you want it, and are there any utilities in the way of the deck or porch? It's a good idea to measure the area of the proposed deck or porch and make

TYPICAL DECK CONSTRUCTION

<u>SUPPORT POST INSTALLATION</u>

<u>JOINING TO BUILDING</u>

<u>FRAMING DETAILS</u>

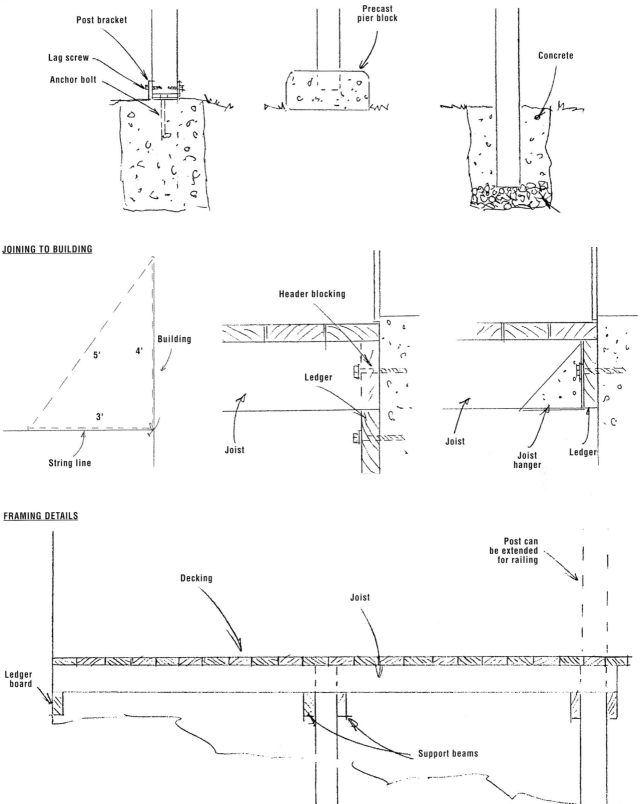

*Use a chalk line to mark out the edge of the deck. Use a circular saw to cut away
the overlapping wood left after laying down the deck boards.*

a rough sketch as to how it fits with the lodge and the landscaping. You probably don't want to remove trees unless you have to and in some cases you can even build around them, but leave plenty of room for the tree to grow. You will have to contact local building authorities in many locales with a sketch or proposed construction and in many instances obtain a permit.

Decks must be made of **rot- and insect-resistant materials**. These may be composite materials or wood, depending on your choice. Wood for decks may be naturally resistant woods such as Western red cedar or redwood or they may be pressure-treated materials. One factor in your choice may be the type of materials available in your area. All fasteners must be corrosion resistant and matched to the decking materials. For instance, if using pressure-

treated materials make sure you use screws and fasteners suited for pressure-treated wood.

The next step is to **lay out the deck**. Outline the deck with **stakes and string lines**. You should also determine level with a line level so you can have an idea of the land slope and height of deck above ground level. Be sure the deck is laid out square. Use the wooden triangle shown in the chapter on foundations or mark 3 and 4 foot length on the house wall and one or two deck sides. The measurement between should be 5 feet (diagram page 185). Move the string line in or out to provide a triangle with a 90-degree angle.

With the deck laid out, mark the locations for the **support posts**. These can be anchored in three ways: set in a **poured concrete hole** with the concrete below frost level; anchored to a **poured concrete footing** with a post bracket; or in **pre-poured pier blocks**, or **poured piers** (diagram page 185). Make sure the support posts are anchored solidly according to code and are anchored and installed plumb. Brace in place with 2 x 4s and stakes. Then determine the height of the deck. If access to the deck is from a door, locate the deck about an inch or two below the threshold. Use lag screws to fasten the ledger board to the house into the foundation or house wall. If the latter, make sure you are anchoring to solid supports such as studs. Be sure the ledger board is level.

Joists are supported in two methods. The first is to place the house ends of the joists on a **ledger board** (diagram page 12). Using a string line or joist, locate the outside end of a joist on the corner deck post, mak-

CONSTRUCTING DECK STEPS

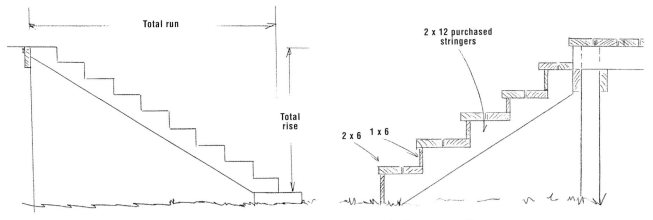

Precut stair stringers can be purchased, or you can lay them out yourself.

ing sure it is level. Mark the level line and place a ledger under the line to support the outer end of the joists. You can also use **joist hangers** (diagram page 185), on ledger boards to support both ends of the joists.

In any case, fasten the joists in place. If placing on a ledger board on the house wall, use header blocking between the joists for additional support. Add additional girder supports as needed to support the joists. Typically these are situated every 4 feet or anchored to the inner posts along the deck sides. Joists are normally located 16 inches on center. You may also wish to add blocking on the outside ends or a header to finish off the ends of the joists.

Then the **deck boards** are installed. These may be composite or wood. A popular deck board is 5/4 pressure-treated wood with rounded edges. Pressure treated or naturally resistant 2 x 6s of Western red cedar or redwood may be used. If using pressure treated wood, don't leave space between the deck boards as the material will shrink as it dries. If using resistant woods, leave a ¼-inch space

Steps and railings are a very important component of decks and must be well designed and sturdily constructed.

RAILING AND BENCH DETAILS

RAILING PATTERNS

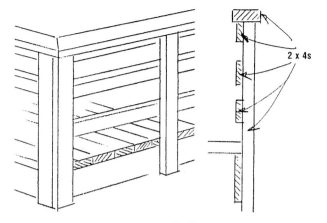

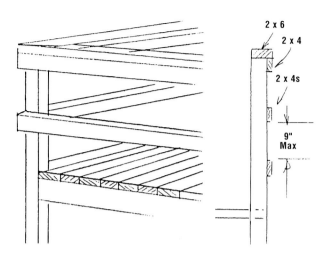

2 x 4s

2 x 6
2 x 4
2 x 4s

9"
Max

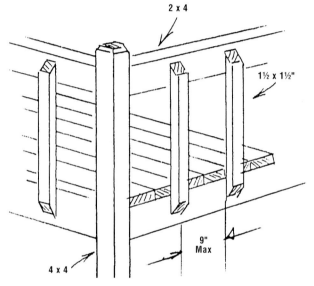

2 x 4

1½ x 1½"

9"
Max

4 x 4

RAILING WITH BUILT-IN BENCH

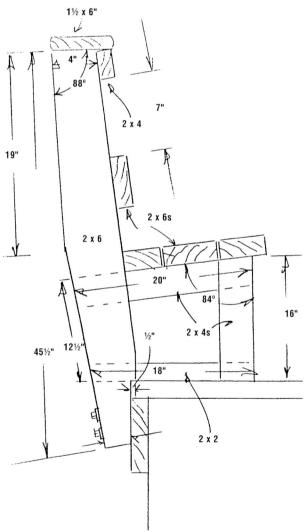

1½ x 6"

4"
88°

7"
2 x 4

19"

2 x 6s

2 x 6

20"
84°

16"

2 x 4s

45½" 12½"   ½"

18"

2 x 2

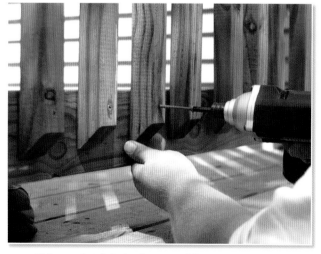

*Make sure that all deck railings are solidly constructed and that
posts are firmly secured with corrosion-resistant screws.*

between the deck boards. Impact drivers make it easy to screw decking down in place, and the Milwaukee Sharp-Fire allows you to stand up and drive screws in place. The Vaughn BoJak is useful for forcing warped deck boards in place until you can fasten them down.

In most instances you will also need steps from the deck to the ground. **Deck steps** consist of **stringers**, **treads** and sometimes a **riser board**. The simplest method of constructing steps is to purchase ready-made pressure-treated stringers. Or you can make up you own stringers from pressure-treated 2 x 12s. The first step in laying out the stringer is to measure the rise or the vertical height from the ground to the top of the deck. To determine how many stair risers are needed, divide this by the stair step rise you desire, usually 7 inches.

To determine the total **run of the stairs**, multiply the number of steps that you require by 11¼ inches. Using a framing square, lay out the risers and then cut them to shape using a portable circular saw. Fasten the risers in place to the deck, supporting their outer ends on **concrete footings or piers**, making sure the treads are level. You can then fasten the first riser board to the front of the risers, and then fasten the treads down on the riser tops. Continue constructing until you have the steps completed.

Railings are the next step in the process. In some instances the posts will be extended above the deck boards so that the railings can be fastened directly to the posts. In other instances, separate post and railing construction is used. This is the case where benches are built in with the railings. Shown on the preceeding page are some typical examples of both railings and benches. If you plan on constructing a roof or sunroof over the deck, the simplest method is to extend the deck support posts to the height needed for the porch roof.

A PATIO, PORCH OR DECK SUNROOF

Decks, porches and patios are a major source of America's entertainment and a great place to relax after the hunt, but they can be hot in the summer sun. They can actually be dangerous if they reflect the sun's ultraviolet rays. Running your grill during a rainstorm that arrives the same time as your hunt guests can be a real frustration. One answer is a **sunroof** over your patio or deck. If designed properly, a sunroof can cut the summer sun, but still allow winter sun rays to warm the house.

Because these projects are always exposed to the weather, they should be constructed of **weather resistant wood** such as Wolmanized Residential Outdoor wood. The wood is southern-pine, pressure-treated with a copper azole preservative. The wood can also be "re-dried" an extra feature that provides extra benefits at a small cost.

When wood is **pressure treated**, it is saturated with a liquid solution of preservative. As the wood dries, it shrinks. That's normal for wood. Treated wood can be re-dried at the treating plant; this may be done naturally through air-drying, or more commonly, in a kiln. **Re-drying** is done, this is indicated on the end tag by ADAT (Air Dried After Treatment)

A porch is basically a covered deck.

The porch roof may be an extension of the building roof, or shed style.

or KDAT (Kiln Dried After Treatment). Drying makes the wood lighter in weight, ready for immediate painting and able to meet building codes (when applicable) for dried material. Perhaps more important, factory drying is done under controlled conditions, unlike the drying that takes place in a project when one side of a deck may be exposed to hot sun while the other faces moist earth. As a result, there is warping (twisting, cupping or bowing) of lumber. Not all wood treaters offer re-drying and many dealers do not sell it because of the extra cost. However, it is an option worth consideration for those who wish to avoid exchanges and warped lumber or who wish to paint their wood without waiting 6 to 12 months for it to dry.

The framing of the sunroof shown was finished with Sikkens Cetol SRD one-coat **wood finish** in Cedar tone. Sikkens is an easy-to-apply, one-coat oil and alkyd resin formula that provides protection from exposure to sun, rain, sleet and snow. And it also acts as a barrier to ultraviolet sun rays, providing further protection and longevity to the wood. Treated wood must be absolutely dry before Cetol SRD is applied, a main reason for the re-dried wood. The finish was applied to each board and allowed to dry before construction.

The **covering** for the sunroof shown is Sequentia Super600 from Crane Composites. The company has several products and it's important to consider your area's **year-round weather conditions** when choosing a covering. The amount of snow, rain and wind you receive as well as the intensity of the sun and range of temperatures are all factors. The building shown is in the Missouri Ozarks where the saying is, "If you don't like the weather today, just wait, it will change tomorrow." And it does, with temperature ranges from over a 100° F to well below zero. And heavy rains, heavy snow, hail and high winds are all common.

Sequentia Super600 is a heavy-duty, commercial-grade fiberglass with a 20-year warranty. It features heavy-duty fiberglass reinforcement and has UV resistant properties. The Sequentia line-up comes in clear plus 6 colors, white, terra cotta, sky blue, yellow, graphite, green and beige. Terra cotta was chosen to blend with the treated wood finish and the Western red cedar siding. The color is a beautiful translucent that provides a moderate light transmission and low heat transmission.

The owners wanted a **sunroof** that would not only provide shade for relaxing and entertaining on the deck, but also to provide more protection to the exposed south wall and the large amount of glass in the window and two patio doors. The owners, however, enjoyed the solar warmth created in the winter so the roof was designed to provide some sun reflection during the low-angle sun location of the winter months.

The result is a sunroof that begins at 10 feet high on the house wall, is 8 feet high at the outside edge, and extends 10 feet from the building. The sunroof shown is 40 feet long. This also allowed for using standard materials, including 10-foot panels of Sequentia Super600 roofing. Before you begin construction of your sunroof, make sure you check local building codes on similar construction, materials and specific construction details. Also check for local zoning requirements and any permits needed.

Construction of the **sunroof framing** is fairly straight forward, but it's important to get the framing square with the building. Otherwise the panels may not align properly, increasing or decreasing in the distance they extend from the rafter front edges. To find the exact location and proper 90-degree angle for the corner posts in relation to the house wall, use a plumb bob on the wall to locate the first outside rafter.

Two methods can be used to **assure a square construction**. The first is to locate the corner post locations with a tape measure and then measure diagonally between a corner post and the opposite starting point on the house wall. Measure the other corner post diagonally to the opposite starting point on the house wall. Adjust the post locations until the measurements are the same.

You can also use the **"triangle" method**. Measure 4 feet on the house wall. Attach a string a line at the starting point and with someone holding the string line, measure and mark 3 feet out from the house wall on the string line. Move the string line in or out until the measurement between the two is 5 feet. Extend the string line to the outside location of the corner post. This creates a 90 degree angle. Because I frequently lay out buildings, I've constructed a lightweight wooden triangle of those measurements. Laying out squared buildings is quick and easy with the triangle. Manufactured squares are also available. Once the corner post locations are determined, run a string line between them and mark

TYPICAL SUNROOF FRAMING

SETTING THE POST

LEVELING THE POST

1. The first step in installing a sun roof is to set the support posts. Use a 4-foot level to make sure the support posts are plumb.

2. It's much easier to prefinish the structural members of the sunroof before assembly.

3. Then the roof support is framed in, you can use the "triangle method to make sure it is square.

4. Holes are drilled into Sequentia Super600 roof covering.

5. Silicone caulking applied.

6. Hex-head neoprene fasteners are used to fasten the materials in place.

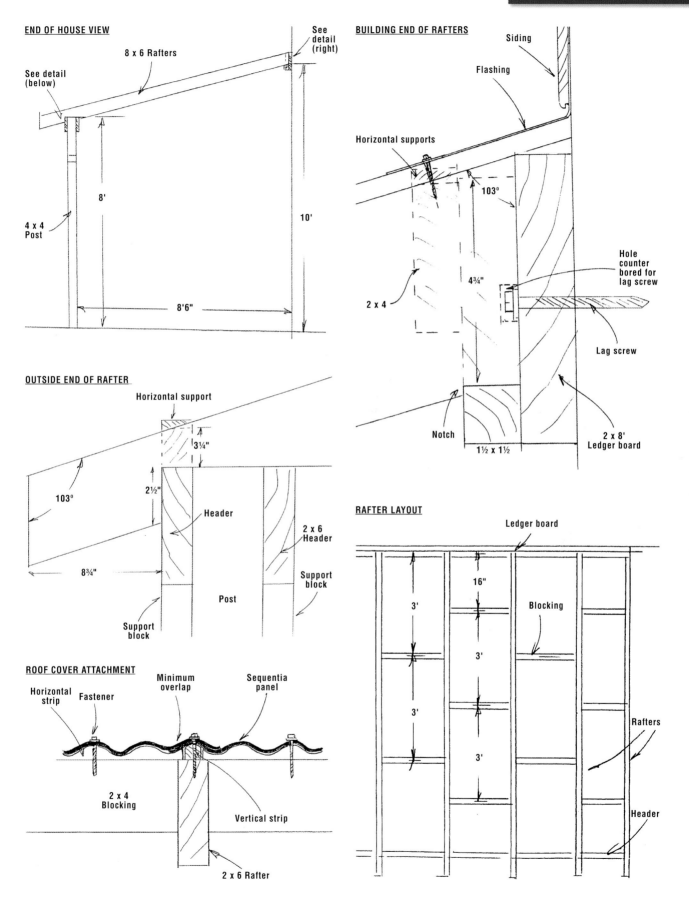

END OF HOUSE VIEW

8 x 6 Rafters

See detail (right)

See detail (below)

8'

10'

4 x 4 Post

8'6"

BUILDING END OF RAFTERS

Siding

Flashing

Horizontal supports

103°

Hole counter bored for lag screw

4¾"

2 x 4

Lag screw

Notch

1½ x 1½

2 x 8' Ledger board

OUTSIDE END OF RAFTER

Horizontal support

3¼"

103°

2½"

Header

2 x 6 Header

8¾"

Support block

Post

Support block

Support block

RAFTER LAYOUT

Ledger board

16"

3'

3'

3'

Blocking

Rafters

Header

ROOF COVER ATTACHMENT

Horizontal strip   Fastener

Minimum overlap

Sequentia panel

2 x 4 Blocking

Vertical strip

2 x 6 Rafter

the inside posts locations.

The **posts** should be set on **slabs and footings** and supported according to local building code regulations. In the project shown the posts were run through the deck to concrete supports below and fastened to the under deck cross member supports as well. The posts should be fastened to concrete slab/footings using approved **steel anchor bolts**. Use a 4-foot level and temporary bracing to hold posts in a plumb upright position during construction. In the project shown, once the posts were plumbed, they were anchored to the under-deck supports. You might wish to check into the Bigfoot Systems concrete tube forms for pouring supports.

The **building end of the rafters** is supported on a **ledger board**. Remove the buildings siding from the ledger board location. In the case shown, the building was being resided and siding was installed up to the ledger board location. The ledger board was installed, leaving space for roof covering, flashing, and siding to be installed above the ledger board. The bottom siding board is temporarily fastened in place in order to insert the metal flashing for the roof cover.

The ledger board was leveled using a string-level for initial location, and then a 4-foot level to adjust as needed. Three-inch deck screws were used for initial fastening of the board in place and then lag screws were installed into the 2x framing of the buildings wall. If fastening to masonry walls, use appropriate wall anchors. The fasteners should be installed on 16-inch centers as required. All **fasteners** used with pressure-treated lumber

must be **corrosion resistant**. Phillips II High Performance DuraFast Coated screws recommended for pressure treated lumber were used for all construction fastening. After years of pressure-treated lumber construction, these are my recommended fasteners. The box comes with a driver head that matches the screws and there is very little head stripping. A 2 x 2 support strip is fastened to the bottom edge of the ledger board to provide support for the rafters.

As with laying out squares, getting the first **rafter** laid out and cut properly is extremely important. I like to use a straight piece of "scrap" board to cut the first rafter. It should be cut and tested, cutting until you get the correct angles and cuts. Once the **trial rafter** is cut, and temporarily installed, again make sure the rafter and house wall are perpendicular or at 90-degree angle. Mark the location, remove the trial rafter and use it as a pattern to cut the first rafter. After cutting, recoat any cut ends with protective finish. Install the **vertical panel support strips** on the rafter tops using galvanized nails. A finish or brad nailer and galvanized nails makes this chore easy.

Temporarily install the first and second rafters. The rafters are located on 24-inch centers. The outside rafter is anchored in place with a screw from the underside of the 2 x 2 support block into the under side of the rafter end. A 22½-inch filler block is placed inside and next to the outside rafter. Fasten the inside rafter against the filler block with a screw from the underside of the support strip. Use a scrap piece of roofing panel on the outer end to test for fit and precise rafter location. Check on the building end as well. Then slide the flashing up under the siding and test it on roof panel and rafters. Once adjusted so all fits properly, permanently anchor the rafters in place with screws through the rafters and into the filler block. An outside filler block is also required and a horizontal cross strip must be fastened to the top of it. The outer ends of the horizontal cross strips must match the crown profiles of the vertical edge strips. Again fasten with brads or galvanized finish nails. I fastened the filler blocks in place by first pre-drilling pocket-hole screw holes on the back side using a Kreg Pocket Hole tool. Anchor the block between the two rafters and then screw the rafters into the filler block.

From this point on, it's a matter of **positioning a rafter**, then screwing it to the outer ends of both filler blocks. Interior filler blocks, again topped with horizontal cross strips are placed between the rafters, spaced as shown in the drawing. You can install the rafters, then cut and fit the individual interior filler strips in place, but on a job of this size, I found it more convenient to "pre-assemble" the components. First all filler blocks were cut to precise lengths using a Ridgid Exactline compound miter saw supported on their Miter Saw Utility Vehicle support. The Repeat-A-Cut fence and a stop block made it quick and easy to cut all of the strips to precise lengths, along with the horizontal panel support strips. All of the strips were then fastened in place.

For ease in placement, the interior support strips were fastened to the rafters before erecting the rafters. The rafters were fastened in place and the loose ends of the interior support strips anchored to the mating rafter. You may need two people to lift and fasten these assemblies. An additional 2 x 4 filler block with horizontal cross strips is installed against the ledger board and as an anchor for the end of the corrugated roof panels and the metal flashing.

Install the first panel making sure it fits precisely over the vertical support strips on the rafters. Start the first panel at the leeward end of the run and work windward. Provide a minimum of one corrugation overlap at the sides. Also provide 8-inch end-laps for roofs with pitch less than 4/12; 6-inch end laps for pitches greater than 4/12. Fasten the crowns of the panels at every second corrugation. **Fasteners** with armored neoprene washers are recommended. Space fasteners 6- to 8-inches on-center along panel edges and 12- to 16-inches on-center for intermediate rafters and blocking.

To **avoid deflection of the panels**, tighten screws until the washers will not rotate and then tighten one more turn. Avoid excess burrs on drilled or punched holes to protect the neoprene sealing face. Always pre-drill panels and molding strips before securing them to your framework in order to prevent cracking or splitting. To help ensure a weatherproof roof, apply a small amount of clear sealer to each hole before installing the fasteners.

Under no circumstances should the panels be allowed to support undistributed loads, such as the weight of a human body. When working, use approved roof ladders and planking. Now it's time for a cool, relaxing drink under your new sunroof.

A SCREENED-IN PORCH

If your hunting or fishing camp is located on a lake or other water source, a screened-in porch can not only add to the enjoyment of your lodge, but may be a necessity to keep off the "skeeters."

A screened-in porch can be constructed in three phases. Many lodge owners have started with a patio or deck, added a sunroof, and then ended up screening in a porch. Or the project can be done as one from beginning to end.

Note: Regardless of whether adding an enclosure to a roofed area, or building from start, in many instances you will be required to provide a building plan for any addition, to local building authorities. You may also be required to obtain a building permit.

Support

Regardless, the first step is to create a **solid base** for the construction of the porch. In some instances decks may be utilized. In this case the area of the deck with the porch must be floored over with a solid material to keep the insects from coming up through the cracks in the deck. Additional support must also be placed under the deck to support the additional weight of the porch, as well as any snow that may accumulate in northern climates. In many instances, however, the porch will be constructed on a concrete or other type of solid patio. The ideal is to pour a **concrete slab** for the porch which can then be further embellished with a slate or quarry tile floor. A screened in porch will have to handle exposure to the elements,

so make sure that all materials used are intended for exterior use.

If using a poured concrete slab, or other solid surface, make sure there is proper **drainage** of water away from the existing building, as water will get into the porch during storms. Most builders consider ¼ inch per foot the proper slope for a concrete patio. For a 12 foot porch, this would be 3 inches, and this is too much for a porch constructed on a slab.

The slab must be laid out and formed. If you do not have experience in, or the tools for concrete work, you may wish to have a contractor do this portion. Pouring a slab of the size shown is do-able, if time is taken in laying out the project so it is square and formed to the proper pitch. Concrete tools can be rented at many rental stores. Do not attempt, however, to mix the concrete for this project. You will need to purchase the necessary concrete in bulk.

Make sure the slab is well **reinforced** and a **footing** is poured around the edge. The footing should be sized to match your geological location. Check with local concrete dealers as to the size and depth. After forming and before pouring, place a **layer of gravel** down, followed by **welded wire reinforcing**. Pour the concrete, level it off with a drag and trowel it smooth. You can hand-trowel, but a power trowel speeds the work and these can also be rented.

If building a screened-in porch on a new slab, place **anchor bolts** around the perimeter in locations for the bottom plate. The plates can then be bolted to the slab to anchor the porch in place. The porch shown was constructed on an existing concrete slab with an awning. The structure

Screening in a porch cuts down on mosquito and other insect problems, often a necessity for lakeside lodges.

was simply framed in and screened. In this case the lower plates were anchored in place with a rented concrete gun that shoots anchors through the plates into the concrete.

Framing

If constructing a totally new screened porch, construct the front wall with a **bottom and top plate**, the 4 x 4 posts, 2 x 4 "studs" and the blocking for the lower framing. Stand the wall upright, make sure it is plumb and then brace it in place. Construct the **side walls**, stand them up and anchor them to the outside wall. Or you can erect the posts, plumb them and add the 2 x 4 framing and blocking. Cut a 2 x 6 inside "plate" and fasten it inside the front wall and flush with the top edge of the plate. This will add strength to the front support, or you can utilize a **double top front plate**. Then cut an inside **support plate** for each side and anchor it as well.

If constructing a **roof**, as opposed to screening in a roofed porch, fasten a **sill plate** to the existing building between the two side walls and flush with their top edges. The **rafters** can then be positioned down on top of this. **Joist hangers** can also be used to help anchor the building ends of the rafters in place. In many instances the roof pitch will match that of the existing building. Or in some cases, the **roof pitch** may be shallower. Make sure the pitch is correct for your area and snow load. Again, check with local authorities. 2 x 6 rafters are suggested for the more shallow-pitched porch roofs. Extend the roof out a foot past the walls. Use blocking on the side to

TYPICAL SCREENING CONSTRUCTION

SIDE OF PORCH

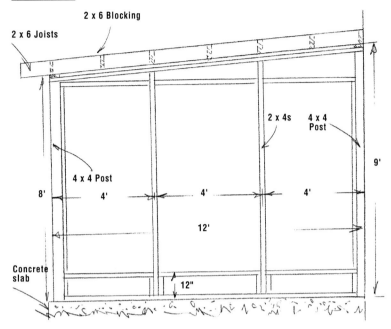

FRONT OF PORCH

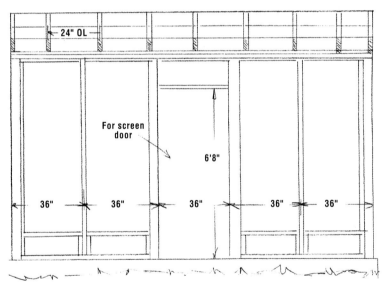

als. Clear or translucent, as well as colored fiberglass panels are available for roofing. These offer **weather protection** and shade, the amount of shade differing depending on the amount of light transference. A number of products are available, including those from Suntuf and Sequentia. These are very tough and impact resistant, withstanding high winds and heavy hailstorms. They have exceptional durability, and do not shatter over time, nor expand or shrink. They are easy to handle, pliable and easy to cut with no special equipment. The porch shown was built with solid roofing materials and the under side was covered with white **vinyl soffit material** to match the white **vinyl siding**. In addition, a ceiling fan with light was added. When installing **ceiling fan/lights** in screened in porches, make sure you utilize a ceiling fan and light unit that is approved for outdoor, wet or damp use.

SCREENING

The next step is to add the screening. Screening is available in a range of materials including **rustproof bronze**, **copper** or **aluminum**, as well as **anodized aluminum** with a baked on finish, and **vinyl**. Vinyl has become increasingly popular because it's easy to work with and durable, although not as durable as some of the metal screens. The traditional method of installing screening on porches is to fasten the screen in place and cover the edges with batten boards. The porch shown was first painted, the screen applied, then the painted batten boards were nailed over the installed screen.

anchor the hanging rafters. A fascia board is fastened to the front edges of the front rafters and to the sides.

The top can be any number of materials, including translucent sheeting or solid roofing materi-

The hardest chore is installing

the screening without having sags or wrinkles. Cut the wire to fit the opening, overlapping by 1 inch. Fasten the top edge in place with staples. Pull the screening down and starting in the middle of the bottom edge, work toward each side, making sure the screening is smooth and not wrinkled. Then begin in the middle of each side and work to the outside edges again smoothing and stapling. Once the screening is fastened, nail the 1 x 2 (¾ x 1½-inch) batten boards over the screen edges.

Finishing

Purchased wooden or prepainted **metal or wood screen doors** may be installed in the door openings, hinging the screen doors to batten boards and overlapping the posts and upper framing. Screen door closures or springs and hooks can be used to hold the door or doors shut. **Splash boards** installed along the bottom of the porch, prevent rainwater and mud from splashing up into the porch. The splash blocks shown were cut from wood siding and fastened to the bottom blocking and posts after the screening was installed.

Screen Tight Porch Screening System

Even with care, it's hard to keep wrinkles and sags from forming in large expanses of porch screening. The Screen Tight Porch Screening System makes it easier to screen in your porch. Screen Tight uses the **spline method** of screening, which every window manufacturer in the country uses. The screen is rolled into place in special holding strips using a spline and screen roller. It's easier than using staples and wood lattice

and also produces a smoother end result. Screen Tight is available at the larger chain stores, such as Lowe's. White, grey, beige and brown colors are available. The caps are standard in 8 foot lengths, 12-foot 1½-inch caps and 10-foot 3½-inch caps can be special ordered. A screen roller for rolling screen and spline, mallet for snapping the cap into place, a utility knife, standard snips or chop saw and a drill/driver for attaching the bases are the tools needed.

The support tracks are available in 1.5 and 3.5 inch tracks which are cut to fit 2 x 4 or 4 x 4 vertical or horizontal framing. Fiberglass screen is recommended.

Installation

Cut the tracks to length with pruning shears. Precision isn't critical and there is no need to miter the corners. Screw or nail the channels over the porch's wood framing. It's a good idea to clean, then stain and finish or paint the surfaces beforehand if desired.

Starting at the top, hold the screen and spline taut in one hand and roll the spline and screen into the track with the other hand, keeping out wrinkles as you go. After installing the spline in two sides, continue with the mid rail if one exists. Make short relief cuts as you go. Trim the excess screen using a utility knife or Screen Tight's multi-purpose roller knife. Tap the trim cap into place over the splined screen using a rubber mallet. Start at one end and work toward the other end. Avoid sliding the cap. Cut the trim caps in place with pruning shears. The butt joint should align with those of the underlying frame members.

SCREENING

Tools
- Staple gun
- Screen roller
- Rubber mallet
- Utility knife
- Standard snips
- Chop saw
- Drill/driver

Materials
- Screen – metal, fiberglass or vinyl
- Batten boards
- Spline

Building Camp Lodge Furniture

Above: You can make your own camp and lodge furniture using wood scraps, saplings, and log slabs.

As a youngster growing up in rural Missouri, I was a reading addict and one of my favorite "reads" was *Boys Life Magazine*. I especially liked the project pages and devoured everything Ben Hunt produced those days. Later I discovered the woodcrafts of Ellsworth Taeger and "Nesmuk." Many of these projects were rustic camp furniture and accessories. I whittled, sawed and glued everything from stools to candle holders.

These days camp or lodge furniture is really big business with large manufacturers constructing rustic furniture to meet a growing desire for more "natural" décor. You can also make your own camp or lodge furniture quite easily with only a few tools and often very economically. If you have access to a woodlot, you can make your own camp or lodge furniture with free materials. Standard tree pruning and woodland management for wildlife creates a great source for materials. If the furniture is to be used indoors, almost any type of wood can be used, however, furniture for outdoor use should be made of a long-lasting wood such as cypress, redwood or cedar. Oak is one of the most common hardwoods milled, and can be used for both indoor and outdoor furniture. Pine, aspen, fir, larch and red cedar are also excellent choices for indoor furniture and all are easy to work. A very popular "style" these days is hickory saplings with the bark left on.

SAPLING FURNITURE

Another material source is **discarded logging and/or sawmill debris**. One of the easiest types of furniture is created from waste sawmill slabs. These trimmings are flat on one side, rounded on the opposite and they are usually free for the asking at smaller mills. **Saplings** are used for the legs and these can often be acquired from tree trimmers. The **slabs** should be from 3 to 6 inches thick at their thickest part, and of the length desired for benches, stools and tables. The saplings for legs should be from 2 to 3 inches in diameter for stools and benches and 3 to 4 inches for eating-height tables.

Other projects, such as beds and chairs, can be made entirely from saplings. For **beds** the saplings should have diameters between four-

and six-inches. You may be able to leave the bark on slabs and saplings of some species, but it's best to **peel the bark** as it will eventually shed from most species. The bark can be removed with a **drawknife or spoke shave**. You can even drive the tip of a large hunting knife into a piece of wood to create a "double-handled" peeling tool. Some slabs may be fairly smooth; others may be rough, depending on the method of milling. A belt sander can be used to smooth up the surface, or a large hand plane can also be used for the chore. Smooth up any rough ends or edges with a belt sander or wood rasp.

The legs of slab furniture are commonly held in place with a tenon cut on the end of the leg and placed in a hole bored in the slab. Use a brace and bit or electric drill with a spade or forstner bit of at

The wagon wheel bench, rustic table and sapling coat rack shown above, were made from unstripped saplings, natural logs and other wood "discards," such as the antique wagon wheel. These items are part of the décor of the Resort at Paws Up in Greenough, Montana.

CONSTRUCTING A STURDY CEDAR BENCH

You can create a sturdy bench for the front porch of your lodge using a cedar slab and cedar saplings.

1. First step is to cut the saplings to rough length and remove the bark and inner cambium layer using a draw knife.

2. A tenoning tool, such as the Veritas Tenon Cutter, is attached to an electric drill to cut round tenons in the ends of the saplings for legs.

3. Bore holes at an angle in the slabs to hold the feet. They should be at about an 80 to 85 degree angle.

4. Try to fit the leg tenons in the holes in the underside of the slab.

5. The tenons are held in place with wedges fitted in slots in their upper ends. Cut the slots with a bandsaw or sharp handsaw, then tap the legs solidly in place in the slab.

6. Drive the wedges in place.

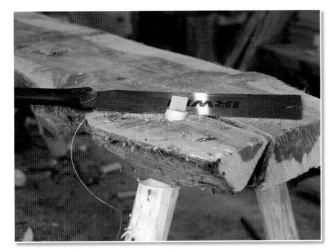

7. Cut off the excess ends of the tenon/wedge.

8. Smooth up the slab top with a belt sander.

Sapling furniture such as beds, chairs and tables are also easy to make using tenons.

OPEN TENON

BLIND TENON

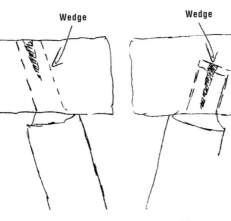

Tenons can be held in place with blind or open tenons. Blind tenons are used on sapling furniture.

Peeled saplings are assembled with a tenoned joint.

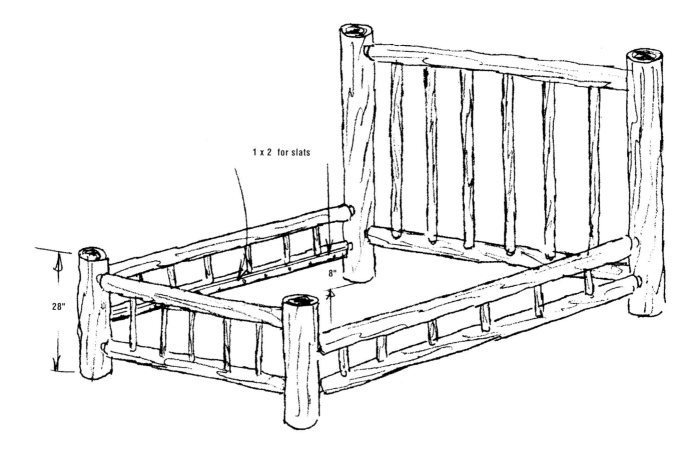

1 x 2 for slats

28"

8"

least 1-inch in diameter to bore a hole through the slab for each leg. The holes should be bored at about an 80- to 85-degree angle in two directions to create the **"splayed" leg** effect. The matching tenons can be cut in several methods. The legs can be held in a vise and the tenons shaped with a drawknife, small hand axe or even large hunting knife. A **tenoning machine** fitted into a portable electric drill makes the chore quick and easy. These are available from Bosworth Tools or Woodworker's Supply. An even easier method, especially for the larger tenons on large tables, chairs and bed frames is to use the Rockler Log Tenon Maker jig with a router. You can also make up your own shop-made tenon cutter to use with your router. In both cases, a bottom

bowl-cutting bit is required.

Regardless, the tenons should be cut to fit snugly into the holes. Rough cut the legs to the approximate size. As the tenons may not all fit with the same exact length, the legs must be cut to final length after fitting the tenons to make sure the furniture sits level. Before inserting the tenons into the holes, cut a saw slot in their top ends. Insert the tenons in place, test the furniture for level, then remove any off the legs and cut excess material off the bottom until the piece is level and doesn't rock. Once you're satisfied the piece sits solidly in place, cut a small **hardwood wedge** and drive into the slot cut in the top of each tenon. Cut off the excess end of the wedge and sand smooth. To "lock" bed tenons in place, bore a hole through the upright posts and the tenons. Then drive a wooden "pin" in place to secure the parts together.

On a simple stool, bench or coffee table, you may wish to stop at this point. **Stretchers**, or **rungs**, however, can make the furniture much stronger and also help prevent undue warping of the furniture components. The stretchers should be slightly smaller than the legs.

To install the stretchers, try-fit the legs in place and make a mark on each leg corresponding to a mark on the bottom side of the slab. This allows you to relocate the legs precisely during assembly. Then measure the distance up from the bottom of the legs you wish to install the stretchers and mark their locations. Bore the holes for the stretchers, cut tenons on the ends of the stretchers and assemble the stretchers to the legs, then the legs into the slab. Pin the stretchers in place with small **wooden pins**.

One of the most common projects is a **tenon-jointed sapling bed**. These can be single or bunk style. The bunks are great for a hunting camp bunkhouse because you can make several quite easily. The old-

timers used rope to hold a mattress in place, topped off with canvas and a goose down feather mattress. These days a bedspring and mattress is more popular with a 2 x 4 fastened inside to hold bed slats. Or you can use 1½ x 1½-inch angle iron strips to support a bed frame.

HALF-LAP FURNITURE

Another method of construction involves using a half-lap design. This is easily created with a hand saw and chisel, or chainsaw and can be used for any of the furniture pieces including chairs and beds. In this type of construction **half-lap joints** are cut with notches in the vertical supports and the ends of the horizontal pieces cut with the half lap. Then bore holes at the joints and fasten together with **carriage bolts**. For a better appearance you can countersink the bolts and even cover them with wooden dowels or pins.

Making your own camp furniture is fun, easy, and can be addictive. You'll probably end up making all kinds of chairs, tables, beds, gun and archery racks, candle holders, and cooking camp equipment.

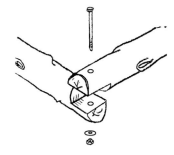

Furniture assembled with half lap joints, illustrated above, requires only basic hand tools and fittings.

Exterior Projects

In addition to the lodge, several other outdoor projects can make your hunting or fishing camp more enjoyable. These include an attached woodshed, small equipment storage shed, a portable shooting house, ladder stands for deer hunting and a privy.

DELUXE DEER POLE

Construct your deer pole from 16-foot, 6x6-inch **pressure-treated** upright poles and a 14-foot (or longer) horizontal beam. You can decide exactly what height you prefer based on the average size of the deer in your area. If you plan to leave deer hanging overnight, the horizontal beam should be high enough to keep them out of reach of animals. The width of your pole may vary, depending on the number of hunters — and their expected success rate!

Wood should be pressure-treated and the poles must be **embedded in concrete**, sunk in the ground. Dig two 24-inch wide, 3½-foot-deep post-holds a little under 14 feet apart. Fill the bottom with about 6 inches of gravel and sink the two **vertical poles** in the ground. Fill in around them with concrete. Use a 4-foot level to make sure the poles are plumb and temporarily brace them in place. Trim the uprights to final height if necessary. Let the concrete dry. If you are unable to dig down the full 3½ feet, seat the uprights as deep as possible, fill with concrete and shore them up with 6x6-inch angle braces.

Above: For any lodge in deer hunting country, a deer (or meat) pole is a useful accessory and a fine source for "bragging rights."

Next, install the **horizontal beam**, consisting of two 14-foot (or longer), 2x6-inch pressure treated boards. Attach the beams to each post with 2, 11- or 12-inch machine bolts with washers, inserted through ½-inch holes. Brace the support beams with 45-degree **angle braces** cut from 4x4s. Attach the braces with one end between the support beams, using a 7- to 8-inch machine bolt. Fasten the other end to the upright with a 6-inch machine bolt countersunk in place. You can add a 7-inch 6x6 reinforcement block between the boards in the center of the horizontal beam. Attach it in place with two 11- or 12-inch machine bolts with washers.

To make moveable **"meat hooks,"** loop several hangers made from heavy-gauge galvanized chain, secured with chain connector and fitted with stainless steel hooks, around the horizontal beam. These can be moved along the beam to suit the needs of a number of successful hunters.

To easily lift your deer to the meat hooks, securely bolt a **hand-cranked boat winch**, available at any boating supply store, to one upright with at least 24 feet of wire cable tipped with a galvanized latch hook. Run the cable to a **pulley** attached to a loose loop of strong chain encircling the crosspiece. The chain can be shifted along the crosspiece to various lifting positions. Add eye lags at intervals along the top of one or both boards of the horizontal beam to make chain stops. The deer can be attached to the hook using hanging straps looped around the antlers or neck, or hung feet first with a gambrel.

MATERIALS

Posts:
   6 x 6" x 16' pressure-treated posts, 2 req'd.
Hanging Pole:
   2 x 6" x 14' (or longer as needed) pressure-treated board, 2 req'd.
Hanging Pole Braces:
   4 x 4" x 3' pressure-treated board, 2 req'd.
Center brace:
   6 x 6 x7" pressure-treated block
Hardware:
   Machine bolts (11" - 12") w/nuts & washers, 6 req'd.
   Machine bolts (7"- 8") w/nuts & washers, 2 req'd.
   Hand-cranked boat winch w/cable & bolts
   Heavy duty galvanized snap hook
   Pulley (single w/swivel)
   Chain & chain connectors

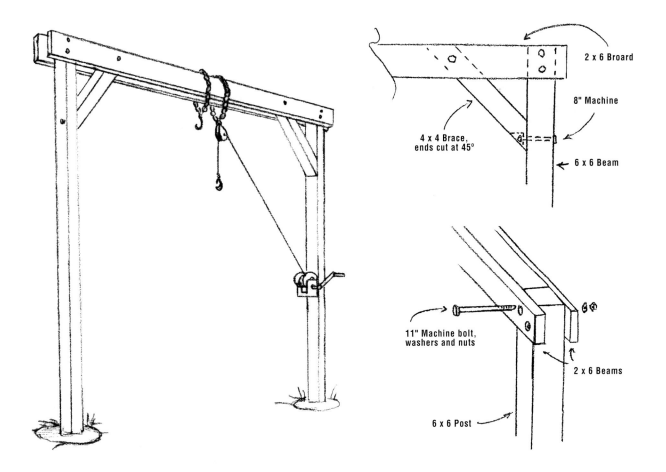

2 x 6 Broard

8" Machine

4 x 4 Brace, ends cut at 45°

6 x 6 Beam

11" Machine bolt, washers and nuts

2 x 6 Beams

6 x 6 Post

MATERIALS

Support posts:
6 x 6" x 10', 2 req'd.
Support log:
6 x 6" x 10', 1 req'd.
Log support beams:
4 x 4" x 10', 4 req'd.
Roof supports:
2 x 4" x 10', 5 req'd.
Roofing:
metal, 10 x 10'

LEAN-TO WOODSHED

A lean-to woodshed attached to the lodge and near a door to the fireplace can add to the ease of burning with wood. The lean-to can be quite simple, but should blend with the building design. If a log home, you will want to construct the lean-to of logs. If a stick construction, you can build the lean-to with pole-barn or post-on-beam construction. Both constructions are similar. The shed should be constructed of **moisture resistant materials** as it will be exposed to the weather. The outer end of the roof is supported by **poles or vertical logs set in concrete**, with a beam, girder or horizontal log supported by the uprights. The sides can be covered with materials to match, logs or with horizontal girts and wooden siding. The roof can be metal, asphalt or be made to match the building roof.

The first step is to determine the upper roof height location and the length of the shed. Mark this on the building wall. Drop string lines with a plumb bob from each end of the proposed roof edge and mark the inside corners of the shed. **Measure** out from the building and mark the support pole locations with stakes. Make sure the layout is square using the steps shown in Chapter Four on foundations. Fasten the rear **ledger board** that supports the roof to the building with lag bolts into the studs or logs. Pour the **concrete supports** and position the posts in place, making sure they are plumb and located properly. Install the **front girder or beam**, and install **diagonal supports** on each corner. Fasten the inner end studs to the building and create the siding support as desired; then add the siding.

If using a **log-wall construction**, the inner ends of the logs should be scribed to fit around the wall logs for appearance and also to keep out blowing snow and rain. Fasten the rafters to the ledger board attached to the wall and down on the front support beam or log. Add the chosen roofing.

A lean-to wood shed for firewood is a practical project that can make your hunt or fishing camp more comfortable.

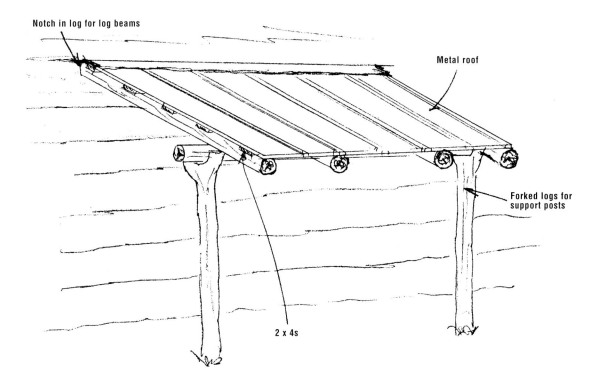

Notch in log for log beams

Metal roof

Forked logs for support posts

2 x 4s

EQUIPMENT SHED

An equipment shed is also important and it should be sturdy, lockable and secure, to deter thieves and keep out the critters. The shed shown has enough space to hold an ATV, or a canoe or small boat, plus other gear stored during the off season, such as wildlife feeders and wildlife habitat maintenance tools.

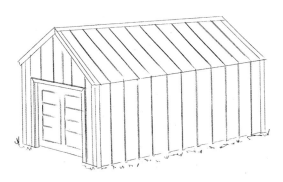

A small pole-barn equipment shed, above, can be easily constructed, diagram below, and can be used to hold ATVs, boats and other gear.

Stick-construction can be but the simplest method is to construct a **pole building** with a concrete floor. Construct the building as per the information on pole structures in Chapter 10. Once the poles and lower girts are in place, pour the concrete floor between the girts, troweling and finishing smooth. Cover the building with the chosen **siding and roofing**. Metal is the quickest, easiest and requires the least maintenance; however, you may wish to add siding and roofing to match other buildings. You can construct wooden doors, but the best method is to use an **overhead garage door**. These are sturdy, tight-fitting and more theft-proof than wooden doors. You can install a window, for light, but these are inviting to thieves.

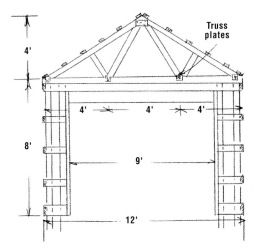

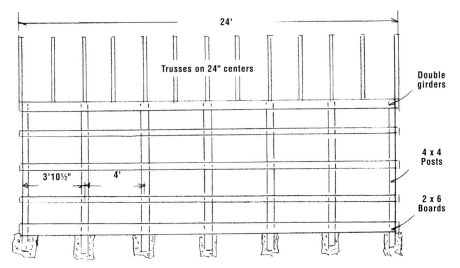

MATERIALS

Posts:
4 x 4" x 10' (or longer as needed), 18 req'd.
Side splash boards:
2 x 6" x 24', 2 req'd.
Rear splash board:
2 x 6" x 12', cut to fit, 1 req'd.
Front splash boards:
2 x 6" x 1½', cut to fit, 2 req'd.
Side girts:
2 x 4" x 24', 6 req'd.
Rear girts:
2 x 4" x 12', cut to fit, 3 req'd.
Front girts:
2 x 4" x 1½', cut to fit, 6 req'd.
Side girders:
2 x 6" x 24', 4 req'd.
Front and rear girders:
2 x 6" x 12', cut to fit, 2 req'd.
Bottom truss boards:
2 x 6" x 12', 13 req'd.
Top truss boards:
2 x 4" x 8', cut to fit, 26 req'd.
Center truss boards:
2 x 4" x 4', cut to fit, 26 req'd.
Outside truss boards:
2 x 4" x 2', cut to fit, 26 req'd.
Truss plates:
91 req'd.
Purlins:
2 x 4" x 24', 12 req'd.
Garage Door:
9', 1 req'd.
Door side blocking:
2 x 4" x 7', 2 req'd.
Metal roofing:
568 square feet req'd.
Metal roof ridge cap:
24' req'd.
Eave metal roof trim:
cut to fit, 30' req'd.
Corner trim:
wood or metal, cut to fit, 32' req'd.
Door trim:
metal or wood, cut to fit, 25' req'd.
Siding:
4 x 8' hardboard or plywood, 20 sheets req'd. or metal siding to fit.

MATERIALS

Skids:
  2 x 6" x 9'6", 2 req'd.
Support posts:
  4 x 4 x 48", 4 req'd.
Side top pieces:
  2 x 6 x 72", 2 req'd.
Upper and lower front and rear support braces:
  2 x 6 x 72", 4 req'd.
Diagonal braces:
  2 x 6 x 24", 8 req'd.
Step brace:
  2 x 6 x 72", 1 req'd.
Step stringers:
  2 x 6 x 53", 2 req'd.
Step supports:
  2 x 2 x 5", 8 req'd.
Steps:
  2 x 6 x 24", 4 req'd.
Floor joists:
  2 x 6 x 72", cut to fit, 2 req'd.
Flooring:
  decking to cover 6' x 6'
Front and rear top and bottom plates:
  2 x 4 x 72", 4 req'd.
Rear studs:
  2 x 4 x 78", 4 req'd.
Front studs:
  2 x 4 x 84", 4 req'd.

PORTABLE SHOOTING HOUSE

Shooting houses are very popular with hunt clubs, hunting lodges and private land owners. These houses provide a comfortable means of **stand hunting** for deer and even turkeys. You're not only out of the weather, but a heater can also be added for those long waits on bitter cold days. Some houses are simply **"tree-houses"** constructed in or against a tree. Others are **free-standing** and placed over food plots, trails and other frequently used deer areas. A portable shooting house, such as the one shown, offers all the benefits of a traditional free-standing shooting house, yet can be moved as needed with a four-wheel drive auto, tractor or even a large size ATV utility vehicle.

You or your hunt-club members can build your own shooting house or houses quite easily. Only basic woodworking skills and a few hand tools are needed. A cordless circular saw, drill and impact driver greatly speed up the work.

Shown is a shooting house built on a **raised platform on skids**. The platform should be constructed of pressure-treated lumber for longevity and strength. Its best if the house is framed in treated materials as well. The house shown was made of recycled Wolmanized Residential Outdoor Wood. The wood is Southern pine, pressure-treated with a copper azole preservative.

The first step is to build the **platform**. Assemble on as level an area as possible. Cut the **skids** from 2 x 6s and cut angles on each end. This prevents the skids from digging into the ground when the house is pulled around. Cut 4 x 4 **support posts** to the correct length and fasten the support posts to the inside of the skids using 3-inch deck screws designed for use with pressure-treated wood. Place the bottom edges of the support posts 2-inches up from the bot-

A shooting house can providing weather protection as well as concealment. The house shown at right is portable and can be moved as needed.

tom edges of the skids. Again, this prevents digging in when the house is pulled. Use a carpenter's square to make sure the posts are installed square with the skids. Cut the side top pieces and fasten in place to the top outside edges of the posts. Stand both post sections upright and brace in place or have someone hold them for you. Cut the front and rear bottom support braces and fasten to the posts down on top of the skids. Cut the top front and rear **support braces** and fasten to the top front and back edges of the posts. Cut the **diagonal braces** and fasten in place, using a carpenter's square to make sure the assembly is square. Cut the 2 x 6 **floor joists** and anchor them in place with screws through the front and rear braces into the ends of the floor joists. Joist hangers can also be used for additional support.

Next construct the steps. Fasten the **step support brace** to the back ends of the skids. Cut the "stringers" to the correct angle and length and fasten to the rear upper support brace and to the step support brace. Cut 2 x 2 step supports and fasten to the inside of the stringers. Then cut the **steps** and anchor them down on the step-support pieces and with screws through the sides of the stringers into the step ends.

The **floor** should also be constructed of a weather- or water-proof material. One half-inch exterior or marine grade plywood can be used, or 5/4-inch pressure-treated decking materials can be used. I had 2 x 6 decking material left over from refurbishing a deck and used them for the floor. Anchor the flooring in place with deck screws.

The **"house"** portion is constructed in the same manner as erecting any standard building, except you're erecting it on the raised platform. Cut the

MATERIALS

Side top and bottom plates:
  2 x 4 x 65", 4 req'd.
Side studs:
  2 x 4 x 84", cut to fit, 8 req'd.
Rear window framing:
  2 x 4 x 26", 2 req'd.
Rear door top frame piece:
  2 x 4 x 30", 1 req'd.
Front and side window framing:
  2 x 4 x 40", 6 req'd.
Jack studs:
  2 x 4 x 33", 9 req'd.
Jack studs:
  2 x 4 x 28", 9 req'd.
Door frame:
  2 x 2 x 18', cut to fit, 1 req'd.
Hinge:
  1 pair req'd.
Knob:
  1 exterior lock set req'd.
Rafters:
  2 x 4" x 6', cut to fit, 5 req'd.
Roofing:
  to cover 6' x 6'
Railing:
  2 x 4 x 48", 1 req'd.
Railing support:
  2 x 4 x 36", 1 req'd.
Siding:
  to cover four sides, 6 x 7½'

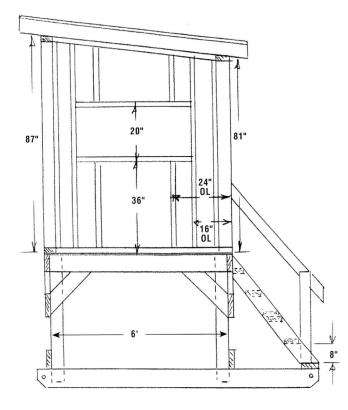

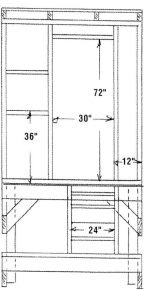

REAR VIEW

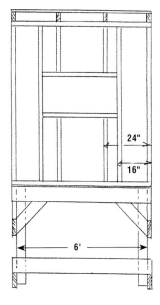

FRONT VIEW

*First step is to create a
raised platform on skids.*

1. Cordless portable power tools make construction easy.

*3. Then construct stud walls for the
house in the same manner as
building a house.*

*Erect the front and back walls and
brace in place.*

*5. Construct the side walls and
anchor between them.*

pieces and build the back wall. Lift the wall into place and temporarily brace with 2 x 4s. Use a carpenter's square to make sure the back wall is square with the floor. Anchor the bottom sill plate of the wall to the platform flooring. Construct the front wall in the same manner and anchor it in place, again bracing temporarily, and making sure it is installed square with the floor. Construct the side walls, measuring so they fit between the front and back walls. Erect the side walls and fasten them to the front and back walls and down on the platform flooring. Cut out the door section sill plate. The 2 x 4 rafters are cut to fit and fastened in place.

The house can be sided in various ways. The quickest method is to purchase **house siding panels**, such as Louisiana Pacific Smart Panel siding. Nail the front and side panels in place. Then, using a portable electric drill bore a starting hole at each corner of the windows from the inside. Use a portable circular saw or reciprocating saw to cut the window openings. Measure the

6. Add the rafters.

7. Install the siding and roofing.

8. Construct and hang the door.

*A Black & Decker airless paint sprayer makes it easy to paint
and camouflage the house.*

cut-out for the door from the rear panel, cut it out and then install the panel in place. Then cut the rear window opening.

An alternative is to use **solid wood siding**, either lap or vertical board and batten. The latter is a good way of utilizing recycled lumber. In this case the individual boards are cut and installed around the doors and windows. The door is assembled in the same manner. The door is made by ripping 2 x 4s into 2 x 2s (1½ x 1½ inches) and creating an inner frame, then covering the frame with siding materials. Hinge the door in place and install an exterior lock set.

Cut ½-inch sheathing or exterior plywood for the roof. Further roof protection can be provided by roll felt or even asphalt shingles.

You may also wish to add a 2 x 4 **railing** for protection when using the steps.

Paint the house and stand, adding the camouflage design of your choice. Camouflage netting stapled to the inside of the windows and with shooting slits, as well as a section of old carpeting (to deaden the sounds) completes the house.

MATERIALS

Legs:
2 x 6" x 14', 2 req'd.
Steps:
2 x 4 x 24", 11 req'd.
Seat braces:
2 x 4 x 36", 2 req'd.
Seat boards:
2 x 6 x 27", 4 req'd.
Top side rails:
2 x 4 x 30", 2 req'd.
Front shooting rail:
2 x 4 x 27", 1 req'd.
Strap iron:
1 x 4", 1 req'd.
Lag screws:
⅜ x 4, 3 req'd.

SHOOTING BAR LADDER STAND

It's fairly quick and easy to build several ladder stands for your hunting property. It's extremely important to construct the stands of **pressure-treated materials** for long life and safety and to use fasteners compatible with pressure-treated lumber. Galvanized lag bolts and/or 3½-inch deck screws are the best choices. The stand shown has a movable shooting bar on the front and safety bars on the sides. The **shooting bar** swings up and out of the way for getting into and out of the stand, and swings down to provide a rifle rest while you're in the stand. Even at that, make sure you always use a safety belt, harness or vest when erecting, climbing into or out of and all the time you're in the stand. It's also important the stand be placed on a **solid, flat surface** and is **securely anchored** to the tree in two places: at the top with ratchet straps and one about midway down the stand legs. These stands are somewhat heavy so it's also important to have someone help you erect them in place. They can be moved, but they're definitely not as easy to move and erect as are the lightweight aluminum tree stands.

The first step is to lay the **legs** side-by-side on a smooth flat surface with their front faces up. Mark the locations for the **steps** on both of the legs at the same time using a square. Cut the steps and anchor them to the legs using lag bolts or the deck screws. Predrill the holes so the ends of the steps don't split. Use a carpenter's square to assure the assembly is square. Cut the **seat board supports** to length and fasten them in place to the outside of the legs. Note they have a slight angle. Cut the **seat boards** and fasten them in place down on the supports. Note the back seat board is notched to provide a better fit to the tree. Cut the back rail supports and attach them in place; then cut and attach the side rails. Cut and fasten the shooting rail in place. The rail has a bolt run through one end and the opposite end sits in a wooden cradle when it is placed in the down position.

Wooden ladder stands are easy to construct, but they must be made of sturdy, pressure-treated materials using sturdy corrosion resistant fasteners. Ladder stands must be solidly anchored in place and equipped with a a safety belt or harness.

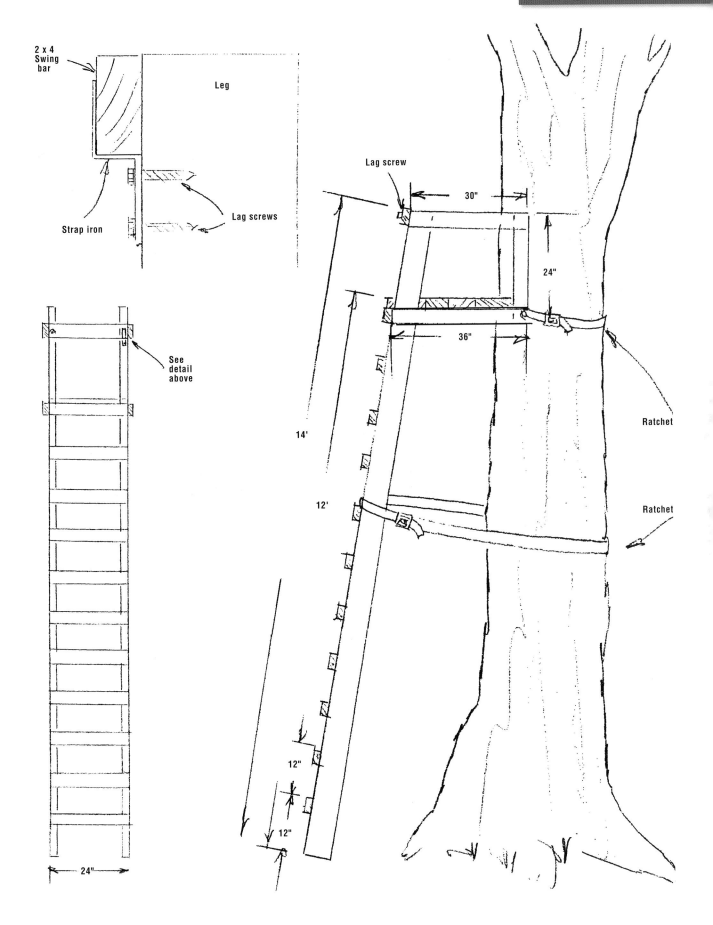

2 x 4
Swing
bar

Leg

Strap iron

Lag screws

See
detail
above

24"

Lag screw

30"

24"

36"

14'

12'

Ratchet

Ratchet

12"

12"

PRIVY

An old-fashioned outhouse or "privy" might bring snickering memories to the old folks, but it's still a practical problem solver for those true backwoods hunt camps. I'll never forget one elk camp high in the Wyoming mountains with a privy about a hundred yards from the bunkhouse. One night the cook made some "mean" chili and the outhouse door never stopped swinging all night, even in a blowing snowstorm and gale winds.

If you don't have running water to your lodge or camp, a privy may be a necessity. Before you build your outhouse, check with local authorities as to whether such a situation is legal.

Construction is fairly straight forward, and the house shown is a "one-holer." I never understood the purpose of a "two-holer," even though I grew up on a farm with just such an outhouse. I guess if two people were desperate enough, and friendly enough, there might be a need. Extend the width to 6 feet if you prefer the "super size" privy.

Because much of the wood will be exposed to the weather, **pressure treated or a naturally decay-resistant wood** is the best choice. The privy shown here is also constructed on pressure-treated 2 x 6 **skids** so it can be moved when a new pit becomes necessary. One of the biggest problems with outhouses is **wasps** getting into them and building nests. This can be a harrowing experience. The building should be constructed as tightly as possible, but with adequate ventilation, covered with **screening**.

The first step in construction is to build the **under support framing** of 2 x 4s attached to the 2 x 6 skids. Note the skids have an angled front and back, and a hole in each end. This allows you to attach a heavy wire and chain for dragging the house to the location or moving it around. The under framing consists of two side joists attached to the skids. A **front filler piece** and **rear filler piece**, along with a **center joist** between the two filler pieces, completes the under-support framing. The floor is then installed down on the floor joists and filler pieces. The two sides are framed in using 2 x 4s. Make sure they are framed square. Position the sides and anchor to the floor. Frame the back and install between the two sides, making sure the building is square. Frame the front and fasten between the two sides.

Cut the **rafters** to the correct length and with the correct angles on their ends. Fasten down on the top plates. Install blocking between the rafters to keep out insects and critters. Fasten the roof in place. The roof can be pressure-treated plywood, solid decking or plywood or OSB board decking covered with asphalt paper and shingles, or you can utilize a metal roof, but it is hotter.

Install the **siding**. Any number of siding materials can be used, including purchased hardboard

An old-fashioned privy may be necessary for those back-in-the woods cabins.

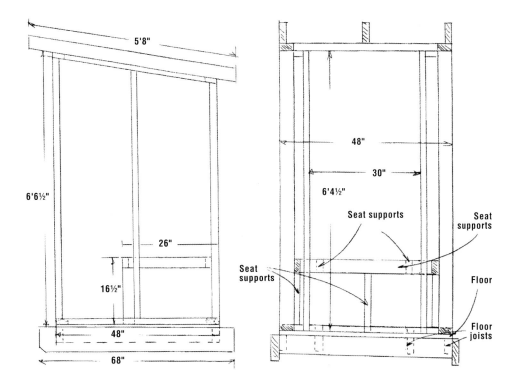

MATERIALS

Skids:
  2 x 6 x 60", 2 req'd.
Front and rear floor supports:
  2 x 4 x 48", 2 req'd.
Floor joists:
  2 x 4 x 45", 4 req'd. Floor, 2 x
  4 x 48", 1 req'd.
Studs:
  2 x 4" x 8', cut to length,
  9 req'd.
Floor plates:
  2 x 4 x 48", cut to length,
  4 req'd.
Top plates:
  2 x 4 x 48", cut to length,
  4 req'd.
Rafters:
  2 x 4 x 5'8", 3 req'd.
Roof:
  ½" exterior plywood,
  48" x 5'10", 1 req'd.
Roof blocking:
  2 x 4 x 24", cut to fit, 4 req'd.
Siding:
  hardboard or plywood, 4 x 8',
  4 sheets req'd, or board and
  batten.
Door:
  covering, cut from siding.
Door framing:
  2 x 2", cut from 2 x 4's,
  18' req'd.
Seat framing, front horizontal:
  2 x 4 x 41", 2 req'd.
Seat framing, front vertical:
  2 x 4 x 12½", 3 req'd.
Seat framing, seat support:
  2 x 4 x 25", 4 req'd.
Seat front:
  ½ x 16½" x 41", 1 req'd.
Seat board:
  ½ x 26" x 41", 1 req'd.
Door hinges, door latches,
  inside and out, and screen
  wire for venting.

such as Louisiana Pacific Smart Panel, pressure-treated plywood, plywood siding or solid wood. Traditionally, outhouses were sided with solid rough-sawn wood. In cases of lazy builders the green sawn boards often shrunk during drying and left lots of cracks. Using board and batten construction with battens over the spaces between the boards solves the problem.

Obviously you'll want plenty of ventilation. The better houses utilized a vent pipe, but a more traditional approach is to leave vent slots around the top of the sides and back and cover with screen wire from the inside. Of course, the door has the **traditional "moon shaped" vent**. The rear has a drop-down **"clean-out" door**. Hinge it at the top and use screen-wire hooks at the bottom to hold it securely shut.

Now it's time to construct the seat portion. Frame the front and add side and rear supports. Install the front covering. Then cut the **seat board** to size. Using a pattern from a modern toilet seat, mark the seat hole shape. Cut by first drilling a starter hole then using a saber saw to make the cut-out. Smooth the cut-out with a wood rasp and sandpaper. Fasten down in place on the framing. The upper-grade outhouses also had a hole cover to again keep down insect, varmint and other problems. A conventional toilet seat can be added for comfort and a cover.

Construct the door. Again, make sure it fits tightly to keep out wasps and other critters. The door was traditionally constructed using solid boards with top and bottom cross pieces and a diagonal cross piece for support. Hinge the door and provide an inside and outside screen door hook to keep the door closed.

Equip with a bucket of lime, and a Penney's or Sears catalog and you're ready for the adventure.

Appendix

INSULATION	
Types	**Detail**
Rolls and Batts (blankets)	Flexible rolls of mineral fiber, such as fiberglass or rock wool that come in continuous rolls with widths measured for the standard spacing of wall studs and attic or floor joists. Rolls and batts are available with or without vapor retarding facings. Batts are available with flame-resistant facings.
Foam Insulation	• Foam insulation is generally made of molded, expanded polystyrene and extruded expanded polystyrene, polyurethane or polyisocyanurate. Some are installed as liquids, while other types are available as rigid foam panels or boards. Foam insulation is effective in buildings with limited space or where higher R-values are needed. Foam insulation R-values range from R-4 to R-6.5 per inch of thickness. • Rigid foam boards are lightweight, and provide structural support and acoustical insulation. They may be faced with a reflective foil to reduce heat flow next to air spaces. Check the local fire codes to find out whether boards must be covered with a fire barrier, such as gypsum wallboard. • Liquid foam insulation is good for use in areas where it would be difficult to fit rigid boards. It can be sprayed into building cavities as a liquid and will conform to seal building cavities.
Loose-Fill Insulation	• Usually made of fiberglass, rock wool or cellulose, loose-fill insulation comes in shreds, granules or nodules that can be blown into spaces using special pneumatic equipment. The blown-in material conforms to building cavities and attics. Additional resistance to air infiltration can be provided if the insulation is sufficiently dense or thick. • Recycled waste materials are used in the production of the main types of loose-fill insulation.
Radiant Barriers	Fabricated from aluminum foils, these reflective insulation systems are generally installed under the roof rafters to reduce heat gain from the sun. They can also be very effective in walls that absorb direct sunlight. Radiant barriers are more effective in hot climates than in cooler areas.
Reflective Insulation Systems	Reflective insulation systems are fabricated from aluminum foils with a variety of backings such as kraft paper, cardboard, plastic film or polyethylene bubbles. This type of insulation is most effective in reducing downward heat flow and is typically located between roof rafters and floor joists. When a reflective surface is used facing an open space, it is called a radiant barrier.
Structural Insulated Panels	These consist of carefully engineered laminate containing a 4- to 8-inch foam core with a structural facing on each side. The most common types of facings are drywall or structural wood sheathing such as plywood and oriented strand board. R-values range from about R-4 to R-6 per inch of thickness, depending on the type of foam core used. Most structural insulated panel foam cores contain expanded polystyrene (beadboard). Some contain polyurethane and isocyanurate as the insulating material.

BEARING CAPABILITIES OF SOILS	
Materials	**Tons per square foot**
Hard rock	40
Soft rock	8
Crystaline bedrock	6
Sedimentary rock	2
Coarse sand	4
Sandy gravel	3.2
Hard, dry clay	3
Fine clay sand	2
Soft clay	1

AVERAGE BTU CONTENT OF FUELS	
Fuel Type	**BTUs/Unit**
Fuel Oil (No. 2)	140,000/gallon
Electricity	3,412/KWH
Natural Gas	1,025,000/thousand cubic feet
Propane	91,330/gallon
Wood (air dried)*	20,000,000/cord or 8,000/pound
Wood pellets (premium)	16,500,000/ton

*Wood heating values can vary significantly according to the moisture content and tree species of the wood. Higher heating values of wood can vary from 8,000 to 10,000 Btu per pound, bone dry. The Btu content of pellet fuels will vary depending on the type of wood that the sawdust is made from.

STANDARD CLEARANCES FOR WOOD-BURNING APPLIANCES*	
Type of Appliance	**Distance From Combustion**
Radiant stoves or room heaters	36"
Circulating stoves or room heaters	12" to 24"
Cooking stoves	36" (18" on non-fired side)
Vent connections, stove pipe	(all types) 18"

*Recommendations provided by the National Fire Protection Association. If manufacturer's specifications differ, follow the manufacturer's recommendations. Clearances are for back and side wall. Front side and loading side clearances should be 36"- 48". Distances can be reduced if a protective shield with 1-inch spacers is installed.

PIPES

Types	Description
Galvanized Steel Pipe	Galvanized steel pipe (zinc coated) comes in standard 21 foot lengths with threaded ends. The pipe can be cut and threaded. Pipe joints are assembled by coating the pipe threads with a small amount of pipe-joint compound and screwing on the fitting. Galvanized steel pipe is suitable for all interior piping. Highly mineralized water greatly reduces the life of steel pipe.
Copper Pipe	• Copper pipe is available in types: K (heavy duty), used for underground piping; L (standard), used for interior plumbing; M (light-weight), used inside buildings behind walls. • Types K and L are available in hard- or soft-tempered form. Hard-tempered pipe is rigid, comes in 10 to 20 foot lengths and is used for exposed piping inside buildings. It requires very little mechanical support. Soft-tempered tubing is flexible and is good for underground use and piping inside existing walls.
Plastic Piping	• Plastic pipe is available in flexible, semi-rigid and rigid forms. Flexible pipe is used for underground water piping because it is inexpensive and easy to install. PVC semi-rigid pipe can be solvent-welded, or glued. Nylon or brass fittings and stainless steel clamps and clamp screws are used for polyethylene pipe joints. For use with drinking water, use only pipe fittings that have the National Sanitation Foundation seal. • There are several classes of plastic pipe and fittings approved by the ASTM for potable household water: **Polyethylene (PE)** This flexible or semi-rigid pipe strength decreases as the temperature rises, therefore it is for cold-water lines only. It has pressure ratings between 80 and 160 psi. PE pipe is available in diameters of up to 6 inches or larger; and it is joined by threads and clamps. **Polyvinyl Chloride (PVC)** This rigid pipe is available with pressure ratings of 50 to 315 psi. PVC should be used for cold-water only. It is used for some household cold water pipes and drains and in some permanent irrigation installations. Pipe for pressure water systems should be rated at least 80 psi. PVC comes in 20 or 10 foot lengths and common diameters; and it is joined with a coupling solvent. It is generally more resistant to crushing or puncturing than PE pipe, and it will stand slightly higher temperatures. **Acrylonitrile Butadene Styrene (ABS)** This semi-rigid pipe has pressure ratings between 80 and 160 psi, and is suitable for sewer pipe. **Chlorinated Polyvinyl Chloride (CPVC)** This material is similar to PVC, but it is better for handling corrosive water at temperatures 40 to 60° F above the limits for other vinyl plastics. It is suitable for hot or cold water lines. Although this type of pipe was developed to handle hot water, the manufacturer's stress and temperature limitations should be checked before installing. Local plumbing codes should be consulted also. **Polybutylene (PB)** Suitable for both hot or cold water lines but the manufacturer's stress and temperature limitations, along with the local plumbing codes, should be checked before installation. **Cross-linked Polyethylene (PEX)** This pipe is suitable for potable water plumbing in hot and cold water lines (limited to temperatures below 180° F), and is resistant to freeze breaks and chemicals found in the plumbing environment. PEX is intended for indoor and buried plumbing applications only and is not recommended for outdoor, above ground use where it will be exposed to direct sunlight. PEX cannot be joined with solvent cement, glues or heat fusion. It is installed using mechanical or compression fittings. PEX is approved in all the current model-plumbing codes but some jurisdictions using older versions of these codes may not include PEX tubing. Check with local authorities to confirm the acceptance of PEX tubing for plumbing applications.

SOFTWOODS USAGE

Types	Usage
Hemlock & Fir	Posts, beams, studs, stringers, joists, floor and roof trusses, rafters and bracing, flooring. Pressure-treated — outdoor structural components and decks.
Pine	• **Southern & Yellow (longleaf, slash, shortleaf, loblolly):** Structural timber, general utility framing, studs, bracing, blocking, rafter, floor and roof trusses, floor and ceiling joists, rafters • **Ponderosa:** Building construction, poles, posts, turnery (balusters, porch columns, dowels) • **White:** Light framing (up to 24' lengths), structural joists and planks • **Western (lodgepole, Western white):** Structural lumber, shelving, millwork, window components, trusses, doors, trim
Spruce	**(Engelmann, Western white, Sitka):** Structural lumber, trusses, prefabricated housing, shelving, millwork, joinery, architectural joinery, window louvers, interior wall paneling, exterior decking, outdoor furniture
Cedar	• **Alaska cedar:** Interior and exterior finish, turnery, posts, shingles, doors • **Western red cedar:** Shingles, siding, poles, posts, ties, decking, trim, doors, window components, outdoor furniture and structures, fencing • **Yellow cedar:** flooring, bridge decking, horse stables, outdoor floors or seating, sauna manufacturing
California Redwood	Siding, sash, doors, fences, decks, outdoor furniture, and shakes
Cypress	Walls, posts, siding, paneling

HARDWOODS USAGE

Types	Usage
Elm	Flooring
Maple (bigleaf, sugar black)	Flooring, interior joinery: stairs, handrails, moldings, and doors
Oak	• **Red:** Heavy construction lumber, millwork, flooring, turnery • **White:** Construction, flooring, architectural joinery, exterior joinery, trim and millwork
Poplar (yellow, tulip)	Light construction
White Ash	Flooring

WIRE SIZE REQUIRED* (computed for maximum of 2-volt drop on two-wire 120-volt circuit)																				
Load Per Circuit	Current 120-volt Circuit	Length of Run (Panel Box to Load Center) — Feet																		
Watts	Amps	30	40	50	60	70	80	90	100	110	120	130	140	150	160	170	180	190	200
500	4.2	14	14	14	14	14	14	12	12	12	12	12	12	10	10	10	10	10	10
600	5.0	14	14	14	14	14	12	12	12	12	10	10	10	10	10	10	10	8	8
700	5.8	14	14	14	14	12	12	12	10	10	10	10	10	10	8	8	8	8	8
800	6.7	14	14	14	12	12	12	10	10	10	10	10	8	8	8	8	8	8	8
900	7.5	14	14	12	12	12	10	10	10	10	8	8	8	8	8	8	8	8	6
1000	8.3	14	14	12	12	10	10	10	10	10	8	8	8	8	8	8	6	6	6
1200	10.0	14	12	12	10	10	10	10	8	8	8	8	8	6	6	6	6	6	6
1400	11.7	14	12	10	10	10	8	8	8	8	8	6	6	6	6	6	6	6	6
1600	13.3	12	12	10	10	8	8	8	8	6	6	6	6	6	6	6	6	4	4
1800	15.0	12	10	10	10	8	8	8	6	6	6	6	6	6	6	4	4	4	4
2000	16.7	12	10	10	8	8	8	6	6	6	6	6	6	4	4	4	4	4	4
2200	18.3	12	10	10	8	8	8	6	6	6	6	6	4	4	4	4	4	4	2
2400	20.0	10	10	8	8	8	6	6	6	6	6	4	4	4	4	4	4	2	2
2600	21.7	10	10	8	8	6	6	6	6	4	4	4	4	4	4	4	4	2	2
2800	23.3	10	8	8	8	6	6	6	6	4	4	4	4	4	4	4	2	2	2
3000	25.0	10	8	8	6	6	6	6	6	4	4	4	4	4	4	2	2	2	2
3500	29.2	10	8	8	6	6	6	4	4	4	4	2	2	2	2	2	2	2	2
4000	33.3	8	8	6	6	6	4	4	4	4	2	2	2	2	2	2	1	1	1
4500	37.5	8	6	6	6	4	4	4	2	2	2	2	2	2	1	1	1	1	1

*Middleton, Roger G. Practical Electricity (Indianapolis, Indiana: Audel and Co., a division of Howard Sams and Co., Inc., 1974).

LOAD BEARING VALUES FOR CONVENTIONAL WOOD FRAME CONSTRUCTION

Load-Bearing Value of Soil (psf)	Minimum Width of Concrete or Masonry Footings (in.)	
	1-story	2-story
1,500	16	19
2,000	12	15
2,500	10	12
3,000	8	10
3,500	7	8
4,000	6	7

SPAN OF JOISTS

Span calculations provide for carrying the live loads shown and the additional weight of the joints and double flooring

Size	Spacing	20 lbs. Live Load	30 lbs. Live Load	40 lbs. Live Load	50 lbs. Live Load	60 lbs. Live Load
2 x 4	12"	8' – 8"				
	16"	7' – 11"				
	24"	6' – 11"				
2 x 6	12"	13' – 3"	14' – 10"	13' – 2"	12' – 0"	11' – 1"
	16"	12' – 1"	12' – 11"	11' – 6"	10' – 5"	9' – 8"
	24"	10' – 8"	10' – 8"	9' – 6"	8' – 7"	7' – 10"
2 x 8	12"	17' – 6"	19' – 7"	17' – 5"	15' – 10"	14' – 8"
	16"	16' – 0"	17' – 1"	15' – 3"	13' – 10"	12' – 9"
	24"	14' – 2"	14' – 2"	12' – 6"	11' – 4"	10' – 6"
2 x 10	12"	21' – 11"	24' – 6"	21' – 10"	19' – 11"	18' – 5"
	16"	20' – 2"	21' – 6"	19' – 2"	17' – 5"	16' – 1"
	24"	17' – 10"	17' – 10"	15' – 10"	14' – 4"	13' – 3"
2 x 12	12"	26' – 3"	29' – 4"	26' – 3"	24' – 0"	22' – 2"
	16"	24' – 3"	25' – 10"	23' – 0"	21' – 0"	19' – 5"
	24"	21' – 6"	21' – 5"	19' – 1"	17' – 4"	16' – 0"

This shows maximum safe spans for high-quality wood joists. Values vary for different species of lumber; always check local building codes for exact data.

SOURCE LIST

American Hardwood Information Center, www.hardwoodinfo.com

American Lumber Standard Committee, www.alsc.org, 301-972-1700

Asphalt Roofing Manufacturing Assoc., ARMA, www.asphaltroofing.org, 800-829-3572

Big Cedar Lodge, www.big-cedar.com, 800-BCLODGE

Bigfoot Systems, Inc., www.bigfootsystems.com, 800-934-0393

Black & Decker, www.blackanddecker.com, 800-544-6986

Bon Tool Company, www.bontool.com, 724-443-7080

Bosch Tools, www.BoschTools.com

Bosworth Tools, www.bosworthtools.com, 406-886-2500

BW Creative Wood, www.bwcreativewood.com. 800-667-8247

C.H. Hanson Pivot Square, www.chhanson.com, 800-827-3398

CMT Orange Tools, www.cmtusa.com, 888-CMT-BITS

California Redwood Association, www.cafredwood.org, 415-382-0662

Chinker's Edge, Sashco, www.sashco.com, 800-767-5656

ChoiceDek, www.choicedek.com. 800-951-5117

Dap, www.dap.com

DeWalt, www.dewalt.com

Dow Great Stuff Window & Door Insulation, www.dowcorning.com

Dupont Tyvek, www.dupont.com

Echo, www.echo-usa.com. 800-673-1558

The Engineered Wood Association, www.apawood.org, 253-620-7400

EPA, Environmental Protection Agency, www.energystar.gov

Forest Applications Training, Inc., www.forestapps.com, 770-222-2511

Formica Brand Laminate, www.formica.com, 800-FORMICA

Freud, www.freudtools,com

Fypon, www.fypon.com, 800-446-3040

Georgia Pacific, www.gp.com

Goldblatt Tool Co., www.goldblatttools.com, 877-876-7652

Granberg International, www.granberg.com, 800-233-6499

GreenFiber, www.cocooninsulation.com, 800-228-0024

Grizzly Industrial, www.grizzlytools.com

Hardwood Plywood & Veneer Assoc., www.hpva.org, 702-435-2900

Hitachi Power Tools, www.hitachipowertools.com, 800-829-4752

Husqvarna, www.husqvarna.com, 800-438-7297

Jeld-Wen Windows & Doors, www.jeld-wen.com

John Deere, www.deere.com, 800-537-8233

Johns Manville, www.jm.com, 800-654-3103

Jonsered, www.jonsered.com, 877-693-7729

Kreg Tool Co., www.kregtool.com, 800-447-8638

Lee Valley Tools & Veritas, www.leevalley.com, 800-267-8735

Log Jam Chinking, Sashco, www.sashco.com, 800-767-5656

Logosol, www.logosol.com, 1,877-LOGOSOL

Louisiana Pacific Corp., www.lpcorp.com

Makita, www.makitatools.com, 800-461-5482

Marshalltown Trowel Company, www.marshalltown.com, 800-888-0127

McFeelys, www.McFeelys.com, 800-443-7937

Milwaukee Tools, www.milwaukeetool.com

National Electric Code, www.neccodebook.com, 800-253-0541

NFRC, National Fenestration Rating Council, www.nfrc.org

NRCS, www.nrcs.usda.gov

Owens Corning, www.owenscorning.com

The Resort at Paws Up, www.pawsup.com, 866-894-7969

Pella, www.pella.com

Phillips DuraFast Fasteners, Phillips Screw Co., www.phillips-screw.com, 774-396-6190

Porter-Cable, www.deltaportercable.com

QUIKRETE, www.quikrete.com, 800-282-5828

Poulan, www.poulan.com, 800-554-6723

Redwood, California Redwood Assoc., www.calredwood.org, 888-CALREDWOOD

Ridgid Power Tools, www.ridgid.com, 800-4-RIDGID

Rockler Woodworking & Hardware, www.rocklerpro.com, 800-233-9359

Ryobi Power Tools, www.ryobitools.com

Screen Tight, www.screentight.com, One Better Way, 800-768-7325

Sears Craftsman, www.sears.com/craftsman, 800-377-7414

Sequentia, Crane Composites, www.sequentia.com, 800-435-0080

Shindaiwa, www.shindaiwa.com, 877-641-3024

Shop Fox Tools, Woodstock International, www.shopfoxtools.com, 800-840-8420

Sikkens, www.sikkens.com, 866-SIKKENS

Stihl, www.stihlusa.com, 800-467-8445

Strong-Tie, Simpson Mfg., www.strongtie.com, 800-999-5099

Southern Pine Council, www.southernpine.com, 504-443-4464

Suntuf, Palram Americas, www.suntuf.com, 800-999-9459

Tanaka, www.tanaka-usa.com, 253-333-1200

Thompson's Waterproofer, www.thompsononline.com, 800-367-6297

TimberKing, www.timberking.com, 800-942-4406

Titebond III waterproof glue, Franklin International, www.titebond.com

Vaughan & Bushnell, www.vaughanmfg.com

Veritas Tools Inc., www.veritastools.com, 613-596-1922

Vermont Castings, www.vermontcastings.com, 800-668-5323

Western Red Cedar, www.WRCLA.org or www.realcedar.org

Weyerhaeuser, www.weyerhaeuser.com, www.ilevel.com

Wilsonart International, www.wilsonart.com

WindsorONE, www.windsorone.com

Wolmanized Outdoor Treated Wood, www.wolmanizedwood.com

Woodmaster Tools, Inc., www.WoodmasterTools.com, 800-821-6651

Wood-Mizer, www.woodmizer.com, 800-553-0182

Woodworker's Supply, Inc., www.woodworker.com, 800-645-9292

Woodworking industry information, www.woodweb.com

Index